The Management of Service

The Management of Service
for the Restaurant Manager

Raymond J.
Goodman, Jr.
Conrad N. Hilton College
Of Hotel and Restaurant Management
University of Houston

wcb
**Wm. C. Brown Company
Publishers**
Dubuque, Iowa

Consulting Editor,
Jerry Vallen

To Louis who always knew
To Carroll who would have been so proud
To Helen, Raymond, and David who had to wait

We may live without poetry,
  music, and art;
We may live without conscience and
  live without heart;
We may live without friends, we may live
  without books;
But civilized man cannot live without
  cooks.
He may live without books—what is
  knowledge but grieving?
He may live without hope—what is
  hope but deceiving?
He may live without love—what is
  passion but pining?
But where is the man that can live
  without dining?

                              Anonymous

Contents

Chapter 5 Equipment Used in Service   77

Chapter 6 Sanitation and Safety in Service   99

**Part 2
Techniques and
Procedures   133**

Contents

Preface

Service in the United States has traditionally been delegated to European-trained maitres d'hotel who were trained through a long apprentice training program. Trained waiters are no longer immigrating to the United States, and the few persons that do immigrate are not trained as waiters. Many are employed for their accents rather than their expertise.

Professor Vance A. Christian at the School of Hotel Administration at Cornell University recognized this fact as well as the fact that even when a food service operator could find skilled waiters and waitresses, he or she did not have the managerial skills to direct the service staffs' efforts. As a result, he asked me to write on and teach a course in service. Certainly there has been instruction in service techniques, yet none was tailored to train future food service, hotel, or hospitality industry executives.

This book is an expansion of the original work which began as a course outline in 1974. Since that time, two hundred and thirty students per year have studied the Management of Service at Cornell University.

This book will serve three purposes: *first, as a textbook for technical schools, colleges,* and *universities* offering courses in hotel and restaurant administration; second, as *a managerial guide for executives involved in food service*; and third, as *a reference for teachers in food service education* who may not have had the opportunity to study service as a separate discipline.

Much of the service-related literature, although mentioning some management topics, deals mainly in generalities. There are few step-by-step procedures for accomplishing the various tasks necessary to the service function. *There are few specific guidelines* for how one should deal with people—customers or employees. The procedures presented in this text can be used in most service systems.

Research for the book began with an extensive review of any literature that pertained to restaurant service. It was also necessary to interview individuals who had considerable experience in service and to incorporate this information in the text. The author held seminars and had personal interviews with these experienced individuals in order to clarify particular shortcomings in the available literature.

The book is divided into two major sections: Part I—Management and Part II—Techniques and Procedures. Chapter 1 discusses the true essence of the hospitality industry— "The Psychology of Service." Chapter 2, "Concepts in Human Relations in Service," is in effect a continuation of chapter 1; however specific references are directed towards the management of service employees as opposed to guest relations. Chapter 2 incorporates a very brief discussion on the historical development of the human relations movement before launching into the practical aspects of human relations in the dining room. "The Personnel Function in Service," chapter 3, addresses itself to the manager's duties of organizing, interviewing, selecting, and training service employees. Additional material in chapter 3 covers the subjects of wages and salaries, tips, performance appraisal, and discipline procedures.

In chapter 4 a discussion on the types of service—plate, platter, cart, etc.—includes managerial advantages and disadvantages of the types of service. The student will be able to determine which type service should be instituted when given a series of guidelines. "Equipment used in Service," chapter 5, is a description of silverware, china, glassware, and other equipment used in the front-of-the-house in a restaurant. In order to present, as far as possible, an unbiased discussion of all equipment, the advantages and disadvantages of each have been cited. In this way the student, the manager, or the teacher may choose the equipment he or she prefers. Chapter 6 on sanitation and safety in service makes no attempt to duplicate the courses presented by NIFI, NRA, and other state and local agencies, but rather proposes to sensitize the student, from yet another perspective, as to how important the subjects of both safety and sanitation are. I honestly feel that we *cannot teach too much* about safety or sanitation.

Part II—Techniques and Procedures departs from a general discussion of managerial topics and plunges directly into the how-to approach. Chapter 7—"Sales as a Service Function"—however, bridges the gap between a general discussion and teaching service personnel how to sell. The chapter is very short, and it is to the point. If all servers were knowledgeable in the areas covered in this chapter, management *as well as service personnel* would certainly profit.

"The Director of Service," chapter 8, was included because a student once came and asked where he could read about how to be a maitre d'hotel. In order to fill the need that exists for such information, this chapter begins with a job description, offers a checklist for opening duties and dining room organization, describes a workable reservation system, and literally teaches one how to be a host—from greeting the guests, to seating the guests, to scheduling service personnel. The specific intent is to describe a system that allows one to manage proactively as opposed to reactively. Chapter 9, "The Service Staff: Responsibilities, Procedures and Techniques" completes the discussion of the system. The chapter begins with job descriptions for all positions in the dining room and subsequently breaks down important standard tasks into step-by-step procedures. A framework is thus established that allows one to complete the breakdown analysis for tasks that may be peculiar to one's operation. This chapter is replete with illustrations that are used to teach proper service procedures.

Chapter 10—"Tableside Service"—is a modern departure from the classical approach to Cart Service discussed in chapter 4. This chapter emphasizes the point that tableside service is not as difficult as the classical approach leads us to believe. Additionally the advantages and disadvantages of the various pieces of equipment used in tableside cookery are discussed. Chapter 11—"Wine and Beverage Service"— not only discusses proper service techniques for serving wine and cocktails, but also provides a short background on wines, spirits, beers, and cordials. This chapter is also replete with illustrations on proper service technique.

The appendices include several interesting sections. The purpose of the glossary and pronunciation guide, Appendix A, is to familiarize the student with both the terminology and the correct pronunciation of menu terms and wines. The presentation in this section is brief. Also included is a myriad of table arrangements, Appendix B, that can be used for banquets, buffets, meetings or conferences, etc. The napkin folding section, Appendix C, includes an *easy-to-understand* guide for folding napkins. Several of the folds are not in any other publication. Appendix D, includes a metric conversion table as well as a guide for how to convert to metric. Appendix E includes a temperature conversion chart.

This book is the culmination of many years of practical experience, research, writing, rewriting and editing, and rewriting. There is no way that I could have done it alone.

I wish first to thank Professor Vance A. Christian for the idea and the opportunity to approach this subject—the management of service. I would be remiss if I did not thank Mrs. Eva Melton for guiding me through the first application of this new approach, and yet I could not have gotten off the ground had it not been for the students and the Cornell Hotel School. My teaching assistants, who have been so close to me and to the course, have given me infinite amounts of feedback— I thank all of you!

I thank Professor James C. White who read the chapter on safety and sanitation and made many helpful suggestions.

I would also like to thank Carol Silvernail, Penny Newland, and Jean Savichky for typing and typing. Jean Pascual, my first editor, was invaluable in giving me encouragement during the early phases; and Janice Lang, my second editor, had to do all the dirty work. Thank you both ever so much.

Joe Durocher has been a sounding board for four years. Sometimes I don't know how he stood it. Thank you, Joe.

I wish to acknowledge my parents, Raymond and Rosalie, who could not be close because they live 1,800 miles away, but who have been an inspiration in my life.

To my two boys Raymond and David, I hope you do not remember when I had to say "Not now honey, Daddy has to work," and to my precious Helen who has lived through an interminable period of writing, writing, writing.

R.J.G.

Part 1

Management

Chapter 1

The Psychology of Service

A discussion of the psychology of service properly begins with an attempt to understand some of the basic needs of man.* Several well-known psychologists and psychiatrists have their theories as to what makes man tick. Most college students are aware of A.H. Maslow's hierarchy of human needs, and management literature almost always includes descriptions of Maslow's needs hierarchy when discussing motivation. Certainly Maslow summarizes what many of the other theorists have postulated, while many others have used Maslow's needs hierarchy as a framework for their ideas. And who can argue with his five basic needs for a normal person: physiological, safety, love, esteem, and self-actualization.

1. The physiological needs include hunger, thirst, sleep, and sex.
2. The safety needs are for protection from danger, threat, or deprivation.
3. The love needs are for satisfactory associations with others, for belonging to groups, receiving affection, and friendship.
4. The esteem needs for self-respect and respect of others could be labeled ego or status needs.
5. The self-actualization (self-fulfillment) needs are to achieve what the individual feels is *his* maximum potential, development, creativity, and expression.

*Throughout this chapter *man* will always imply man or woman unless specifically designated otherwise.

Maslow feels that the more basic needs must be significantly satisfied before needs at the next level can be satisfied. However, one may be satisfying portions of two need levels simultaneously. The need exerting more influence will elicit behavior in response to that need. None of the needs are ever completely satisfied as they tend to recur, yet a satisfied (albeit temporarily) need does not motivate behavior. Esteem and self-actualization are rarely satisfied; yet, they move people to strive for more satisfaction from esteem and self-actualization once they become important.

The need for self-esteem, status, and success are needs that a service individual can help satisfy for the guest. People need to feel recognized, respected, and approved by friends, and even by enemies. In short, man needs to be recognized by all of those with whom he comes in contact. When these needs are not satisfied, man feels inferior, rejected, isolated, worthless, and resentful. Incidentally, the quest for power, wealth, prestige, and other symbols of status are universal in all societies, but the means of attaining them differ from society to society.[1]

Maslow's notion of self-esteem is related to Hamachek's ideas regarding the self. Modal people (used in lieu of *normal* people) tend to relate to others with whom they agree. This fact is one of the most consistent findings in mass communications research.[2]

Communications about ourselves are thus either biased in a generally favorable direction or are so ambiguous that our own biases are free to operate.

That is the case suggested by the responses of some adolescent subjects to the question: "What do most people think of you?" Nearly ninety-seven percent said that most people thought well or fairly well of them, and only three percent said poorly or very poorly. Even two-thirds of those with low self-esteem attributed such benevolent attitudes towards others. They may, of course, be right. It is possible that a vast wave of mutual love and good engulfs the world. One cannot, however, evade the suspicion that, with the ambiguity inherent in determining another's attitudes, a great many people are giving themselves the benefit of the doubt.[3]

1. D. McClelland, *The Achieving Society* (New York: Van Nostrand, 1961).

2. Don E. Hamachek, *Encounters with the Self* (New York: Holt, Rinehart, and Winston, 1971), p. 244.

3. M. Rosenberg, "Psychological Selectivity in Self-Esteem Formation," in *Attitudes, Ego Involvement and Change,* ed. by C.W. Sherif and M. Sherif (New York: Wiley, 1967), p. 47.

People find friends and acquaintances and tend to associate with people who think well of them and support their self-concept. They also tend not to make friends or to associate with people whom they dislike or who dislike them. Typically, people like others because they feel liked by that person or persons. Research on groups and on individuals relating to groups corroborates the research findings mentioned above.

People cannot create their own environments, but they can select them. They choose experiences and environments in which they have a fair chance of success. Many select occupations in which their particular interests and skills will be utilized and appreciated. The need for support influences people to choose social gatherings, courses in college, lectures, religions, and even places to take their business.

Jourard, in *The Transparent Self,* raises an ethical point in psychology: As a result of increased technology, people can control or manipulate behavior. When someone comes into your restaurant he is looking for something more than satisfying the basic hunger or thirst need. The responsibility of satisfying that "something else" is up to the service personnel and the manager. It is incumbent upon the manager (for his survival, as well as that of his employees) to manipulate the guest so that he has a pleasant experience and returns to that establishment.

Esteem Needs Related to the Restaurant Industry

The lifeline of the restaurant business is return guests. Even a restaurant along a toll road depends on repeat customers. Certainly different tourists travel the roads, but the majority of the people who travel the toll roads travel the same road frequently. Perhaps some of the few restaurants that do not depend on repeat business are restaurants in a theme park (i.e., Disneyland, Six Flags, Astro World). Any one guest usually goes to a theme park on an infrequent basis, usually spends enough time to see the attractions, and eats in different food establishments during his stay.

In order to develop return guests, certain techniques may be used to manipulate the guest's behavior by supporting his self-concept, self-esteem, self-image, etc. In *How to Win Friends and Influence People,* Dale Carnegie has outlined techniques for making people like you, and these techniques can be used by the manager and the employees toward the guest.

The restaurant industry is a people business and those working in the front of the house must be interested in people—sincerely interested. One of the most important and emphasized techniques for demonstrating interest and concern is a smile:

It is easy enough to be pleasant
When life flows along like a song,
But the man worth while
Is the man who can smile
When everything goes dead wrong.

—Anonymous

Remembering Names and Faces

A manager should teach the service personnel the techniques of remembering names and faces. It is all well and good to *tell* someone to remember names and faces, but telling them *how* to do it is the better approach.

(1) *Get the person's name clearly and distinctly.* Many times when one is introduced to a person the person mumbles his name. It is very difficult to remember a name you do not know. Look at the person's face while repeating his name when introduced.

(2) *Repeat the name as often as possible in conversation.* This does not mean to conspicuously repeat the name several times, but to use the person's name in conversation as much as possible. "That is really a good idea, John." "Where did you say you were from, David?" Each time you repeat a person's name, look at his face and make a positive connection or association. In other words, make a concerted, overt effort to record the person's name and face in your mind.

(3) *Attach a meaning to the person's name.* The meaning one attaches to the name could be a city, Tom Jackson (Jackson, Mississippi), etc.; an object, Byron Moore (imagine a moor); an animal, Fred Lyons; or a nationality/religion, David Campione, Bill McMannis, etc.

(4) *Write the person's name down—but not in front of him.* This is great assistance in remembering someone's name. After getting the person's name clearly and distinctly, looking at the name written will make another positive connection.

Satisfying the Need for Esteem

Be a good listener. When handling guest complaints or just conversing with a person, a good service manager should listen attentively and let the other person talk about himself. Two things will result: The person will enjoy listening to himself, and the manager will take less chance of saying the wrong thing. The manager may practice active listening by encouraging the other person to talk more about himself. "That is very interesting, could you tell me more?" "I'm sorry you didn't like the vegetable, sir, what would you have liked?" Sometimes the manager should remain silent, simply give an affirmative nod or some other encouraging gesture.

Do not interrupt, and let the other person finish his thought completely. When you speak, talk about the other person's interest. Find something interesting about the person and explore it; even if you have limited experience in the other person's interest, relate your experiences based on his interest.

Make the other person feel important. This *is* as easily said as done! Remembering a person's name does make him feel important. Praise also makes another person feel important, for people love to hear about themselves. There are three types of praise one can use and use sincerely.

—*Physical Praise.* Find something on or about the person that you like. It could be a piece of jewelry, a tie, a scarf, a hat, a fragrance, etc. The important thing is to find something that you, in fact, do like so that you can be sincere.

—*Familial Praise.* If a family comes into your establishment, comment to the parents about their children. In a recent informal survey, many waiters/waitresses mentioned how important and how effective it was for them to cater to the children in a family. The parents are certainly flattered at the attention given their child(ren), and thankful that you have entertained the child(ren). One caution here: praise another's spouse or date only if you are the same sex as the person you are praising. If you are a waitress, do not praise a man in front of his wife. However, if you are a male in your mid-thirties, and the female you are praising is a senior citizen, there is little chance for misunderstanding.

—*Praise by Inference.* This form of praise is perhaps the best form to use in a restaurant. If you recognize a person from a picture in a newspaper or any other way, make a favorable remark to the person about this. If someone's relative comes in, you need not compliment him, but you may mention how favorably his grandfather had spoken of him. This form of praise is seldom recognized by the person being praised, but it makes him feel good.

Giving Good Service

—Perform side duties as required by the particular establishment.
—Follow order of service as specified.
—Follow acceptable service procedures as specified.
—Serve condiments to accompany items before guest needs to ask.
—Have water glass always 2/3 to 7/8 full.
—Make sure that bread and butter supply are adequate.
—Clear trays with soiled dishes frequently from dining room.
—Serve food the way *each* guest ordered it.
—Help the guest(s) order if necessary.
—Remove unnecessary glassware and dishes from guest's table.
—Refill wine glasses (half full for red and 3/4 full for white).
—Order more cocktails or wine if guest desires.
—Check buffet table or salad bar for food, appearance, and heat or cold.
—Continue to follow up with service.
—Smile.

A Waiter/Waitresse's Tips for Good Service

—Never stand around in groups of more than two—stay at your station.
—Always greet your guests; make eye contact with guests, greet them cordially and smile.
—Avoid conversations with other employees, especially in the presence of guests.
—Do not give loud orders.
—Never argue with anyone—especially a guest.
—Observe side towel rules:
  —Do not mop your face with towel.
  —Never carry towel under your arm or on your shoulder.
  —Take a clean towel once in a while.

—Never wipe silverware or glassware with towel in front of guest.

—Use a clean, sanitary towel to polish silver or glassware only before opening or when out of guest's view.

—Do not lean on chairs or put your foot on a chair rung. Stand erect or bend from the waist to hear.

—If the guest spills something or you spill something on a guest, apologize, clean it up, and advise your supervisor.

—If a guest drops a napkin, replace it with a clean one.

—Talk only as necessary for politeness.

—Do not smoke in areas where not allowed and never during the serving period or in guest's view.

—Do not holler in the kitchen.

—Never use bad language.

—Take guest complaints to your supervisor.

—Say "thank you" when tipped; regardless of the amount.

—Do not count money or jingle coins in pockets.

—Never hurry your guests.

—Never eat during service.

—Do not carry pencils, books, etc., where visible, i.e., in pockets, behind ears, etc.

—Carry menus in your hands—not under arms or in a shirt, blouse, apron or jacket.

—Do not lean on walls or sidestands.

—Do not put hands in pockets or on hips.

—Do not cross arms in front of chest.

—Cross arms behind you or grasp hands in front or behind you.

—Do not add checks in view of any guests.

—Do not complain about food to kitchen personnel—tell your supervisor.

—Do not point in the dining room or gesture at a table.

—Always be courteous.

—Walk briskly, but never run.

—Do not walk briskly when leading guests to their seats.

Special Service Situations

It is impossible to comment about all special service situations. Yet a few words in each category will help.

Children require some additional or special service. The children's ages will dictate how much special attention they require, but children generally enjoy being treated as adults, and the service person should try as much as possible to do this. Do not ignore a child, and do not resort to baby talk. Offer a high chair or booster chair if required. Suggest a child's portion of a popular dish—spaghetti, hamburger, hot dog, or peanut butter and jelly sandwich, and bring it to the table as quickly as possible. If the child is irritable, food may sometimes quiet him. The service personnel should never reprimand the child if he misbehaves. Waiters/waitresses who handle children effectively, usually fare better in gratuities.

Ill guests should be offered any assistance necessary to comfort them, but do not move an ill guest. The manager should summon professional assistance quietly, and the service personnel should try not to embarrass the person or arouse commotion in his area. Any accidents should be quickly wiped clean as this may ruin the appetite of other guests.

Recently, a restaurant was held liable and required to pay damages to a widow whose husband became ill in the restaurant. All the employees as well as the managers assumed that the man was drunk. They treated him accordingly—quietly escorted him out of the restaurant, propped him against a wall outside, and left him unattended. The man died of an illness, found after an autopsy, that perhaps could have been checked had the restaurant exercised *reasonable care* in handling this situation.

Senior citizens are generally very set in their ways and make many demands on the service person. Managers should instruct hosts not to seat too many senior citizens in one section, as they are generally noted for being poor tippers and tend to complain more than the average guest. This upsets other guests *and* the service person.

Blind or deaf guests should be treated with as little extra fanfare as possible. Blind guests should be led to their seats by the host/hostess or waiter/waitress. Most blind guests will follow by grasping the host/hostesses elbow. A blind guest may ask to have the menu read, and a deaf guest may ask for a menu explanation. Blind guests should be verbally notified when being served. The service person should assist as necessary, and it may be necessary to cut or portion larger items for the blind guest. This service should be specifically requested by the guest.

VIPs (very important persons) deserve some special considerations, but this should not be observed by other guests in the establishment as the other guests may feel discriminated against. VIP guests may not be good tippers, but nonetheless should be given the best waiter/waitress. In a real case a waitress brought some of her homemade strawberry jelly to one of her regular guests who had asked for fresh strawberries, which were out of season. This incident caused many problems in the dining room as other guests requested strawberry jelly and there was none to be had. *One* guest was quite happy, but many of the other regulars were upset. Perhaps in this instance, the waitress should have cleared this with her supervisor *before* serving the guest, and the manager should have disapproved. The restaurant can be held for damages should the guest become ill as a result of unwholesome food. This anecdote highlights how other guests feel when someone gets special treatment. VIPs should be served in private dining rooms or in areas of the restaurant that are not visible to other guests.

Inebriated guests should not be seated if this can be accomplished without offending the guest. Remember that the other guests in the restaurant deserve a quiet meal, and a drunken guest can ruin their evening as well as yours. Drunk VIPs pose an additional problem as they are more difficult to turn away. If a private area is available, it would be an excellent alternative.

Guests who arrive near closing time deserve the same service as guests arriving at the opening, and management should plan for late customers. A waiter/waitress could be brought in later than the regular shift in order to service late guests, but if a party lingers unnecessarily, it would be more appropriate for the manager to approach the guests, and offer a suitable substitute: a cup of coffee or a cocktail in the lounge on the house. Closing time procedures should be explained in an open manner, rather than having the service staff make obvious indirect gestures, such as dimming or increasing illumination of the lights. This is inexcusable behavior.

If a party arrives near closing time, the host/hostess or waiter/waitress may do several things: (1) Politely inform the guests that you *have* closed, but you will make *every* effort to service them. (2) Politely inform guests that you must check with the manager or the chef to see if they can be seated. The host/hostess or waiter/waitress may delay *briefly* in the kitchen (whether or not he/she asks the manager or chef) and then inform the guests that you will serve them. This sets the stage for politely asking them to leave as soon as they have finished their meals. (3) Ignore the fact that the restaurant is near closing, seat the guests and do not ask them to leave. This is *not recommended* as the service personnel may serve in haste and make a dissatisfied patron.

When the dining room is filled to capacity the manager should try to keep the waiting customers from leaving. He may offer a complimentary cocktail, and regular guests should be given seating preference if this practice can go undetected by the transient guests. If an establishment offers reservations, this is definitely possible, but if not, preferential treatment for regular guests is difficult to accomplish. If the property is a multiunit food operation, the guest should be encouraged to stay in house.

The capacity of the dining room depends on the capabilities of the staff, not the number of seats in the house. The guest will remember poor service, but may not look disfavorably on the establishment for turning him away especially if the situation is explained. Frequently the guest who says, "I'm not in a rush," is the most adamant and complains more about slow service.

Let us assume that we have a 100-seat restaurant with three waiters/waitresses on duty. For the type of service we are using, plate service, one waiter/waitress can efficiently serve fourteen to eighteen guests at one time. What is the maximum capacity of the dining room in these conditions? Fifty-four guests.

We could over-seat the room, but the guests in any station with more than eighteen patrons will get less efficient service. Eighteen plus guests will be upset rather than the few guests who were politely turned away. Seeing empty tables, some guests will complain, "What about that table over there?" The host/hostess must then explain the service situation and that they cannot be seated in the dining room, but that they could wait in the cocktail lounge. When this situation occurs, the unoccupied tables can be used for turnovers, obviating the need to reset. The dirty tables *must* be cleared, however, they do not need to be reset until needed for the second turn.

The manager and the waiter should be aware of certain cautions in practicing the techniques presented. Praising people in order to make them feel good, and in turn like you, must be done subtly. If the guest feels that the praises are not sincere, the technique can backfire. Moreover, persons who do not think highly of themselves tend to overrespond to praise and flattery, while others are embarrassed when another person praises or flatters them.

In a restaurant there is such a thing as over-service. A family-type restaurant typically offers friendly service, but the waiter is not expected to fill water glasses after each sip or empty the ashtray after each flick of an ash. Correspondingly, if one were eating at a very elegant, expensive restaurant, the guest would expect and perhaps demand this sort of service. Another caution that a manager and a service person should take is to not be overly familiar. Frequently, friends of employees may come into an establishment and although the host/hostess, waiter/waitress should greet their friends warmly, they should not be too loud or overly demonstrative. Selection of words and tone of voice go hand in hand, but are also important separately. For example, "What do you want?" even if uttered in a nice way is not a proper selection of words. However, "May I take your order?" may be uttered in an impolite manner and, therefore, be unacceptable. Service personnel should always remain low key and should be courteous at all times.

Giving compliments, praise, and flattery is very helpful, but accepting compliments properly is equally important. A celebrity once gave a waiter quite a compliment on his service technique, his manner, and his style. The waiter jumped at this opportunity, monopolized the celebrity and his guests for five minutes, talked very loudly, and ignored his other guests. Certainly this behavior did considerable damage to this establishment.

Service persons should not belittle themselves, the establishment, nor the chef; nor should they be boisterous. They should say, "Thank you very much," and quietly back away.

Additional Readings

Carnegie, Dale. *How to Win Friends and Influence People*. New York: Pocket Books, 1972.

Hamachek, Don E. *Encounters with the Self*. New York: Holt, Rinehart & Winston, 1971.

Jourard, S. *Personal Adjustment*. New York: Macmillan Co., 1963.

———. *The Transparent Self*. New York: Van Nostrand, 1964.

McClelland, D. *The Achieving Society*. New York: Van Nostrand, 1961.

Rosenberg, M. "Psychological Selectivity in Self Esteem Formation." in *Attitudes Ego Involvement and Change*. edited by C.W. Sherif and M. Sherif, New York: Wiley, 1967.

Chapter 2

Concepts in Human Relations in Service

With respect to management literature, the term *human relations* applies to the interaction of management and labor. The early human relationists had two primary concerns: concern for man in an organization and concern for the use of knowledge gained in studying organizational behavior.

The objective of a business is to realize a fair return on an investment. In order that a business may succeed in the long run, many subgoals must be specified and accomplished: good working conditions for employees, community involvement, satisfied customers, and fulfilled government requirements. The hospitality industry is no different except that it offers an intangible product. We sell *service*. Good food, comfortable surroundings, and fair price all contribute to the success of an operation, but we are still selling service!

An Historical Background

A discussion of human relations would lose impact unless an historical perspective of management is developed. During the early twentieth century, Frederick Taylor (1856–1915) began writing about management and developed the scientific management movement. Taylor was influenced by the Protestant work ethic of the time and emphasized hard work, economic rationality, individualism, and the view that each person has a particular role in society. He did not develop a general theory of management, but rather emphasized an engineering or mechanistic approach to increase a worker's productivity. Taylor felt that by increasing productivity both the employer and the employee would benefit.

By maximizing the productive efficiency of each worker, scientific management would also maximize the earnings (piece rate) of workers and employers. Hence all conflict between capital and labor would be resolved by the findings of science.[1]

Taylor sought to: (1) develop a science for each element of a person's work; (2) scientifically select, train, teach, and develop the worker; (3) cooperate with workers so all work would be done on scientific principles; and (4) divide responsibility between workers and managers. There was some opposition to Taylor's approach at that time, as managers felt their knowledge was being usurped and the unions felt that its objectives threatened their existence.

At the same time that Frederick Taylor was recording his ideas on management in the United States, Henry Fayol, a leading French industrialist, was developing his general management theory. In fact, he has been described as the father of management theory. Fayol published *Administration Industrielle et Generale* in 1916 in which he defined administration in terms of five primary elements: planning, organization, command, coordination, and control. These elements have come to be seen as the functions of management. Fayol advanced fourteen principles providing the basic foundation for his school of thought. Some of his principles include: (1) division of work, (2) authority commensurate with responsibility, (3) unity of command, (4) unity of direction, and (5) the scalar principle (i.e., the organizational hierarchy).

Although both Taylor and Fayol began developing basic management theory, Mary Parker Follet emphasized the psychological and sociological aspects of management. Management to Follet was a social process and the organization was the social system. She emphasized the acceptance of authority, importance of lateral coordination, and the integration of organizational participants. Perhaps more than anyone else, Mary Parker Follet can be viewed as the link between classical administrative management theorists and the behaviorists.

Max Weber's bureaucratic model was a significant contribution to economic, social, and administrative thought. He traced the changes in political views, discussed their impact upon the growth of capitalism, and examined the effect of industrialization on organizational structure.

1. Frederick Winslow Taylor, "The Principles of Scientific Management," in *Scientific Management* (New York: Harper & Row, 1947), p. 140.

The behavioral model emphasized the psychosocial system and the human aspects of administration. Several forces contributed to the development of this model: (1) heterogeneous operations, (2) diversity of products and objectives, and (3) technological change. At this point the movement shifted from Scientific Management to Management Science, which included the behavioral sciences—psychology, sociology, and anthropology. The behavioral scientists approached management from yet a different perspective. They dealt with human behavior and used a scientific method.[2]

Elton Mayo was one of the first behavioral science researchers in industry. Prior to his work, employees had been considered mechanistic elements in the production system. Mayo and his associates began a study in 1927 in the Hawthorne Plant of the Western Electric Company to determine the effects on output of working conditions, length of working day, frequency and length of rest periods, and other factors relating to the physical environment.

The researchers were astounded when production continued to increase regardless of conditions. Mayo felt that the increased production was a result of the changed social situation of the workers and the different pattern of supervision. Others felt that the recognition given the experimental group (test group) was the main cause of increased productivity. Social and psychological factors were now seen to be important factors in determining productivity. These early human relationists are responsible for developing the basic concern for employees in an organization and the use of the scientific method in studying organizations.

In spite of these contributions, the human relations movement has been criticized as being a basically closed system because it does not address economic, political, or environmental factors.

More recently, management thought has centered on the theories of A.H. Maslow, Douglas M. McGregor, Peter Drucker, and Frederick Hertzberg. Maslow's theory of motivation has strongly influenced concepts in organizational behavior. "His hierarchy of needs directed the emphasis away from the satisfac-

2. "Scientific Method—principles and procedures for the systematic pursuit of knowledge involving the recognition and formulation of a problem, the collection of data through observation and experiment, and the formulation and testing of hypotheses." By permission. From Webster's New Collegiate Dictionary © 1977 by G. & C. Merriam Co., Publishers of the Merriam-Webster Dictionaries.

tion of basic economic and survival needs toward higher level needs of status, social satisfaction, and self-actualization."[3]

McGregor's Theory X and Theory Y advances two views of personnel within an organization:

Theory X: (1) Management is responsible for organizing elements of productive enterprise in the interest of economic trends. (2) Management is the process of directing people's efforts, motivating, controlling, and modifying behavior. (3) People are passive and therefore must be persuaded and coerced—management must get things done through other people.

Theory Y: (1) Management is responsible for organizing elements of productive enterprise in the interest of economic trends. (2) People are not passive but have become so because of organizations. (3) Motivation is present; management's task is to develop motivation by recognizing human characteristics. (4) Management must arrange organizational conditions so that people can achieve their own goals best by directing their own efforts toward organizational objectives.[4]

Drucker has popularized Management by Objectives (MBO), a technique by which managers and their employees sit down and jointly set specific objectives to be accomplished within a certain time frame.[5] Hertzberg advances a two factor theory: Hygiene factors (maintenance) and Motivators.[6] He includes pay, vacations, and working conditions as hygiene factors, and as true motivators he includes achievement, responsibility, job satisfaction, and advancement.

The most recent organizational theory, Organization Development (OD), is a collaborative effort on the part of management and labor to direct the culture of the organization so that individual, group, and organizational goals are accomplished simultaneously. OD utilizes and applies behavioral science principles and practices within an organization in order to effect change. OD is planned, directed change, and functions as a self-renewal process for the organization.

3. Fremont E. Kast and James E. Rosenzweig, *Organization and Management: A Systems Approach* (New York: McGraw-Hill Book Co., 1970), p. 92.

4. Douglas McGregor, *The Human Side of Enterprise* (New York: McGraw-Hill Book Co., 1960), pp. 33-57.

5. Peter F. Drucker, *The Practice of Management* (New York: Harper & Row, 1954), pp. 121-136.

6. Frederick Hertzberg, *Work and the Nature of Man* (Cleveland, Ohio: World Publishing Co., 1966), pp. 72-75.

The birth of any business venture begins with an idea that is transformed into reality. Food service dates back to the days of primitive society when individuals first travelled from their dwellings. The food service industry has always been associated with travel, and the increase in travel during the last thirty to forty years has brought the food service industry to number four rank in the national census on industry sales volume.

Historically, restaurants were started by a Mom and Pop organization. One ran the kitchen and the other waited tables. As the business grew, Mom and Pop had to hire employees to perform some of the functions. As the business grew even larger, Mom and Pop no longer cooked, washed dishes, and waited tables, but found themselves planning, organizing, commanding, coordinating, and controlling the business. Perhaps their lack of training in those areas accounts somewhat for the high rate of failure of restaurants.

. . . For every ten restaurants which open for business in a given month, five will have closed their doors by the end of one year. At the end of five years only two of the original ten will remain in business.[7]

The need for professional management in the industry is vital. The food service industry can no longer operate as it did in the past: the art of managing a food service operation requires professional management with professional skills and professional abilities.

The study of human relations in theory and the practice of good human relations is necessary for the success of a professional manager. This is true for all industries, but in the food service industry it is vital to the *immediate* success of the operation, for in no other industry is the philosophy of management and the attitude of the employees displayed so vividly to the consumer. Don Roth, owner-manager of the Blackhawk Restaurant, Chicago, says:

The two major ingredients of Blackhawk service are the showmanship in presentation, and enthusiasm on the part of the waiter. This involves more than just proper training. The desire to please the customer must come from the top and middle management, and must permeate each department, including the back of the house as well as the dining

7. John W. Stokes, *How to Manage a Restaurant* (Dubuque, Ia.: Wm.C. Brown Company Publishers, 1967), p. 4.

rooms. Any lack of integrity or sincerity on management's part will be felt by the customers, but first noted by our employees.[8]

The preparation of food—especially fine food—is regarded by the chef as a work of art; by the nutritionist as therapy; and by the menu planner and the menu designer as an outlet for creative imagination. The industry permits direct contact with people, which intrigues many food service employees.

The food service industry has always had difficulty in attracting and retaining employees because of the many strains imposed on personnel during busy periods. Typically, the food service employee is of the lowest socioeconomic background; therefore, pay and fringe benefits may be of greater importance to him in order to satisfy his basic needs.

Training as a Means of Promoting Effective Human Relations

Training can provide needed job security. A new employee on the job should be introduced to his immediate supervisor, and his supervisor should introduce him to the job. Care should be taken to instruct supervisors in how to introduce the job to the new employee since first impressions are very meaningful. The supervisor should renew the new employee's job description at this time. Job descriptions must be accurate as they can be as binding on management as on the employee.

The training of a food service employee should be done, systematically, by the most qualified individuals. On-the-job training is preferable to training *only* during slack periods, but this does not mean that slack periods should not be used to the trainer's advantage. Proper steps must be followed in training all personnel. (1) *Prepare the trainee* to learn, make him feel at ease, and prepare the learning environment. (2) *Make the presentation* as clear and as brief as possible. (3) *Allow the trainee to perform* under careful supervision. Once these three processes are accomplished a (4) *follow-up* should be planned. During the follow-up phase, emphasis should be placed on the proper method to insure that the trainee has not picked up any bad habits. This training method can be utilized for dining room employees as well as kitchen employees.

8. Don Roth, "Restaurant Merchandising," *The Cornell Hotel and Restaurant Administration Quarterly* 13, no. 4 (February 1973), p. 91.

In training dining room personnel, the teacher has an enviable position. Not only will prompt and personal service make the restaurant look good, but an effective waiter/waitress will also earn more in tips. Proper training in sales techniques (i.e., selling wines, desserts, and beverages) increases the check average as well as the waiter's/waitresses' tips. It behooves both management and labor to increase sales. (See chapter 7.) There are several objectives to training: (1) to broaden an individual's knowledge, (2) to improve his skill, and (3) to change his attitude. (A change in attitude usually follows when one is more knowledgeable and proficient in one's job.) Yet it is most important for the manager or trainer to know what is expected to be accomplished before setting up elaborate training programs.

A positive method of approaching employee relations is for the manager to consciously determine his goals and objectives. The objectives should include the importance of employee involvement and understanding to the success of the business.

Participative Management

Although participative management should be practiced to the furthest extent possible, performance standards must be set. An effort should be made so functional and behavioral standards are clearly definable. Dr. Fritz Redl uses an analogy in children's psychology that states

. . . Behavior falls into three color zones—green, yellow, and red. The green area consists of behavior that is wanted and sanctioned, the area where "yes" is given freely and graciously. The yellow zone includes behavior that is not sanctioned but tolerated for specific reasons. . . . The red zone covers conduct that cannot be tolerated at all and must be stopped.[9]

Richard Wienmann says that in a thousand arbitration cases, many disciplinary action cases are lost by management because of the failure to communicate management's policies and intentions to its employees with sufficient clarity, or because management has been inconsistent in its application with regard to lateness, absence, smoking, drinking, or the like.

People working in restaurants form social organizations, and existing relationships and the standing of individuals in the orga-

9. Dr. Haim G. Ginott, *Between Parent and Child* (New York: Avon Books, 1969), p. 114.

Management

nization have a very important bearing on customer service and efficiency, on satisfaction, and on the morale of both workers and supervisors. Conflict can result when lower status employees (dining room attendants, for example) ask higher status employees (cooks) to perform certain functions.

So far this discussion has centered around the improvement of employee relations at the functional level. At this point something must be said about the managerial level. To ensure an orderly succession of management, the modern business enterprise needs to recruit the ablest, best educated, and most dedicated men. Some companies feel that extensive management training may invite raids from other companies, and, therefore, that they cannot afford investment for executive development. But the industry can no longer tolerate this feeling; progressive companies must build an adequate base for replacement as vacancies are created by retirement, promotion, and expansion. To delay creates instability in the organization and the possible demise of the business.

The college graduate in modern food service is being sought more and more. Historically, very few formally educated people have gone into food service, but the last fifteen years have shown a tremendous growth in hotel and restaurant schools. The industry is also in search of professional managers, and this places the college graduate in food service in great demand. Many companies feel the pressure of hiring college men and women for their company. Many, however, do not know how to cope with this new phenomenon, which, unfortunately, has led to many graduates leaving the service industries. College graduates anticipate a participative environment in the work world. They bring in fresh approaches, but many managers do not listen to their ideas because of the college graduate's lack of experience.

Recent experiments have been conducted by several corporations in search of professional food service personnel. These corporations place college juniors and seniors in supervisory positions, which gives the corporation an opportunity to see how these individuals would fare in an operational environment. It also gives the students an opportunity to see the corporation and to decide whether they, in turn, would want to work there. Some corporations have students occasionally meet with vice-presidents of the corporation, and the students are allowed to brainstorm on solving problems they have noticed. These brainstorming sessions give top management the opportunity to get a composite, first-hand view of the workings of operations and to gather valuable information. The students obviously were spouting ideas they had learned in the classroom and playing on the knowledge given them by a host of professors.

Loyalty must be *earned* by the company. The company cannot demand it. If top management uses participative management, especially with the college graduate, both the company and the new manager will gain from this experience. The college graduate will then empathize with top management and the organization, and with empathy comes company loyalty. The college graduate has an intense desire to succeed, since he has been in an academic environment for four or more years and is anxious to try his wares in the real world.

Dr. William P. Fisher, past executive vice-president of the National Restaurant Association, in discussing the industry's recruiting problem and the National Restaurant Associations' (NRA) Institute for Certification of Job Skills and Training, said, "The industry is paying more attention to making entry jobs part of a career progression to improve position and pay better wages."

Major Causes of Restaurant Failure

—Unfriendly personnel
—Poor service/disorganization
—Poor food
—Excessive prices (with decreasing value to the guest and profits to the owner)

Unfriendly personnel reflects the management's attitude generally. Friendly personnel are not overfamiliar with guests; they are courteous.

If one has an employee in the kitchen who is upset with the manager, but continues to put out a good product, the job continues to be done. But what happens if the service person on the floor is upset with management? He is management's contact with the guest. If he is upset, this attitude is *directly* conveyed to the guest. Additionally, if management is not responsive to guest needs, this attitude too can be conveyed to the guest through the service person.

Managers must maintain a good relationship with their service employees, but this should not be confused with poor discipline. Good discipline creates a smooth running operation. Management's attitude in the service industries directly affects the success or failure of the business.

Strains on the Service Staff

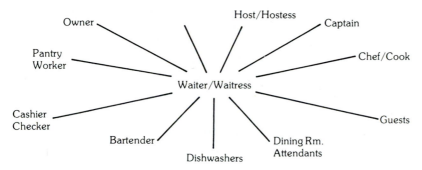

It may appear that service is an easy job. The cook thinks the waiter has nice working conditions while he or she sweats over a hot range or broiler. The dishwashers think the service person has a "fat" job. The bartender cannot understand why the waiter/waitress cannot remember the drinks. The cashier or the checker needs the "dupe" before the food goes out the door. The dining room attendant has enough to do, so the waitress cannot depend on him for help. Management thinks she should be able to handle fifty guests because "they are only having sandwiches." The host/hostess is yelling for tables to be set because guests are breaking down the door, and the manager wonders why Susie or Harry is not smiling at his/her guests.

The difficulty in service is not in the particular tasks that must be performed (although the tasks are not simple). The difficulty is in the number of people that the service person must satisfy. Each person places a different demand on the service person which pulls the service person in different directions, and in the face of it all, the service person is supposed to smile!

Personal Characteristics of the Successful Service Manager

How can the manager establish a good rapport with service personnel? Managers must respect the position of the service person. In the United States a restaurant waiter ranks approximately eightieth (lowest ten) of ninety occupations rated for prestige. Although the restaurant manager cannot change the prestige ratings of the people of the United States, he must understand and empathize with the position of his service employees. This prestige rating is quite different in Europe. A waiter in a fine establishment is respected, and the job is prestigious.

The following guidelines may be used when dealing with people in general, however, the references made here are specifically intended to help the manager in his relations with his service staff.

When beginning a conversation with a waiter or waitress, begin in a friendly manner. This sets the mood of the conversation, and even if harsher words follow, they will be taken better if the individual feels you are sincere. Try to avoid a demeaning tone, and say things that will be agreeable to the person (as much as possible). This is not to imply that one should use ridiculous questions, such as "Well, Jan, wouldn't you like to make more tips?" This in itself belittles the individual.

Next, if at all possible, let your staff use their own ideas to implement service. However, do take caution here as their ideas must be consistent with the establishment's standards. A feeling of trust results when certain assignments are controlled by the service group. Station rotation, side duties, as well as scheduling, could be accomplished by the service staff. This would take some of the responsibility away from management without affecting the flow or efficiency of the operation.

Be sympathetic to others' problems and ideas and try to see things from their perspective. This idea is especially important when handling guest complaints, and management should always make the attempt to let the guest think he is right. However, a manager should never belittle the service person, or embarrass him in the guest's presence. Management should defend service personnel whenever possible, but not in front of the guest. The manager should make his support clear in PRIVATE to the waiter/waitress as well as in general and reinforce this idea after specific incidents. Remember that whatever an individual's feelings are, they are his and he is proud of them. Listen, and attempt to see his point of view.

Above all, if someone has an idea, do not tell him that he is wrong. This immediately places the individual on the defensive and the remainder of the discussion is apt to be negative. Consider the idea, weigh its relative merits; and if you disagree, do not tell the person. Present *your* idea by picking up on one of his ideas that you find agreeable and adding to it. If you find that you are wrong during a discussion, admit it and admit it quickly. Your staff will respect you for it and know that you are sincere. Do not pretend to know everything.

Conclusion

Management's task is to get the job done with and through other people. Hopefully, management can get the job done through others because the others enjoy doing their work. Management's job is to help people enjoy their work and to provide leadership and guidance. In order to best accomplish this, a manager must know his staff personally, and realize the difficulty of the job. He or she must know where these individuals are in society and must possess the personal leadership characteristics to motivate the service staff in a positive way. Doing so will cure one, and perhaps two, of the major causes of restaurant failure: unfriendly personnel and poor service. It will directly effect the success of the business.

Questions

1. What were the two primary ideas that the early human relationists had, and how do they apply to the hospitality (service) industry?
2. What are the major causes of restaurant failure?
3. What is meant by "Strains on the Service Staff"?
4. List five personal characteristics the successful service manager should possess and discuss each one.

Chapter 3

The Personnel Function in Service Management

Dining Room Organization

A food service establishment depends upon the performance of the employees in order for the organization to function effectively. The formal and informal organizations that are formed in the work environment strongly influence this effectiveness. These organizations form the psychosocial make-up, which directs the establishment or the larger organization toward specific goal accomplishment. A well-designed, formal organization will take into account the informal organization, and channel these two organizations, as well as individual goals, to maximize productivity.

The organizational structure is a depiction of the lines of communication within the establishment. In other words, in viewing the organizational chart, one should be able to locate himself and trace the hierarchy to the top manager (up the chart) and down the chart to the lowest level within the organization. These lines also indicate that responsibility *commensurate with authority* should flow down the chart to the lowest competent level, and correspondingly information about job or task accomplishment should flow up the chart.

The objective of the organization is to establish the structure required to implement the goals of the organization and to facilitate communications. There are two lines of development in classical organization thought:

1. Frederick Taylor—scientific management
2. Luther Gulick and Lyndall Urwick—administrative management

Taylor's idea is functional (i.e., he divides the organization into functions) and fits the person to the machines (i.e., people are seen as adjuncts to the machines in the performance of routine tasks). He analyzed the interaction between the characteristics of humans and the social and task environments created by the organization and, among other things, proposed that for efficient work management must: (1) find the best way, (2) provide monetary incentive, and (3) use functional foremen.

Gulick and Urwick thought along the lines of giving the organization a purpose and identifying the unit tasks necessary for that purpose. They felt that: (1) tasks should be grouped into jobs (productive, service, coordinative, and supervisory), (2) jobs should then be grouped into administrative units, (3) units should be grouped into larger units, and (4) top-level departments should be established. Gulick and Urwick also disregarded human behavior in the organization and viewed members as inert instruments performing assigned tasks and as givens rather than variables.

Both classical organizational theories, however, dissolve when placed in practice. So where does this leave the restaurant operator, or dining room supervisor, who is trying to organize his department for effective goal accomplishment? A combination of the two classical thoughts can serve as a framework from which one can begin to organize personnel in a dining room.

1. Find the best possible way (most efficient and most effective) to accomplish each task.
2. Group tasks into jobs so that the individuals accomplishing these tasks (i.e., the particular job description) can perform them efficiently and effectively.
3. Place a person (functional foreman) in charge of the various jobs.

In order to sketch the organization of a formal dining room, some definitions must be clarified. A comparison of the European and American terminology must also be identified.

American Terminology	French Terminology
Food and Beverage Manager	Maître d'Hôtel
Director of Service	Chef de Service
Wine Steward	Chef de Vin/Chef Sommelier
Headwaiter	Chef de Salle
Captain	Chef d' Etage
Waiter	Chef de rang/Demi chef de rang
Bus Boy (dining room attendant)	Commis de rang/Apprentice

The comparison of dining room terminologies is confused by modern meanings of the same terms. With the exception of *Maître d'Hôtel, Sommelier, Chef de rang* and *Commis de rang*, the other terms are rarely used; and the term *Maître d'Hôtel* or *Maitre d'* is used synonomously with Director of Service, Headwaiter, or Host, depending upon his tasks or duties. A *Chef de rang* is synonomous with Captain, and a *Commis de rang* may be a waiter *or* a dining room attendant.

In a discussion of the classical dining room staff, all reference is made to males. This is quite antiquated, however, and in this text the term "host" will always include the female title—hostess. This title and position will reflect the supervisory duties of a person responsible for service (e.g., employee scheduling, etc.) in the dining room (see job description for Director of Service in chapter 8, which may also encompass the job of host/hostess*). The host or hostess may report to or could be synonymous with a dining room manager, service director or assistant restaurant manager, all of whom in turn report to the restaurant manager (depending upon the size of the establishment). "Captain" is a suitable title for both males and females, and she may be responsible for a section of the dining room or responsible for the service of two waiters. "Waiter" or "waitress" will be used interchangeably and reference to one sex will always include references to the other. "Dining room attendant" is the standard United States Government (nonsexist) terminology for what was known previously as a bus boy.

*Some establishments utilize young, inexperienced, perhaps nice-looking individuals to serve as hosts or hostesses to seat guests. This arrangement can work well. It is important to realize that someone else *in authority* must be at the entrance, greeting guests, assigning tables, and handling guest complaints. This is a most demanding and difficult task, and it should not be left to one who is not capable of shouldering this responsibility.

Dining Room Organization Chart for Formal A La Carte Service

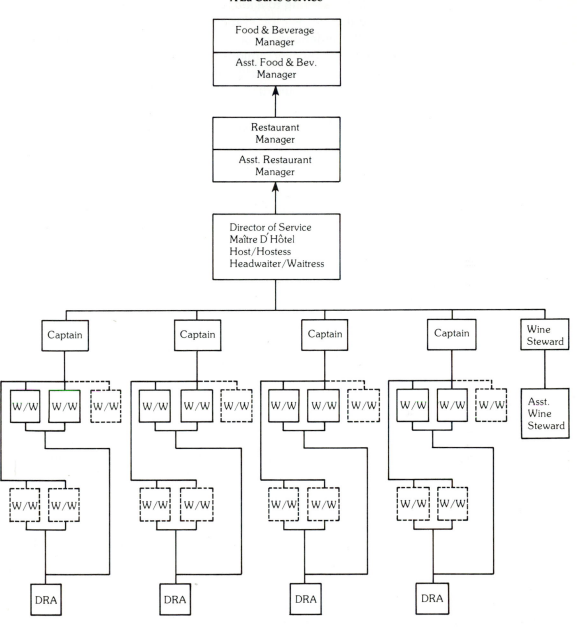

W/W—Waiter/Waitress
DRA—Dining Room Attendant

Figure 1.1

It is important to emphasize that these titles are standard terminology referring to a *job,* and a job is a cluster of tasks used to define the job. Although there are tasks that *are* used to define jobs, the independent operator should not feel bound by terminology. However, unions and some government regulations may require more specific information for classifying the jobs; and under these jurisdictions, the operator must comply.

As can be seen, lines of *authority commensurate with responsibility* flow down the chart, while formal channels of communication follow the lines *up and down the chart.* A dining room attendant may be able to service up to four waiters, and, therefore, there are four lines drawn to the dining room attendant. However, one captain can service only two, or at best three, waitresses. For this reason, the third waiter from the captain is depicted with a dotted line. If classical management principles are adhered to, eight to ten persons at maximum is the *span of control* for one person to supervise at the skill level (in this case the hostess). Also each person on the chart should report and is responsible to only one supervisor. This principle is termed *unity of command.* Ideally, the host could pass instructions only to the captains and they, in turn, down the line. This is most difficult if not impossible to accomplish in an a la carte dining room as each person takes direct instruction from the hostess.

Above or beyond the principles of unity of command, span of control, authority commensurate with responsibility, etc., a manager must realize that the organization is comprised of many different elements. For one to assume that the organization chart gives her license to dictate to the staff is a false assumption. It is

A Typical Banquet Organization Chart

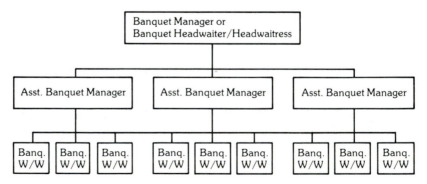

Figure 1.2 A typical banquet organization chart

Management

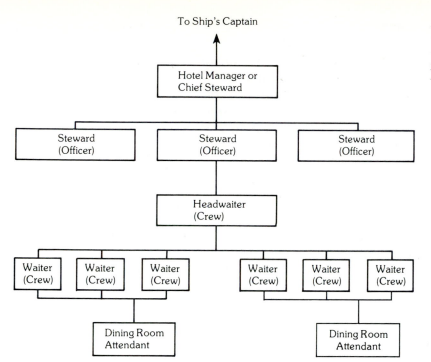

To Ship's Captain

Hotel Manager or
Chief Steward

Steward
(Officer)

Steward
(Officer)

Steward
(Officer)

Headwaiter
(Crew)

Waiter
(Crew)

Waiter
(Crew)

Waiter
(Crew)

Waiter
(Crew)

Waiter
(Crew)

Waiter
(Crew)

Dining Room
Attendant

Dining Room
Attendant

Figure 1.3 Dining room organization aboard the luxury liner m/s Sagafjord—Norwegian American Line

important that a manager work with her employees and provide leadership so that the group accomplishes the organization's goals, the group's goals, *and* the individual's goals.

Managing people can be compared to trying to move a rope or a chain: *pushing* a rope or chain will net you little, if any, results, while *pulling* the rope or chain will be much more effective.

Recruiting and Selecting Service Employees

In some labor markets it is most difficult to recruit waiters and waitresses, while in other labor markets it is quite easy. For example, it is difficult to find adequate service personnel in Washington, D.C.; while in a small town with a large university, finding service personnel may be very simple. In the absence of labor unions who supply service personnel, many reference sources suggest that by placing notices in local newspapers, an operator would attract inquiries for the jobs advertised. Yet another reputable source indicates that low skilled employees (all service personnel do not fit into this category) seldom read newspapers, and that advertisements placed in newspapers in a commercial environment, as compared to a college town, are, for the most part, useless.

In any case, the best way to attract service personnel, as well as other restaurant personnel, is by word-of-mouth. All employees in the establishment should be made aware of job openings. Employees may want to transfer to other departments in order to increase their career possibilities (which could decrease turnover rate); or they may have friends or relatives who may be well qualified for the jobs. This approach also may help the workers accept the new employee. One operator actually "sets-up-shop" on a street corner in a high unemployment area in order to attract prospective employees; and perhaps the best employees (and sometimes the greatest number of applicants) simply come to the establishment (walk-ins) and ask for a job.

No one expressing an interest in working should be turned away. The more applications that are accepted and kept on file, the greater is the probability of finding a qualified or motivated worker. The establishment should have a standard procedure for accepting and encouraging job applicants, and this procedure *must comply* with Equal Employment Opportunity Commission (EEOC) considerations and requirements. When employee turnover in general is as high as it is in the industry, and when good employees are so hard to find for the hospitality industry, it pays to have a pool of applicants who are waiting to be hired, lest individuals be hired hastily off the streets. In most operations, a small, unobtrusive sign may be posted inviting applications from the general public as guests may also be a good labor source. "The Management of 'Richard's' welcomes anyone interested in applying for employment." However, an elite restaurant could not attract employees from its clientele. The obtrusive and obnoxious "Help Wanted" sign posted (usually permanently) in an establishment's window hardly attracts quality applicants, and can serve as a deterent for guests. "I'll probably get poor food or poor service if they are short of help."

There are advantages to hiring inexperienced or untrained waiters and waitresses. They arrive with no preconceived notions about the nature of the work, and their behavior can be shaped more easily. However an effective training program is required, which has many benefits over letting the operation run "as is."

Additional sources include radio and television, which are ideal for locating part-time employees. One whose children have started school may be looking for additional income or a change in life-style. It would be wise to advertise over radio and TV *at the exact time you need* the part-time help. Employment agencies, both public and private, are also sources; however, these applicants may need to be screened, depending upon the reputation of the employment agency. Organizations for the handicapped, military organizations, as well as schools and colleges are also sources for job applicants. With the advent and increase of technical schools and community colleges, it is surprising that more operators do not take advantage of these sources, which support the industry's efforts by providing well-motivated, well-trained employees.

Minimum requirements for the job in the form of job specifications must be established, but *desirable* qualifications should also be specified. (Precaution must be taken with those who are too well qualified for the job; they may take the job only temporarily and move on to better things when openings occur.)

Dr. Robert McMurry suggests some desirable qualifications for a good waitress:

1. Good health and physical stamina; the ability to work long hours on one's feet under conditions that call for a high energy level.
2. Higher than average drive; waitressing is not for the lazy or lethargic.
3. Pleasant physical appearance; neatness and freedom from obvious blemishes are especially important.
4. Inherent friendliness and courtesy; these traits are the product of a lifetime of personality development, contributed to by family relations, past successes and failures, and physical condition.
5. A need for money; a waitress who must support a family or pay off debts will be motivated to work hard.
6. Self-confidence and self-reliance; a waitress must project a competent exterior, and impress both the customer and other personnel as capable of taking care of herself in any situation.
7. Relative freedom from poor habits, such as overdrinking, causing friction with customers, being chronically late, or avoiding side work.[1]

1. Donald E. Lundberg and James P. Armatas, *The Management of People in Hotels, Restaurants, and Clubs,* 3rd ed. (Dubuque, Ia.: Wm. C. Brown Company Publishers, 1974), p. 105.

Dr. Ward Jenssen, a psychologist and management consultant, designed a test for waitress applicants for Van de Kamp Restaurants and found four key factors for successful job performance: (1) attention to detail, (2) speed of work, (3) effect on coworkers, and (4) customer service.[2]

Outline for a Job Specification

Job Title: _____

   A. *Age:*
   B. *Family Status:*
   C. *Education:*
   D. *Job Knowledge:*
   E. *Character:*
   F. *Judgment:*
   G. *Ingenuity and Initiative:*
   H. *Mental Ability:*
   I. *Physical Requirements:*
   J. *Skill:*
   K. *Training and/or Experience:*
       Minimum Required:
       Desired:
   L. *Personality Traits:*
   M. *Personal Appearance:*
   N. *Motivations:*

Job specifications for all jobs in the industry can be developed from *The Dictionary of Occupational Titles* (DOT) and decoded by using *The Handbook for Analyzing Jobs.* The DOT can be found in any school or public library, and the *Handbook* may be purchased from the Superintendent of Documents for $2.50.

The recruiting effort should continually be evaluated to determine which sources yield the best employees and which sources do not. The following factors, among other things, can be used to measure employee effectiveness: test and interview scores, training program performance, pay, performance appraisal (on-the-job), promotion, turnover, absenteeism, and accident rates.

After the job application has been analyzed, the applicant should be given an interview. All too often too little time is spent

2. Peter Dukas and Donald E. Lundberg, *How to Operate a Restaurant* (New York: Ahrens Publishing Company, 1960), p. 162.

training supervisors in techniques for interviewing, and too much is spent on various psychological tests. The tests provide excellent background information, but the individual responsible for the employee's performance should have final say as to the hiring of the individual after an interview.

Interview Techniques

Three widely accepted reasons for interviewing are: (1) to get information (attitudes, feelings, personality, general temperament, appearance, speech patterns, etc.); (2) to give information (i.e., to sell the job and the establishment); and (3) to make a friend (the applicant may become an employee or a guest).

The interview should be viewed as a two-way process, as each of the participants has something to sell. Many interviewers use their roles to intimidate the applicant and to delve further than necessary into the applicant's life. This attitude on the part of the interviewer can ruin the reputation of the business; and if the applicant is hired, there may be resentment towards the supervisor if he or she is the person who conducted the interview.

When interviewing prospective employees, the environment should be as pleasant as possible; this may be the interviewee's first impression of the establishment. If possible, the room should not suggest intimacy although privacy is required. It should be well lighted, adequately furnished, and large enough for ease of movement. The interviewer should prepare for the interview by becoming familiar with the applicant's employment application, as well as with the specifications for the job or jobs for which the person may be interviewing. The interview should be held at a time convenient for both, and ample time should be allowed for each interview. A short interview made in haste in order to "fill the squares" may result in short-term employment, which wastes the establishment's time and money.

Tips on Interviewing

1. Have a plan or pattern for the interview.
2. Put the interviewee at ease.
3. Be attentive and interested in what the applicant has to say.
4. Allow ample opportunity for the interviewee to respond to your questions and to volunteer information.

5. Avoid discriminatory remarks (regarding race, color, religion, sex, or nationality).
6. Take as few notes as possible during the interview.
7. Do not interrupt. Make use of *how, why, when, what, where, who;* and *for example, for instance, in what way;* do not be afraid to probe.
8. Acknowledge the applicant's ideas; "uh-huh," "yes," "and what else can you add to that?"
9. Use summaries and do not be judgmental.
10. Before you close the interview, let the applicant ask you any questions he wishes.
11. Immediately after the interview, record your impressions on an interview response sheet.

Interviewed by _____   Date _____

Remarks _____

Neatness_____   Character_____

Personality _____   Ability _____

Position _____   Reporting Date _____

Salary or Wage _____

After the interview and before hiring, there are several subtle things one can do to test the suitability of one applying for a service job in a restaurant. Before conducting the interview, invite the applicant to have a seat in the dining room and to order whatever he would like. Notice where he sits—does he pick a table and a seat where he can see what's going on? Or ask the interviewee, "Were you born happy?" If the applicant smiles, the person probably is well-suited as a waiter, has a sense of humor, and will be pleasant with guests. One restaurant operator asks the applicant to follow him somewhere. He intentionally walks fast; if the applicant keeps up, he is more apt to be alert and fast on his feet. Another operator is especially aware of body odors. If applicants have an odor on the interview, he assumes they will have an odor on the job.[3]

3. Dukas and Lundberg, *How to Operate a Restaurant*, pp. 160-61.

Dr. Robert Murray suggests using a series of questions relating to the factors listed below in selecting waitresses. (He also estimates that ten people should be interviewed in order to get one good waitress.)

1. Willingness to work the hours and under the conditions required by the job.
2. Acceptability of wages and benefits to the candidate.
3. Willingness to take a physical exam.
4. Time required getting to and from work (some surveys show anyone living more than an hour from the place of work is unsuitable).
5. Length of time in the community (to determine whether or not the candidate is a wanderer).
6. Number of preschool children (more than one makes it almost impossible for success on the job without unusual arrangements).
7. Vocational stability (number of jobs held in the last year).[4]

Eugene Laitala conducted research on 2,000 waitresses who were college students working in resorts and found that:

1. Girls under eighteen were not successful as waitresses in one-third of the cases.
2. Those who came from cities with populations over 100,000 did not work out in forty percent of the cases.
3. Women over twenty-two, who had finished college and were on their "last fling," were problems in one-third of the cases.
4. Those away from home for the first time were a greater problem than those who had lived on the campus.[5]

Interviewing is a difficult task. Perhaps this short vignette will highlight how perceptive one must be when conducting interviews.

. . . Consider the unskilled inner-city black looking for a job. His handling of time and space alone is sufficiently different from the white middle-class pattern to create great misunderstandings on both sides. The black is told to appear for a job interview at a certain time. He arrives late. The white interviewer concludes from his tardy arrival that the

4. Lundberg and Armatas, *The Management of People*, p. 105.
5. Ibid., p. 107.

black is irresponsible and not really interested in the job. What the interviewer doesn't know is that the black time system (often referred to by blacks as C.P.T.—colored people's time) isn't the same as that of whites. . . .

The black job applicant, having arrived late for his interview, may further antagonize the white interviewer by his posture and his eye behavior. Perhaps he slouches and avoids looking at the interviewer; to him, this is playing it cool. To the interviewer, however, he may well look shifty and sound uninterested. The interviewer has failed to notice the actual signs of interest and eagerness in the black's behavior, such as the subtle shift in the quality of the voice—a gentle and tentative excitement—an almost imperceptible change in the cast of the eyes and a relaxing of the jaw muscles.[6]

Conducting Reference Checks

The most convenient method of conducting a reference check is by the telephone. It is preferable to talk directly to three previous employers if possible or all supervisors during the last few years, as well as to personal references. Telephone references are easier to record for the person collecting the information as well as for the person giving information. Additionally, those giving information by phone are apt to give a more candid response than if they were to write the information via correspondence. The cost of the phone call is small in comparison to the time invested in the hiring process or the costs incurred if the employee is not suitable. Some questions that can be asked of previous employers include: name of employer, job title, tasks performed, pay, length and dates of employment, reasons for leaving, quality and quantity of work, absenteeism and punctuality, accidents, personal characteristics, strengths, weaknesses, overall effectiveness, would you rehire? if not, why not? The police in the cities where the applicant lives can give a record of convictions, if any. Credit reporting agencies may also be used, but one must be knowledgeable of the provisions of the Fair Conduct Reporting Act. A full listing of the provisions is available from a local credit reporting agency.

6. Edward T. Hall and Mildred Reed Hall, "The Sounds of Silence," in *Conformity and Conflict: Readings in Cultural Anthropology,* ed. by James P. Spradley and David W. McCurdy (Boston: Little, Brown and Company, 1977), p. 141. Originally appeared in *Playboy Magazine;* © 1971 by *Playboy.*

1. Notify the employee within three days after ordering the investigation that a report will be made that will include information about her character as well as her mode of living.
2. If the applicant is denied employment on the basis of the information supplied by the agency, the applicant must be notified, and the name and address of the agency making the report must be given.

Using the knowledge gleaned from the employment application, the personal interview and the reference checks, the supervisor is now in a position to decide which applicant to choose, or whether or not to hire a particular applicant under consideration.

It is a good idea to hire employees on probation whenever possible. The importance of the job or the level at which the person was hired will determine the length of the probationary period. For example, a dining room hostess may require a one- or two-month probationary period, while an upper level management position may require a six-month probationary period. Dining room attendants would require three or four weeks. In this amount of time, the employee's supervisors should be able to determine whether the new employee with required training is capable of handling the job.

Wages and Salaries

Any discussion of wages and salaries for tipped employees would doubtless be outdated in a very short time as the United States Congress is considering abolishing tip credit.[7] Presently, employers are allowed to pay only one-half of the minimum wage to employees who receive more than twenty dollars per month in tips. This provision has been most helpful to restaurant operators, employees, and guests. For the restaurant operator, labor costs, which typically run quite high, can be kept under control. Wages paid to service employees are approximately ten percent of sales for the restaurants surveyed by Laventhol and Horwath; this cost would be increased considerably if Congress were to abolish tip credit. The alternative would be to increase menu prices accordingly, which would reduce the number of

7. An excellent discussion of wage and salary administration can be found in chapter 14 of Lundberg and Armatas, *The Management of People.*

people eating out in food service establishments. For the employee, all earnings will be reported, which will decrease his disposable income; the job will be less desirable for this reason, as well as for the fact that the money will not come in as fast (i.e., instead of daily cash payments, the employee will receive a weekly or biweekly payment). Employers will somehow have to make up this difference, which will further erode profits, increase menu prices, and decrease the number of people eating out. For the guests, the abolishment of tip credit will increase the price they must pay, as well as decrease the amount of service they receive. Despite modern management thought, a tip, or the anticipation of receiving tips, motivates service employees. Additionally, the guest may feel that he has less control over the waiter.

The government has legislation that will decrease the amount of tip credit an employer may claim for tipped employees. In 1979 the minimum wage will be $2.90; in 1980 it will rise to $3.10; and $3.35 in 1981. In 1979 tip credit will be reduced from fifty percent to forty-five percent, and in 1980 tip credit will drop to forty percent of the minimum hourly rate. As a result of these actions, minimum wages for a full-time employee will increase forty-five percent over the next few years, while pay for waiters, waitresses, and other tipped employees will rise seventy-five percent in this same period. This scheduled reduction in tip credit allowance that begins in 1979 will add 100 to 250 million dollars to restaurant payroll expense each year throughout the industry. The impact of this legislation is overwhelming.

The hospitality industry has historically combined low wages and salaries with long hours. Traditionally, entry level positions have been filled by immigrants and minority groups who were happy to fill these positions. Because of various restrictions on immigration, laws restricting young people from working, and government compensations, this situation is changing rapidly. Wages will have to move upward.

Employees are usually satisfied with the absolute amount of pay they receive if the job provides a sense of achievement and satisfaction for the work performed. The worker's demands vary with the individual's expectation, life-style, social background, and financial obligations, and an employee may not be satisfied or motivated to do a good job unless he or she feels the wage or salary is equitable. The major source for discontent, however, is comparative pay—"how much is Fred (in my establishment) making for equal work?" or how much does Mary, who works across town in the same job make?"

Since the anticipation of getting paid has a greater motivating force than the pay itself, regular increases in pay are helpful, but should be related, whenever possible, to the employee's performance. Ideally, an effective employee should see that effective performance is rewarded, while poor performance is not rewarded.

In the absence of minimum wages enforced by federal or state governments or labor unions, wages in the hospitality industry are low. Across the board enforcement may be helpful for both employers and employees. For employers it will set standards, while raising employees' standards of living. Difficulties arise, however, when only selective establishments, such as those grossing more than $275,000, are affected. The small operator is allowed to pay a lower rate for equal work than the chain or affiliated operator. Chains enjoy other economies of scale,[8] but the independent restaurateur operating in a large hotel may not receive either of these advantages.

The tip credit legislation could drastically and negatively affect the industry (depending upon final form and degree of enforcement), while minimum wage legislation, if applied across the board, may cause the operator to pass the increase to the guests. The industry as a whole stands to gain as the standard of living and status for each employee, many of whom are disadvantaged, can be elevated.

On the other side of the picture, as wages and salaries in general in the United States have risen, so has productivity (i.e., the contribution one employee makes towards sales). In the labor-intensive food service industry, productivity has not kept pace with the rise in wages. The food service operator must investigate new methods for decreasing payroll costs by increasing productivity. Layout and design, equipment, menu design, and employee scheduling will become critical factors for keeping costs in line.

8. An economic term used to describe advantageous (quantity) buying power or combination of functions (e.g., accounting, advertising, etc.).

Pooling Tips

Some operations pool tips, a practice that has both pros and cons. Each employee is given points that are determined by the function of his job. For example, the maître d'hôtel and chef may receive four points, the first cook or sous chef and captains may receive three points, and the waiters and cooks two points, and the dining room attendants and cook's assistants one point. All tips are totalled for the shift, and this total is divided by the total number of points. The money is then awarded on the number of points each employee has. Although all operations do not include production employees, some restaurants do. In some restaurants one point on a good evening may be worth $25 or $35!

This system has an advantage when employee turnover is very low, promotions come from within the organization, the management enjoys a good working relationship with the staff, and the staff works well together. The disadvantage to pooling tips is that it may reduce individual incentive. The workhorse does not feel that she is being adequately compensated, while the loafer is reaping benefits from the efforts of her coworkers.

Performance Appraisal (Rating Systems)

It is difficult to limit a discussion of performance appraisal strictly to service employees, yet it is important to do so because service employees enjoy a unique and pivotal job. A service employee cannot be evaluated strictly on his relations with guests, or strictly on his relations with other employees, or strictly on his relations with his supervisors. He must be rated on all factors. As a result, standard rating forms are inadequate for rating waiters, waitresses, captains, or dining room attendants.

Rating employees should be accomplished with as much objectivity as possible. Rating, in and of itself, is always biased or subjective, as it is the rater's perception of the ratee that is being recorded. Rating employees, however, offers a tool by which management can communicate with employees about their performance in specific job functions. Some accuse rating systems of producing resentment on the part of the ratee. Although this may be true, many employers would agree that communicating to the employee about poor or excellent performance is preferable to keeping things in the dark. The employee is being rated anyway, whether in the supervisor's mind or on paper.

The job description (i.e., a complete job description listing all tasks and responsibilities) should be both the basis for training and for any rating system. The rating form or procedure should be simple enough so that the employee can understand the basis for the rating. The various factors may be weighed, since some factors may be more important than others.

Types of Rating Scales. There are various types of rating systems against which an employee's performance may be measured.

Critical Incident research is being concluded that will establish, as much as possible, an objective employee rating system.[9] In contrast to an absolute rating system, in which arbitrary values are assigned to task accomplishment, the critical incident rating system describes specifically an employee's behavior in a specific incident in several categories and at different levels of effectiveness. Although the rater can subvert the objectivity of this system, the opportunity is available for her to objectively evaluate an employee.

Mark this form where the employee being evaluated has performed. When taking an order this particular waiter/waitress:

1	2	3	4	5	6	7	8
Does not smile; stands in one place while taking the order for the entire table.			Smiles and stands in one place while taking the order for the entire table.		Smiles and walks around the table speaking individually to each guest.		

Perhaps fifty of this type question in various categories would be asked for each employee.

Absolute Rating Scale—an arbitrary value assigned to a trait or behavior.

1	2	3	4	5	6	7	8
Dislikes Work				Shows Interest		Shows intense enthusiasm and interest in all work.	

This system is very susceptible to subjective ratings since a definition of the individual factors is vague.

Ranking is another system used within the industry to evaluate employee performance. Individuals are ranked and may be assigned points for their particular position in the ranking. It is most difficult to measure the real effects of this type of rating

9. This research has been done by the author.

system, and it does not allow for effective employee counseling. An additional disadvantage to the ranking system is that many good employees are rewarded insufficiently.

The following form is helpful for rating service employees. The person closest to the individual's job should complete the rating form. It has been found that as a person rises within an organization, he loses touch with the specific aspects of a job. In a large dining room the captains may be called on to rate waiters. A better system allows a second level supervisor to focus his evaluation of an employee for a given day, spreading his evaluations out over the course of a year. He only needs to evaluate one person per day. This accumulated rating system will provide a broader overview of an individual's performance evaluation as compared to a point-in-time evaluation. The total can be transferred and recorded on the employee's permanent record, and the tally sheet (Service Manager's Rating Sheet) can be destroyed.

The following categories outline the areas for which service employees can be held accountable:

Appearance—neat and in good taste, tidy, clean.

Accuracy—correctness of service procedures whenever possible.

Quantity of Work—amount of service given during meal as well as amount of guests the individual could efficiently serve.

Dependability—punctuality, attendance, ability to perform required tasks with a minimum of supervision.

Cooperation (employees)—willingness to work with fellow employees; sociability and warmth to fellow employees and supervisors.

Courtesy (guests)—sociability, warmth, and attention given to guests.

Initiative—demonstrates the ability to be a self-starter.

Judgment—ability to make proper decisions.

Stability—ability to withstand pressure and remain calm under crisis.

Housekeeping and Sanitation—ability to keep his/her station and tray orderly and clean; removes dirty trays regularly; follows rules of sanitation.

Service Manager's Rating Sheet

_____ Circle One: Luncheon / Dinner
Employee's Name

Host/Hostess _____
(Rating Official)

_____
(Reviewing Official)

Rate the member of the service staff on his/her performance for the day's operation. Total the scores for each day. Fill in this form for each employee at least once per month. This form should be completed at the end of each year.

Use this scale for point values:

0-65 pts. = unsatisfactory   84- 94 = above average
66-73 pts. = satisfactory   95-100 = absolutely superior
74-83 pts. = average

Day/Date	Appearance	Accuracy	Quantity of Work	Attendance and Dependability	Cooperation with (Employees)	Courtesy Towards (Guests)	Initiative	Judgment	Stability	Housekeeping & Sanitation	Total Points for Overall Evaluation
1.											
2.											
3.											
4.											
5.											
6.											
7.											
8.											
9.											
10.											
11.											
12.											
Totals											

Rating Errors

The halo effect is the tendency of a rater to prejudge the ratee (e.g., on one or two factors) and mark the form indicating superior performance or poor performance.

The leniency error is the tendency to be a "nice guy" and rate each employee higher than her actual performance in the job. This syndrome has forced the military rating system to dispense with the absolute system, and adopt the forced choice ranking.

The error of central tendency exists when the rater does not differentiate between effective or ineffective job performance and rates all employees as average.

Promotion

Whenever openings occur, it is wise to search for replacements within the organization. This effort utilizes the experience and proven abilities of present personnel. Offering advancement opportunities within the firm increases employee incentive by demonstrating a career ladder. Yet before one from within the establishment is promoted, she must possess the same minimum qualifications as anyone applying for the job. It is important to establish job specifications and to adhere to these specifications even when promoting from within the organization. Promotion on seniority alone is perhaps one of the worst measures for managerial success. Seniority should be considered, but as a factor only, not as the sole determinant for promotion. The practice of adhering to specifications will decrease the amount of favoritism that may damage morale and incentive among other employees. Whenever possible, present employees should be given the opportunity to practice for promotion. Assigning the safety director's job to a present employee gives upper management a good look at that individual's organizational and managerial skills. This and similar assignments will make it easier to identify management potential in the present work force.

Discipline

The management establishes rules and regulations and expects employees to follow them. The rules should define not only restrictions on the employees, but their rights as well. It is an excellent idea to post the rules and regulations, and to have each employee read them and review them at regular intervals.

Mr. Alan Katz of White's Coffee Pot Restaurants in Baltimore, Maryland, lists twenty-three rules and regulations in the employee's manual. Corrective action (counsel, dismissal, warning, etc.) is listed along side each regulation, and employees are required to read, sign, and date a form indicating that they read and understand the rules. Employees are required to review the rules every six months. At each six-month period, the employee must initial and date the original document indicating that he has again reviewed the rules and regulations.

In some cases it is necessary to document any disciplinary action. A memorandum should be sent to the employee and should indicate:

1. Action taken for particular offense
2. Time period given for improvement
3. Further action if no noticeable improvement
4. Specific performance incidents for which the action was taken
5. Provision for the employee to acknowledge receipt of the warning

The memorandum should exclude extraneous matter and should be short and to the point. One copy should be sent to the next level of supervision, one to central personnel, and one kept for the writer's record as well as one for the employee.

Terminations

Terminating employees is rapidly becoming obsolete as a management alternative. If a decision is made to fire an employee, the supervisor should insure that every opportunity has been given to the employee for enabling him to do his job correctly. Firing is an unpleasant managerial task; and should this task become too simple or too frequent, the individual manager should take a closer look at herself. The following procedures should be followed when an employee must be terminated:

1. Terminate in private. Do not apologize, and do not embarrass the employee.
2. Give the person several reasons for termination, but also highlight his strong points and offer to help him find another job. The termination process should not be long (15 minutes maximum).

3. Make sure that the offense is serious, or that the person has been warned previously.
4. Ask if he has any questions. Offer any assistance, and tell him that you will give him the best reference possible.
5. Pay him for all work to this point and ask him to take all his personal belongings from the establishment.

Training

Every restaurant has a training program; however, many operations are not actively involved in training, which is most unfortunate. How can standards be met? How do the employees know what is expected of them? How can accidents be decreased? How do employees learn the correct serving procedures? How do they learn to sell in the dining room? How do they learn to provide correct wine service? How do they learn about safety and sanitation? How can they learn how to satisfy the guest? How can employees learn to adapt to today's rapid changes?

Employees learn the answers to these questions in an organized training program. Many restaurants advertise an "on- the-job training program" which is often a farce. Perhaps many on-the-job training programs should be called "earn-as-you-learn . . ." (the hard way) or "on-the-job-work;" for very few of these training programs are really training programs. "But training costs a lot of money and a lot of time!" an operator will say. "My people get enough in one week when they follow one of my regulars around. I give them a small station to see if they can hack it. If they can, they've got the job!"

This attitude is all too prevalent in the industry, which should recognize that operators *cannot afford **not** to train*. A concentrated training effort translates to a positive attitude on the employee's part, and the necessary skills are more easily learned. Dr. Michael Gallagher[10] charts a trainability curve and a cost curve.

It can be seen from these charts that an operator achieves maximum training at minimum cost when training new employees. The trainability curve shows that employees with more time in the job are more difficult to train, and the cost curve shows that

10. Michael C. Gallagher, "The Economics of Training Food Service Employees," *The CHRAQ*, Ithaca, New York, May 1977.

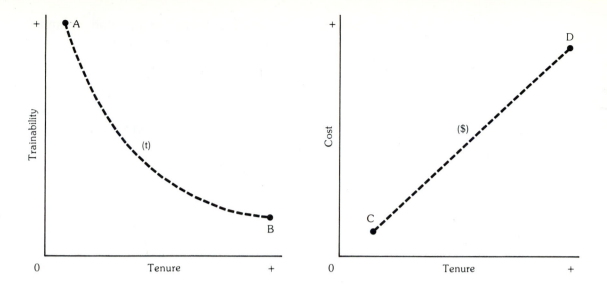

Figure 3.1 The Trainability Curve (t)

Figure 3.2 The Cost Curve (S)

it is more expensive to train employees who have more tenure on the job. As will be discussed later in this text, accidents result from or are caused by new employees in fifty percent of the occurrences. Yet training not only reduces accidents, it has been proven that good training programs also reduce absenteeism and short term illnesses, employee turnover, spoilage and waste, damage to equipment, overhead and labor cost; and increase employee morale, productivity, job knowledge, sales, and customer satisfaction. People are not perfect with respect to organizational goals, and training continues to develop both supervisory and technical skills in an ever-changing organization. Every persn who is hired must go through an orientation program. Many new employees are most uncomfortable in a new job, and the orientation program should serve, among other things, as a gradual introduction to the organization and the job. During the orientation phase of training, the new employee will be given such things as:

1. Company history, the *objectives* of the organization, as well as *how* the organization works
2. What her hours, wages or salary, and benefits are; when the regular pay periods occur, and when can she expect her first check
3. A brief description of her duties (including a basic direction in the job)

4. Policies and procedures forms (e.g., work permits W-4 withholding form, completed time card if applicable, rules and regulations)
5. Uniform and dress code
6. Introduction to supervisor and coworkers
7. Information about her work station, where the break area is, when she will be taking breaks, and where the restrooms are
8. An overview of what (top) management thinks is important
9. Ample time for any questions

After orientation the employee must be trained at a minimum level of proficiency in order for her to be able to perform her job. For example, if trays are used, she must learn how to carry a tray, pour water, serve butter, serve cocktails, etc., before being allowed in the dining room. After this initial training, which is intended to bring the new employee to a minimum level of proficiency, the new employee should be allowed to work for several shifts and then allowed to ask questions of her supervisor on procedures she does not understand. After the initial training, which must be a well-planned and organized effort, the employee should attend refresher or continuation training with *all* other members of the service staff at regular intervals.

This whole process can be viewed as a wheel, with refresher training sessions offered on a biweekly or monthly basis. The frequency or repetition of the various programs should be determined by: (1) the employee turnover rate, (2) the level of intelligence of trainees (i.e., the ability each has to retain knowledge, and (3) the complexity of the tasks. However, before entering this wheel, each employee must attend an orientation training program as well as an introductory training program for minimum proficiency. Some employees may need not attend the introductory training program, but every new employee must attend the orientation program.

All too often establishments with training programs bombard a new employee with all of the things he is expected to know for his entire tenure in the particular job. This overwhelms the person, and sometimes very little information is in fact communicated.

Minimum Proficiency
Training Program

Route for New Employee
Who *Does Not* Demonstrate
Minimum Proficiency

Employee Is
Hired

Orientation
Program

Route for
New Employee Who
Can Demonstrate
Minimum Proficiency

Continuation
Training Program
FOR ALL EMPLOYEES

- Sales Techniques in General
- Basic Service Procedures
- Wine Service and Wine Sales Techniques
- Use of Equipment
- Table Settings

- Psychology of Service
- Cooperation with Other Staff Members
- Sanitation
- Safety
- Etc.

A Systems Approach to Training

The development of a training program should follow the process outlined here. A whole book could be written to describe this topic, but such detailed treatment is beyond the scope of this text.

The first step when developing a training program is to assess needs. Ask the questions: *Do we have a training problem? Could he do it (the task) if his life depended on it?* It must be remembered that training is not an end, but a *means to an end.* Yet training cannot be a one-shot approach. As mentioned in the model, training must be an ongoing effort.

Organization analysis is the first consideration within the assessment phase. Training must be started from the top down, as the major emphasis is to help the individual achieve the organization's goals (both long term and short term) and objectives. Many a trainee has come away from a training program saying, "I wish my boss would take this course." The organization's resources must also be analyzed as to finances, facilities, and human resources. Consider this example of an inadequate analysis from the organizational perspective. In two separate actions a manager mentions to his kitchen steward or training director that the

Figure 3.3 Model for Service Training

dish machine operators need to speed up the number of pieces through the machine. He also talks to the purchasing agent about the same problem. The steward or training director perceives this as a training need, while the purchasing agent views this as a cue to begin looking for a new dish machine. Each expends considerable effort before the manager's desires are known. In a well-designed assessment phase, the training director would quickly cease efforts or clarify organizational goals.

The second investigation in the assessment phase is a complete *task or operations analysis,* and the third is the *human performance analysis.* The discussion of task analysis focuses on task unit job descriptions, which is discussed in detail in the very next section. The human performance phase deals with comments such as: "I've got to teach her." "He's got to change his attitude." "We need a course to teach people. . . ." "Our waitresses can't sell wine." An excellent book that addresses itself to this subject is *Analyzing Performance Problems* by Robert F. Mager and Peter Pipe.

A job description, complete with *all tasks* required in performing the job, must be written.[11] The sources listed plus the job descriptions contained in this text will serve as excellent guidelines. Additionally these descriptions must be tailored to the particular establishment by observing the employees *on the job and in the establishment.* The job description can be used not only as a guideline for the training program, but also for performance appraisal and for wage and salary administration.

From the job description, behavioral objectives should be determined. These objectives should indicate *what the trainee will be able to do* at the completion of the training.[12] Behavioral objectives must be written for *each* desired task, for example, "The student will be able to demonstrate the correct procedure (as printed) for carrying, presenting, opening, and serving red wine." From the objectives, questions, and other forms of examination, an evaluation must be developed in order to measure instructional intent. Before designing the lesson plan, the trainer will select and sequence the units of instruction. In selecting units of instruction, trainers should remember that the content must be

11. *A Hospitality Industry Guide for Writing and Using Task Unit Job Descriptions.* Tourism Education Corporation (Boston: Cohners Publishing Company, 1976).

12. For an excellent book on writing objectives, the reader is directed to *Preparing Instructional Objectives* by Robert F. Mager published by Fearon Publishers, Belmont, California.

relevant to the job in order to facilitate the transfer of knowledge from the training setting to the job. Content must make a *significant* contribution to attaining the organization's objectives, as well as the human performance objectives. When *sequencing* instruction consideration should be given to the arrangement of material based on: (1) chronology (e.g., the order of service); (2) general to specific (e.g., wine knowledge to wine service); (3) specific to general (e.g., basic wine service to knowledge of wines), and (4) simple to complex (e.g., taking a basic order to taking the order with embellishments of menu items and subtle sales techniques).

The lesson plan is the blueprint from which the instructor works. It is the point at which the ideals of what the trainer would like to accomplish meet the realities of time, space, equipment, and money. A good instructor will combine all the resources available to have the best training program for the least expense. The lesson plan describes how all factors will be combined so that the largest number of trainees will develop the highest degree of skill with respect to the facilities, time, instructor(s), and content. Planning the lesson is a time of reckoning—determining how to fit what needs to be done within the time and money restrictions. The lesson plan calls for what the trainee will be doing during each phase of instruction, as well as the type of instruction (lecture, demonstration, or four-step method, etc.) that will be used.

An evaluation scheme of the training program should be developed *before training begins*. This is necessary so that the content of the evaluation plan is not diverted by any occurrences during the actual training.

Standard measures for measuring instruction in training programs are inadequate (e.g., rank, standard scores, percentile scores, percentage, or "passing grades"). The best measure in a training program is a criterion based exam (i.e., derived from the objectives after a detailed analysis). The learner must meet or exceed the level of performance described in the objectives (criteria). If the learner cannot attain this level, either the objectives are unrealistic or the trainee should not be placed in the work situation. Information gathered in the evaluation process must then be routed back to the development phase of the program where updates, changes, and modifications in the training program will be necessary.

Information from the evaluation process should come from: (1) trainees while in the training program, (2) graduates of the training programs at different phases or times after training (e.g., one year after completion, two years after completion, five years after completion, etc.), (3) supervisors of the graduates of the training programs.

The Four-step Training Process

1. *Prepare the Worker*
   A. For the job itself
      1. Select the right person to do the training and make sure he knows how to train—the ability to do, to impart, to inspire, to appraise.
      2. Have necessary tools at hand.
      3. Make sure the work place is in good order.
      4. Provide ample time.
   B. For the training process
      1. Put the learner at ease. A nervous, jumpy learner is in no mental condition to receive or absorb new ideas.
      2. Have a friendly, helpful, interested, unhurried attitude.
      3. Arouse the learner's interest.
      4. Check what the learner already knows.
      5. Build up the learner's self-confidence.
      6. Place in correct position.
2. *Explain the Job*
   A. Give him any preliminary information that will be helpful.
   B. Show him how to do the job at full production speed.
   C. Then demonstrate how it is done, slowly if possible—illustrate and question carefully and patiently.
   D. Stress and explain key points—give reasons.
   E. Point out safety precautions.
   F. Explain clearly and completely, taking one point at a time.
   G. Repeat operation full speed.
3. *Get Him Started (Tryout Performance)*
   A. Let him do the easy parts—you do the hard ones.
   B. Let him add the difficult parts—one by one.
   C. Have him tell and show you how the job is done; have him explain the key points.

D. Point out where he may run into difficulties.
E. Ask questions and correct errors.
F. Continue until you know HE knows.
4. *Put Him on His Own*
    A. Let him take over the entire job—but watch him. See that he is forming safe and correct habits.
    B. Leave him alone but encourage him to come to you if anything bothers him.
    C. As he progresses, explain any additional fine points that may have been deferred at the start.
    D. Review his progress frequently.
    E. Check safety, quality, and quantity of production.

Conducting Meetings with the Service Staff

Regular meetings with the service staff must be conducted in order that managers receive first-hand knowledge of guest reaction and guest desires. An agenda for each meeting must be compiled by the supervisor conducting the meeting. Otherwise, the meeting lacks direction and results in a boring affair for all employees. Groups should not exceed thirty or so members. If the group is too large, exchange among the members may be minimal. An effective method to begin a meeting is to introduce *nonthreatening* directives from management, as it has a settling effect on the group. Compliments should be extended to those individuals who have performed well, especially when guests have recognized the performance of one of the waiters. When necessary, negative comments should be covered next, but specific comments directed towards individuals should be avoided.

From this point forward, a round-the-table discussion can be encouraged by the supervisor. Rather than saying, "Mary, anything to add?" the group leader may pick a specific thing that she knows Mary can talk about and say, "Mary, tell us about the guest who came in wearing a hat and refused to take it off." After the round table discussion, the supervisor may read or distribute a short incident or role play. An effort must be made by the supervisor to w thhold judgment of any employee's handling of the situation. Invariably the other employees will offer suggestions that are acceptable, and the person who took an outlandish position will probably modify her thinking. Good ideas are usually embellished, while mistakes are pointed out. If the group is generally nonresponsive, this may indicate tension within the group. A cohesive team will tend to work together.

The following role-play exercises and incidents may be used to stimulate group discussion. These situations are easy to develop, and any supervisor should be able to generate one good incident per day.

Role-play Exercises

Role Play 1:

Customer: You waited 10 minutes for your order to be taken, your coffee was not hot when served, your main course was undercooked, you did not get any butter for your rolls, and you were offered a refill on coffee only once. Your check is $4.59 and you do not feel like you got either the food or service promised in the advertising. The restaurant is near your work and you would like to return again, but not if it is going to be like this time.

Cashier: You have had an extremely busy rush, the head waitress is home sick, and there are several new people on the schedule. This customer comes in to the restaurant often and usually finds something to complain about.

Role Play 2:

Manager: One of your best waitresses is coming in for work 1/2 hour early this evening so she can talk to you. She sounded upset on the phone. Mary does an excellent job. She is honest, reliable, and has helped you train other waitresses.

Waitress: The new waitress, Polly, is a thief. Ever since she started working, your tips and the tips of the other waitresses have been decreasing. Polly always seems to cash in large sums of change at the end of the night. You have not actually caught her in the act, but one of the other waittresses said she saw Polly take a tip off a table that was not hers. You think your manager should know.

Incident

You are an assistant restaurant manager. Your host is incapable of handling a large crowd, and there are convention delegates swarming into your restaurant. You were helping seat guests and answering the phone for reservations.

Mr. Alexander's secretary called for reservations, and you told her you were filled to capacity. She informed you that Mr. Alexander was already on his way over! He is a regular and important customer. When Mr. Alexander entered you told him that you could not seat him or his five guests. He became quite indignant. To make matters worse, the host remarked to you in Mr. Alexander's presence, "You could have seated Mr. Alexander if you had just planned things a little better." The host has always been envious of you. What do you do?

Incident

You are a shift supervisor in a coffee shop. A guest just got up from his table and grabbed a handful of paper napkins from the counter. Gladys (a middle-aged waitress with ten years longevity) proceeded to *reprimand* the guest and remove the napkins. The guest explained that his two children were messy eaters, and he needed the napkins. Gladys showed no sympathy to the guest. The guest registered a complaint to you personally.

1. How do you handle the guest?
2. How do you handle Gladys?

Incident

You are a young assistant food and beverage manager at a 125-seat American service restaurant. In addition to your responsibility for supervising dinner (6:30 P.M.–10:30 P.M.), you volunteered to supervise the training program your corporate headquarters has designed for service personnel. You have great rapport with almost all of your service staff. However, Gertrude has refused to cooperate with the standardized system you are teaching. She informs you that she has been "quite successfully" waiting tables for twenty-two years. Her tips are better than your average person's tips. Your manager has told you "Get Gerdy up to standard or get rid of her!" Firing Gerdy is not an alternative. What would you do? What factors need to be taken into consideration?

Conclusion

The personnel function in service management is multifaceted. Consideration to the organizational structure, recruiting and selecting service employees, interviewing, and conducting reference checks weigh heavily on the manager. The techniques listed will assist the service manager in selecting and organizing her service staff.

Compensation for tipped employees will undoubtedly go through several changes before Congress settles its debate. Yet the outlook for the industry in this area is dim. Rating systems for tipped employees seldom reflect wages paid as they do for supervisory personnel, but the ratings are important for evaluating the individual's worth to the organization. It is important for managers and employees to know their strengths and weaknesses.

Promotion from within the organization provides career opportunities within the organization. This may decrease employee turnover, which will stabilize the work environment. While discipline and termination are difficult to deal with, it is important that management develop guidelines for treating each of these areas.

Training is a very necessary function. Many operators feel that they do not have enough time or money to train when they really can not afford not to train. The guidelines for conducting employee meetings will assist supervisors in this effort, and conducting an effective meeting is an excellent training session.

Additional Readings

Lundberg, Donald E., and Armatas, James P. *The Management of People in Hotels, Restaurants, and Clubs.* 3rd ed. Dubuque, Ia.: Wm. C. Brown Company Publishers, 1974.

Gallagher, Michael C. "The Economics of Training Food Service Employees." *The CHRAQ,* Ithaca, New York, May 1977.

A Hospitality Industry Guide for Writing and Using Task Unit Job Descriptions. Tourism Education Corporation. Boston: Cahner's Publishing Company, 1976.

Mager, Robert F. *Analyzing Performance Problems.* Belmont, Calif.: Fearon Publishers, Belmont, 1962.

———. *Preparing Instructional Objectives.* Belmont, Calif.: Fearon Publishers, Belmont, 1962.

Chapter 4

The Types of Service

Food service establishments in the United States have, perhaps by tradition only, adopted European terminology for naming the types of service. The European terms refer to the various forms as French, Russian, American, and English. There seems to be some confusion when these service terms are used. In an informal survey of approximately 100 European students taken a few years ago, it was found that what the service was called depended on where the individuals naming them were trained. People have been known to argue vehemently that French Service was this and Russian Service was that, etc. Each was correct from his perspective, but the arguments seem futile. It is easier to name the type of service by the function being performed. To highlight this confusion, when applying for a banquet job a waiter/waitress is asked if he/she knows French Service. What is really being asked is, "Do you know how to use a fork and spoon in order to transfer food from a platter to a guest's plate?" Yet some texts make it clear that Russian Service is erroneously called "French Service." In this text, therefore, the major types of service will be referred to as: Cart Service (tableside cookery and service), Platter Service, Plate Service, and Family Service. Additionally, Buffet and Banquet Service will also be discussed.

Yet even this discussion as to the types of service is academic. Rarely will one see a restaurant in the United States, except in large cities or formal banquets, that strictly adheres to a particular type of service. In order to plan and to make decisions it is important to define the types of service, as a well-educated restauranteur should be aware of the advantages and disadvantages of each.

Cart Service (Gueridon/Trolley)

Cart Service is called "French Service" in the United States and in Germany; yet in France, Cart Service is referred to as "Russian Service." What distinguishes this type of service from the others is that the food is brought to the guests' table in either a raw state or a semiprepared state and finished in front of the guests in the dining room on a cart. This type of service is the most elaborate and offers the greatest personal attention to the guest. The final food preparation is performed by the chef de rang, and he/she is assisted by a commis de rang. Although the chef de rang has been called a captain or a waiter, he performs some of the tasks performed by a waiter and some of the tasks a captain usually performs. The commis de rang is referred to as a bus boy, but he performs many more service related functions than is usually given a bus boy. A demichef de rang is a commis de rang who has recently been promoted and is given a small station and the assistance of a commis.

The chef de rang and the commis work together as a team in a station of approximately twenty guests. The chef de rang prepares the food and places the food on the plates, while the commis actually serves the guest. Each of these two individuals must be highly skilled, since the chef de rang is performing many of the functions in the dining room that the cook performs in the kitchen.[1]

Duties of the Staff

In a classical restaurant the headwaiter (chef de salle) or maître d'hôtel will greet the guests at the door and pass the party to a *chef de rang,* who will also greet the guests, lead them to a table in his station, and seat them. He will then take the order for cocktails or appetizer wines. He may pass the order to the commis, especially if cocktails will be served, or he/she may serve the cocktails or wine himself. In the absence of a wine steward (sommelier), the chef de rang will serve the dinner wines. He must be able to cook menu items at the tableside, and he also needs to be able to flame these foods, carve meat, and bone fish and poultry. After he prepares the food, the chef de rang will plate and garnish the food while the commis serves the guests.

1. Please see the departure from this classical discussion in chapter 00 on Tableside Cookery and Service.

The *commis de rang* assists the chef de rang in seating the guests; and while the chef takes the order, he offers service to guests by serving relishes, butter (informal meal), and water (customary in the United States). After the chef takes the order from the guests, the commis will place the order with the expediter or ennunciator in the kitchen (pantry and range). When the food is ready for serving, the commis brings the food either to the guests (i.e., preplated appetizers) or to the chef for preparation. As mentioned previously, after the chef prepares the food, the commis actually serves the guests.

Characteristics of Cart Service

Cart service is characterized by a cart at tableside as well as quality personalized professional attention and service. Since there is very low guest turnover, menu items must be priced higher in order to cover the restaurant's fixed costs. Additionally, more service personnel are needed per guest. Food is served from the right side of the guest with the waiter/waitresses' right hand. In cart service a minimum cover usually consisting of a dinner knife and a dinner fork (see chapter 9 for detail on place settings) is set, and additional silver is brought with the specific course being served.

Advantages and Disadvantages of Cart Service

If it were determined by survey or in a feasibility study that there is a market for elite clientele and the restaurant owners wanted to attract this type of guest, then Cart Service would be the best type of service to employ. In fact, when menu prices exceed twenty dollars per cover something more than Plate Service is expected. In Europe and in other parts of the world guests would not accept having a plated meal brought from the kitchen and placed in front of them in a restaurant of any caliber. Plate Service is associated with a cafe.

From the managerial point of view there is an additional advantage to Cart Service. It may be used only on slow nights and therefore some of the kitchen staff may be released. This is beneficial, since salaries paid to service personnel are generally lower than those paid production personnel, and service personnel are compensated via gratuities.

Of all the major types of service, Cart Service has more disadvantages than the other types. In other words, it costs management more money to institute and maintain this type of service system. Cart Service, in the classical approach, requires a highly skilled staff, and skilled waiters and waitresses may be either difficult to find or nonexistent in some locales. This means that if it is determined to use Cart Service in an establishment, an extensive service training program must be planned and maintained.

Another disadvantage to Cart Service is that more space is required per guest. A general rule used in planning restaurants is to allow fifteen square feet per person in the dining area (i.e., if the restaurant seats 150 people, 2,250 square feet are required). In restaurants offering Cart Service, eighteen square feet per person is required. More room is needed to roll carts around the dining room, and additional space is required to keep a safe distance between the cart and the table during food preparation. Menu pricing must be adjusted upward since there is a higher cost on rent or on the mortgage.

As an example: A 150-seat restaurant offering cart service would require 2,700 square feet or 450 square feet *more* than if plate service were offered. Dining space rule-of-thumb costs run approximately $40 per square foot.[2] *For the space only* the cost is increased by $18,000.

Menu pricing must also be adjusted upward since cart service is slow, with leisurely service (increased residence time) resulting in fewer turnovers. A 150-seat restaurant with a busy plate service could expect three turns while the same restaurant offering cart service may only expect two turns. If a certain sales figure is required to cover costs plus profit (and it usually is), the menu price must reflect the fewer number of turnovers. A 150-seat plate service restaurant with an $8 cover average and three turns would bring in $3,600 for an evening. The cart service restaurant with two turns would need to increase the cover average to $12 to bring in the same sales volume.

Besides these two factors there will be some additional costs required to purchase carts, flaming lamps (rechauds), pans, platters, etc. These costs will not be as substantial as the rent or mortgage or the lower turnover, but must nonetheless be calculated into the pricing. Also these equipment costs will be slightly less than the platters required for Platter Service. However, the pro-

2. Professor Richard Penner, Architect at the School of Hotel Administration at Cornell University.

duction of food in the dining room may decrease the amount of kitchen equipment (stoves, ovens, etc.) required.

Another small disadvantage in performing tableside cookery in the dining area is that unless it is aired out or vented, the room may smell of stale food. This is especially noticeable if the room has large draperies or tapestries that tend to absorb the odors.

Since there are several individuals in a dimly lit dining room, as compared to only a few in a well-lit kitchen preparing food, the managerial control over product quality is reduced in Cart Service. In other words, a Cart Service restaurant has poor quality control. *Poor quality control* should not be confused with *poor quality*. Many restaurants offering cart service have the finest quality available. However, it is more difficult for management to observe the production of each item, the plating of each menu item, etc. It is also more difficult for the chef de rang to determine degrees of doneness of meat, adjust seasonings or thickness of sauces, etc., in the dining room. In short, it is difficult to cover up any mistakes while in the presence of the guests. Each dish prepared in the kitchen may be inspected before presentation to the guest. It would be ludicrous to have each dish prepared at tableside inspected before presentation to the guest. Portion control can be poorer than in Plate Service, although the high-food- cost items such as steak can be controlled with minimum effort.

Sequential Service for Formal à la Carte Meal

—Settings (minimum cover).
—Maître d'hôtel or chef de rang seats guests and presents menu.
—Water served (optional).
—Take food order.
—Offer wine list and/or suggestions.
—Serve appetizer (in center of cover) on cover (service) plate.
—Remove first-course dish (leave cover plate).
—Serve soup from cart in center of cover on cover plate; offer soup garnish.
—Remove soup dishes and cover plate.
—Food (fish course) served from platter or plates filled from gueridon and placed in center of cover.
—Clear fish course.
—Main course served as fish course.

—Remove main course dishes, order as follows:
1. Relish dish
2. Condiments
3. Dinner plates
4. Vegetables dishes
5. Empty wine glasses
6. Extra silver

—Serve salad (formal service) in center of cover with fork at right (refrigerated forks are impressive).
—Remove salad dish.
—Crumb table.
—Silver for dessert course placed right of cover.
—Serve dessert in center of cover.
—Remove dessert course.
—Serve coffee (may be served with dessert).
—Offer brandy or cordials.
—Present check at a reasonable time after cordials (or coffee), insuring that guest does not feel hurried.
—Take guest's money or card to cashier and return change or card on dish (if card, offer pen for signature). Thank guest for tip.
—Waiter helps guests as they rise to leave and checks that nothing is left behind.
—Remove tip and tray.
—Clear table and relay.

Platter Service

Platter service is generally referred to as Russian Service in the United States and in Germany. In France it is referred to as French Service or Silver Service. Platter Service is universally accepted in fine restaurants the world over. As mentioned earlier, many restaurant patrons would not accept Plate Service in standard service restaurants; and when Cart Service is not feasible, Platter Service is implemented.

Characteristics of Platter Service

In Platter Service the food is fully prepared in the kitchen by a cook or chef and placed on platters for service to the guest. The waiter brings the platter of food—entrees, vegetables, sauces, etc.—from the kitchen into the dining room and may place the food at or on a secondary warming surface. He/she then places

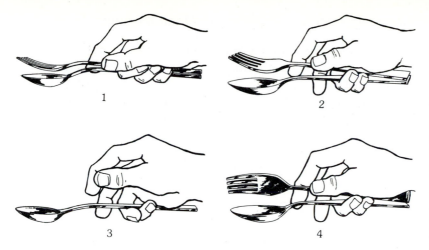

Figure 4.1 The Types of Service. (1) Place the fork on top of the serving spoon and grasp both utensils as one unit with the pads of your index finger and thumb (not at the first joint of the index finger). Slide the fork to the right of the spoon on the same plane. This position may be used for lifting fish or crepes. (2) Lift the fork while simultaneously moving the fork over the spoon. Notice that the index finger is not folded under the fork handle. (3) This is the position of the spoon without a fork (this drawing is for instruction only, as one would not hold the spoon alone in this manner). Notice that the spoon is balanced with three fingers on one side and the pad of the hand on the other. (4) The fork can be rotated with the thumb and the index finger; when the fork and spoon surfaces are facing one another, they may be used to lift round items (e.g., stuffed whole tomato).

hot empty plates (usually kept hot in a warming stand in the dining room) in front of each guest and then serves the food by transferring the product from the platter to the guest's plate. The hot plates are placed from the guest's *right* side, and the waiter/waitress walks around the table *clockwise* as he/she places the plates. This movement around the table makes the flow more fluid as he/she need not stop and back up for each guest. The waiter/waitress serves the food by manipulating a fork and spoon in the right hand from the left side of the guest while holding the platter in the left hand (close to the guest's plate) with the left foot advanced forward for balance. The waiter/waitress moves around the table counterclockwise while serving the food.

Soup is served in a silver soup cup, which may be brought to the table in a soup bowl on an underliner. After the soup is placed on the service plate, the waiter/waitress inverts the silver cup, allowing the soup to fill the bowl. He/she then removes the silver cup and the guest may begin eating. An alternate method for serving soup is similar to the Cart Service method, where a small tureen is brought to the table and the waiter/waitress ladles soup into the empty bowl that has previously been placed in the center of the cover.

It is customary to set a complete place setting (i.e., all silverware required for the particular meal) for Platter Service. It would be quite cumbersome and time consuming for the waiter/waitress to present silverware as well as placing the plates and serving from the platters.

Advantages and Disadvantages of Platter Service

As a formal presentation and service of food, Platter Service has many advantages. Although slightly less personalized for the guest than Cart Service, Platter Service gives more attention to the guest than Plate Service. This form of service may be quite elaborate and showy if ornate silver platters are used. Less space per guest is required in the dining room than in Cart Service, as additional space is not required to roll carts around the dining room. The tables should be slightly larger than for Plate Service (i.e., thirty inches per cover is usually allowed as compared to twenty-four for Plate Service). Service personnel must be able to move comfortably between guests for service. If larger tables are required, special consideration must be given to the placement of these tables in the dining room. Adding an extra foot along the length of a wall may make space for an additional row of tables, whereas removing a foot may not make the dining room any more crowded. It is difficult to serve banquette or booth tables from a platter.

Although service personnel must be well trained, the level of proficiency needed for waiters/waitresses need not be as high as that required for Cart Service. The difficulty arises not from the manipulative skills (fork and spoon), but the speed with which one must serve as a result of the numerous tasks required. One service person can handle more guests in an evening than if Cart Service were being used, since Platter Service allows for more turnovers (i.e., it is a faster form of service). Yet the station size for Platter Service should not be any larger than the stations for Cart Service. If service is à la carte (as opposed to banquet service with a preset menu), one waiter/waitress should be able to serve ten guests efficiently. On one hand, Platter Service is not particularly suitable for a la carte service, as it is time consuming to take the orders, place orders at the range, pick up orders at the range, enter the dining room and place the platters on a secondary heating surface or cavity, pick up hot plates (usually kept in the dining room), place hot plates in the center of the cover, return to secondary heating area and pick up platters, and finally serve the guests their food. On the other hand, it is an excellent type of service for banquets or for preset menus, and is therefore frequently used for formal banquets. The rules of thumb change for banquets or preset menus, and a waiter/waitress should be able to serve up to twenty guests efficiently. Management must assist the waiter/waitress in giving good service by having all necessary equipment, utensils, and silverware available and handy.

Platter Service offers excellent quality rontrol, as each dish is prepared, plated on a platter, and garnished in the kitchen. The waiter/waitress must only transfer food from the platter to the plate since he/she does not have to prepare food at the table-side as is necessary in Cart Service. There can be good portion control; however, in practice, more food is placed on the platter than is required (or purchased by the guest), which ultimately results in waste and higher food costs.

There are some inherent disadvantages to any form of service and Platter Service is no exception. A high initial investment in silver (platters) must be considered, although alternative metals/china (polished aluminum, polished pewter, stainless steel, etc.), which are less expensive, may also be used. It is also difficult to control the silver (platter) inventory, and replacement as well as repairs and maintenance (soldering, replating, etc.) may be costly. Another notable disadvantage is the appearance of the platter after serving has begun. If each person in a party of four ordered Beef Wellington, the cook would plate the entree and vegetables, and garnish the platter for presentation in the dining room. By the time the fourth guest to be served saw the platter, he would be looking at a picked-over, unappetizing plate.

Plate Service

Although Plate Service can be referred to as German Service, most agree that serving food that has been preplated in the kitchen is *American Service*. In order to remain consistent, the term Plate Service will be used throughout this text, but the reader should be aware that Plate Service and American Service are synonymous and are accepted as such universally. The distinguishing characteristic is that food placed on the plate in the kitchen will ultimately be placed in the center of the cover in front of the guest. The service stations are usually arranged to give *fast service*. The particular emphasis with this type service is speed. A characteristic of Plate Service is that food is *served from the left* and *removed from the right*, while all *beverages* (coffee, tea, iced tea, milk, soft drinks, water, cocktails, and wine) are *served and removed from the right.* Perhaps this rule (serve from the left) came about because Americans consume more and more of a variety of beverages than do Europeans. Hence with the positioning of the cups and water glasses, etc., it is easier to serve from the left.

Restaurants offering Plate Service primarily borrow from the other types of service for certain items, such as (1) Cart Service—flaming entrees, desserts, and beverages and (2) Platter Service—planked platters (wooden boards usually decorated with potatoes and vegetables) and casseroles that are plated in front of the guests).

Advantages and Disadvantages of Plate Service

To the author's knowledge, Plate Service only has two disadvantages. First, it is not as elaborate or as personal as Cart Service or Platter Service, and hence may not be acceptable in certain types of restaurants or in certain parts of the world. Second, the service personnel may be bored with their tasks since no special skill is required.[3] This may lead to a more difficult job on the part of management, since the manager must motivate his staff. The operator may experience a higher employee turnover rate (number of people hired for a particular job), as well as a higher absenteeism rate and higher number of short-term illnesses.

Plate Service is simple to perform as compared to Cart or Platter Service, since the service personnel only need to place a plate in front of the guest. As a result, a skilled staff is not required, which makes hiring easier (larger pool of labor) and training for specific tasks less time consuming. Service is incredibly fast since many of the classical waiter's/waitresses functions have been eliminated.

Again the rule of thumb for staffing a Plate Service restaurant changes. One person can serve up to eighteen guests efficiently, and the range of fourteen to eighteen is possible for most service personnel. This rule of thumb applies to a la carte service, as a waiter/waitress should be able to serve twenty-five guests efficiently when a preset menu (banquet) with Plate Service is being used.

3. Waiters/waitresses or managers are unaware of the vast amount of "people skills" required to be an effective waiter/waitress. Management has an easier task motivating his/her service staff when there are more motor skills involved (i.e., handling a fork and spoon, preparing foods at tableside, or opening a bottle of wine).

For Plate Service less dining room space is required for each guest. Fifteen square feet per person is the general rule used for design purposes. The individual cover size, smaller than the size used for Platter Service, should be twenty-four inches across by fifteen inches deep. The smaller covers allow for smaller tables, which translates into more seats within a given area. Since more people can be seated in a given area (lower rent or mortgage payments) and the service is considerably faster than Cart or Platter Service, the menu prices for a given quality food product should be lower than the same quality product in a restaurant offering Cart or Platter Service.

Plate Service offers excellent portion control. Since every food item the guest has ordered for his main course is plated in the kitchen and served to the guest, he pays for what he gets and gets what he pays for. Whatever leaves the kitchen is controlled, so there is less chance for any "shrinkage" between the kitchen and the dining room. In this way it is easier to control a plate than items on a platter or cart. The same degree of control over the quality of the product exists in Plate Service as well as Platter Service. Quality control is excellent since all food is prepared and plated in the kitchen.

An additional point must be made for Plate Service. In a remote area or developing area where there is an excessive amount of unskilled labor, it would be foolish for managers to institute or require a formal service system. Some hotels in developing countries who cater to the European market have tried to use Cart and Platter Service with difficulty, when Plate Service would ease the pressures on both the staff and management. Also if management desires elaborate service and there are too few waiters/waitresses on the floor able to serve the guests efficiently, the elaborate service turns into poor service. It may be well advised to use Plate Service where the service personnel could quickly accomplish their tasks, place the food (on a preplated plate) in front of the guest, and have more time to give some other fine points of service.

Sequential Plate Service

—Settings (standard American—two forks, two knives, two spoons).
—Host seats guests and presents menus.
—Pour water for each guest and place butter.

—Take cocktail order.
—Serve cocktail from right (beverage).
—Take food order.
—Bread is placed on table.
—Offer wine list and/or suggestions.
—Remove cocktail glasses if finished.
—Serve appetizer (center of cover).
—Remove first-course dish.
—Serve soup in center of cover.
—Remove soup dishes and show plates (if used).
—Serve salad, remove salad dishes.
—Serve main course, place in center of cover.
—Clear Table, Order as follows:
    Condiments
    Dinner plates
    Vegetable dishes
    Empty wine glasses
    Extra silver
—Crumb table.
—Present dessert and cordial menu.
—Serve dessert course (center of cover).
—Remove dessert course.
—Serve coffee (if not served with dessert).
—Serve cordials.
—Present check.
—Thank guest.
—Help guests as they rise to leave and check that no personal articles are left behind.
—Remove tip and plate (tray). (Don't count tip.)
—Clear table and relay if necessary. Refill water glasses when less than 2/3 full. Be sure to refill all water glasses to same level when refilling one.

Family-style Service

Family-style Service has been referred to as French or Russian Service in some areas, but it is more commonly called English Service. The particular characteristic of this type of service is that all food is brought to the table where all the guests are seated in dishes or on platters. The food is carved, dished, or plated and passed to each individual at the table, or the food is passed and each guest helps himself. In a home where domestic help is available, the maids or butlers may pass the dishes, approaching each guest from his/her left and allowing the guest to serve himself/herself while the maid holds the platter. This form of Family-style Service may be used in commercial establishments, but this author knows of none. Several restaurants use the form of Family-style Service where the plates and platters with food are placed on the table, and the guests help themselves. This type of service can be compared to an American Thanksgiving Dinner where all the guests are seated at one time, the turkey is carved (before or after all have been seated), and the food is passed around the table.

Oriental restaurants typically use a modified form of Family-style Service, as the various entrees in an Oriental restaurant are shared by the guests at the table. Yet in finer Oriental restaurants the guests do not plate their own food, but a waiter/waitress portions the various entrees at tableside, usually working from a cart.

Service à la Ritz is sometimes referred to as *Luxury English Service* and is very similar to Family-style Service. The host/hostess or waiter/waitresses duties, however, are assumed by a highly skilled server who makes a show of serving the food.

Advantages and Disadvantages of Family-style Service

The necessity of hiring a fully qualified staff is not required when Family-style Service is being used. For example, a restaurant operator could hire high-school aged waiters/waitresses in his/her restaurant, since they only need to place empty plates on the table and place large platters of food on the table. Even the skill required to serve a particular guest the meal he/she ordered is no longer necessary. Additionally, this type of service can be very fast. No time is required to mix and match entrees and vegetables either at the range or from a cart. As a result, menu prices can be lower, which with all other things being equal and a healthy market to draw from, will increase the volume of business. Since all the food is prepared in the kitchen, Family Service offers excellent quality control; however, portion control is likely to be quite poor. Tables should be as large as for Platter Service, since additional table space is required for the dishes that are placed on the table. As with Platter Service, Family-style Service can require dining room space of more than fifteen square feet per person unless the larger tables are carefully arranged. Turnover is apt to be high since the service is fast, and this fast service decreases residence time for the guest.

Depending on the length of the menu (i.e., appetizers, soups, fish, entrees, salads, desserts, etc.), one waiter/waitress could efficiently serve more than the standard fourteen to eighteen guests; however much more than twenty guests at one time (à la carte) would be doubtful.

The most notable disadvantage for Family Service in a commercial establishment is that the guest may not get the feeling that he/she is being waited on, since food is placed on the table and the guests help themselves. Also, the dirty dishes at the table will make the table look messy, and again the guest may not feel he is in a restaurant. These disadvantages are not as critical in an Oriental restaurant mainly because a precedent has been established in Oriental restaurants and guests are accustomed to this form.

This author does not find Family-style Service as a viable alternative as a type of service for a commercial establishment excluding Oriental restaurants. There are however, successful restaurants offering this style of service when there is a market.

Buffet Service

In Buffet Service the guest helps himself from the buffet table. The buffet itself (i.e., the display of food on the table) can range from a very simple buffet, such as a soup and salad bar, to an elaborate buffet, such as those seen aboard luxury cruise liners. Many commercial restaurants build their reputations on the elaborate buffet table they offer.

Buffets are effective sales tools and can be used to the operator's benefit if offered during holidays or Sundays. Since fewer production and service staff are required to efficiently serve a given number of guests as compared to à la carte service, both production and service staffs may be given days off without damaging the reputation of the business. The food quality can be high and each waiter/waitress can serve more guests efficiently for buffet service, since the guest is performing some of the waiter/waitresses functions.

Food production workers can also be more productive as food preparation can be spread over a longer period of time and produced in quantity versus "made-to-order" individual portions.

Service personnel may enjoy working buffets since they can

serve more people and earn more in gratuities. The guest seldom distinguishes between Buffet and Plate Service and usually tips 15%. Yet managers and waiters/waitresses should be aware of an additional responsibility when working buffets. Menu items can be changed or substitutions can occur during the course of the meal and it is each waiter/waitresses' responsibility to check the table for these changes in order to keep the guests informed. The service staff or a designated runner should watch the buffet table to be sure the food stays hot and appears appetizing.

Some Disadvantages of Buffet Service

Unless the service and production staffs are made aware of the appearance of the buffet table, the food can become unappetizing while sitting on the buffet line. One cure for this problem, however, is to produce food in smaller batches and regularly change the dishes on the buffet. Food cost can be high, as there is excessive waste when the food becomes unusable due to exposure. New laws regarding sanitation are making stringent requirements for buffet lines. Food must be covered (sneeze guards), and top heat as well as bottom heat is essential in order to keep food hot and out of the danger zone (45° F to 140° F). Before installing a buffet or soup and salad bar, the restauranteur should investigate the state and local or county laws regarding the service of wholesome food to the consumer.

Banquet Service

No other type of service requires as much planning as Banquet Service. There are many advantages to this form of service, which will be explored here along with some characteristics.

Since Banquet Service is simultaneous service, that is, guests being served at the same time, all arrangements, menus, beverages, wines, and timing must be made in advance. A staff briefing is essential to insure that arrangements are communicated to *each* staff member. Banquet Service usually involves a preset menu with place settings that reflect it. For example, if the menu calls for soup, salad, main course, dessert, two wines, and coffee, the place setting should have a soup spoon, a fork for the salad, a fork and knife for the main course plus steak knife if required, a butter knife, a utensil for dessert (spoon or fork as required), teaspoon for coffee, a water goblet (in the

United States), and two wine glasses. In addition to having each place setting designed for the meal, the tables should also be set for the menu to include any accompaniments. Accompaniments to the meal, which should not be preset on the table, should be ready before service begins. If a waiter forgets to set butter for service during a la carte dining room operations, some delays will result; however this will not completely destroy the timing of the meal. If someone forgets to set the butter for service during a banquet for 400, the delay could ruin the banquet.

The same rules of service apply during a banquet as during a la carte service except that waiters/waitresses seldom engage in conversation with the guests. For à la carte service the waiter/waitress must converse with the guest if not for just taking the order. As mentioned previously, service should be simultaneous. The rule of thumb for simultaneous service is that from the time the first guest is served any particular course until the last guest is served, no more than seven minutes should elapse. If production cannot plate 400 meals in seven minutes, they should preplate some of the meals, keep the food warm, and serve these meals first while continuing to plate the remainder.

Advantages and Disadvantages of Banquet Service

As an addition to à la carte service in an establishment, Banquet Service can be very profitable on many scales. Banquet Service is very fast—one waiter/waitress can serve almost twice as many guests efficiently as compared to à la carte Plate Service. Employee morale among the service staff employees may increase as their efforts are well rewarded in gratuities. Since the number of people to be served (allowing for minor adjustments) is established, the staff wastes little time in setting up. A staff member may come on shift at 10:30 A.M., set up the tables and the accompaniments in one hour, take a twenty-minute lunch break, finish setup, serve the meal, break down, and be out by 2:30 P.M. Meanwhile, she could have served twenty-eight guests an eighteen dollar meal and collected seventy-five dollars for her efforts!

The fact that the number of covers is known in advance makes scheduling much easier than for à la carte. The fact that additional part-time help can be scheduled solely on the known volume rather than the estimated volume makes this much more efficient. Banquet sales can be considered plus sales and can be very profitable since food cost is easily precalculated and waste due to overproduction is minimal. Operators can give better value to the consumer because of the above mentioned factors.

Some Disadvantages

Kitchen personnel usually have little to gain from the additional banquet sales. Equipment in the kitchen is sometimes overused in order to prepare for a banquet. Managers seldom add production personnel in order to cover the banquets, and as a result production personnel morale declines. Additionally, many of the other types of equipment used by service personnel, such as water pitchers, silverware, and glassware, are in short supply during a large banquet, thus the ongoing operation may suffer if each a la carte guest receives poor service.

Conclusion

All too often service is given little attention during the planning phases of a food service establishment and, as pointed out, there are some definite advantages and disadvantages to the various types of service. The formal types of service present more disadvantages on the surface, yet this added touch may be that single factor that distinguishes one's success from another's failure.

Before the decision is made, surveys should be conducted as part of the feasibility study to determine the market for such a venture.

For Review: Complete This Matrix for a Review of This Chapter

Factors	Plate	Platter	Cart	Buffet	Banquet
Selling price for menu items					
Caliber of service					
Turnover available					
Skill required of service personnel					
Amount of training required					
Physical space in dining room					
Quality control					
Portion control					
Rules of thumb for staffing requirements					
Cost to implement					
Place setting required					
Quality of food					
Staff motivation					
Best for à la carte					
Advisability for areas with inexperienced staff (i.e., developing countries)					
Equipment inventory					
Presentation of food					

Chapter 5

Equipment Used in Service

The subject of equipment is approached with disdain by many restaurant managers, while others approach the subject with enthusiasm. Many owners/managers become so totally involved in the selection and purchase of equipment that they neglect other important areas of concern for effective management.

Equipment is quite expensive and many are appalled at the high cost to the purchaser, even though he/she may be purchasing in quantity and at wholesale prices. For example, one chair costs upwards of $100, with many models costing upwards of $150. This means that the chairs alone in a small 60-75-seat dining room may have cost $8,000 or more. This should bring two considerations to the manager's attention: (1) What is my initial cost? (2) Can I replace the items I purchase, and how much will these items cost in the future? In fact, a manager should always be aware of his initial cost and replaceability. Some operations use personalized china, silverware, and glassware, which may lend a touch of class to the operation. Yet personalized equipment and utensils are more expensive than open stock items and personalized items may be taken by guests and employees as souvenirs. The manager must decide if the additional cost is worth the investment. The following discussion of restaurant equipment will be limited to the dining room or front of the house. Specifically, discussion will focus on china, silverware, glassware, holloware (pitchers, wine buckets, etc.), and accessories, such as linen, tables, chairs, and buffet equipment.

China

As with other types of equipment, the initial purchase or replacement of china is most important. Perhaps the managerial considerations in the initial purchase and replacement of china is *more* important than the purchase of other types of equipment. China may have a shorter life than silverware, but it usually has a longer life than glassware.

China is quite expensive; for example, a standard dinner plate costs from $45 to $60 per dozen, and a standard place setting (dinner plate, cup and saucer, butter plate, and two miscellaneous dishes) may cost upwards of $15. When you consider that for each seat in the restaurant you may have to purchase three place settings, the cost per seat for china alone approaches $50.

In order to determine the proper quantity however, several factors must be considered:

1. turnover rate
2. type of dish machine (i.e., rate at which items can be washed)
3. number and type of menu items and frequency of service of particular items
4. which dishes can be used for more than one purpose or more than one menu item.

When a manager of an existing operation decides to add more of the same pattern to his present stock, he must also consider several other factors. His restaurant may have been renovated and the present pattern no longer fits the restaurant's decor. Since the particular pattern in use may be very costly, it might be wiser to retire the present stock, reserve it for special or private parties, and purchase an entirely new pattern for daily use. A particularly well known restaurant purchased gold-rimmed china several years ago when the price of gold and the price of labor was lower. Before a decision was made to purchase more of the same pattern, an enterprising manager investigated the costs and found that it would be less expensive to purchase a new pattern than it would be to bring the pattern in use up to par stock levels. Yet another exclusive restaurant keeps the molds for *their* unique design under lock, and the replacement costs are doubtless quite high.

"Many educators feel that children and adolescents should be brought up with china—particularly in schools and other "eating out" situations as an aid to both social development and discipline. It has been found that meals served on china not only promote better table manners, but can act as a psychological deterrent to rowdiness."[1]

Selection of China

No one can dispute that restaurants are selling a product (food) to the guest, and the guest purchases this product in a package. Admittedly, it is not a cardboard or plastic package, but nonetheless the presentation of the meal on a plate or the transfer from a platter to the plate can be considered a package. How the guest perceives this package preconditions his acceptance or rejection of that product. The restaurant caters to a specific type of customer, and the restauranteur should choose the product that appeals to the largest number of the type guests he/she expects to serve. (This may be determined by a survey or by market research.)

Good restaurant china is very resistant to breakage, chipping, and scratching, but is usually broken by china hitting china. Seventy-five to eighty percent of all breakage occurs in the soiled dish area. The manager should consider the durability of the china before purchasing a particular pattern or brand. Salesmen can be excellent sources of information, but tend to overrate their line over a competitor's line. It would be a good idea to use (on a trial basis) china in one's establishment before purchase, but this is not always possible. Another idea would be to ask other restauranteurs about their experiences with either the pattern, the manufacturer, or both. Local or regional associations offer the opportunity to exchange ideas with other operators.

Heavy or thick plates are not necessarily more durable or more resistant to breakage, however heavy china holds heat longer. The manager may consider the following considerations with regard to thickness and weight:

1. the ease of handling for servers, dishwashers, and other kitchen staff
2. the extra storage space required for thicker china

---

1. From a publication by American Restaurant China Council.

3. freight costs
4. the suitability of the china for the individual restaurant[2]

There are many other factors that a manager must look for in order to make wise decisions in the purchase of china. When replacement costs for china and glassware on an annual basis range from .7% to .3% of sales, it behooves one to know as much as possible about the product he/she is purchasing.[3]

Factors for functional considerations of particular concern include durability, chemical composition, thickness and weight, engineering and construction, resiliency to shock, resistance to warping, scratching, and fading, porosity, cleanability, thermal characteristics, microwave usage, and breakage patterns. Design concerns include size, shape, thickness, and pattern and color.[4] Certainly one of the most important factors in the selection, purchase, and replacement of china is the cost considerations and replacement. Open stock items are less expensive and are held for immediate delivery by manufacturers and can usually be replaced within a month. Undecorated china costs less than decorated china, and china with a sprayed-on design, print decorated, decal decorated, and hand decorated follow in that order in cost.[5] Machine prints are lower in cost, while anything requiring hand painting is more expensive. Since gold and silver designs are painted on after glazing, they do not wear as well.

Item	Amount (multiply number of seats by)
Dinner Plates	2.5-3
Salad Plates	3-4
Bread and Butter Plates	3-4
Cups	3-4
Saucers	3-4

Source: American Restaurant China Council, *Questions and Answers—Purchasing Tableware* (Alexandria, Va.: The American Restaurant China Council), p. 2.

2. Emily M. Bowden, "Managerial Considerations in the Selection of Restaurant China," *The Cornell Hotel and Restaurant Administration Quarterly* (May 1977): 43.

3. National Restaurant Association, *Tableservice Restaurant Operations Report 1976* (Philadelphia, Pa.: Laventhol and Horwath, 1976), p. 22.

4. Bowden, "Managerial Considerations."

5. Lendal H. Kotcshevar, *Quantity Food Purchasing,* 2nd ed. (New York: 1975), p. 647.

China breakage may run to two percent of gross sales per year, and this is a *direct* increase in expense and correspondingly a loss of profit. If breakage can be cut to even one percent, an operation with a million dollars in sales could realize *$10,000 more in profit!* Perhaps one-half of this $10,000, or $5,000, can be passed on to the dish crew as an incentive. The *restaurant still profits* by $5,000 that would otherwise not be there!

China can be cared for and breakage can be reduced by:

—Reducing handling as much as possible by having good storage facilities in order to avoid cross traffic; and by having an adequate inventory in order to prevent rushing to get the china back in service.

—Have a good kitchen design with proper equipment to unload, sort, and store the china as it is cleaned.

—A well-trained dish crew with proper guidelines for unloading, sorting, and stacking as well as incentives for reducing breakage.

Glassware

The factors and considerations mentioned previously in the discussion of china also apply to the selection and purchase of glassware. Replaceability costs on the average for glassware are in the same range as those of china. However, the percentage for glassware could be considerably higher for an individual operation if expensive lead crystal were being used in service. Although some lead crystal goblets may cost twenty-five dollars or more, most restaurants do not use this type crystal in their dining rooms.

As with china, but perhaps to even a greater extent, glassware is a package that the food service operator is using for his/her product. Appearance and durability play equally important roles in the selection of glassware. Yet in an effort to have individual glasses for *every* different wine or cocktail on the menu, the manager is forced to spend excessive time keeping inventory at par stock levels for each different style, and additional time training the beverage and service staff as to which glass should be used for which drink or cocktail. Some operations use brandy snifters or brandy inhalers for all cocktails, and this practice has both advantages and disadvantages. Because of the size of brandy snifters, it is difficult for guests or employees to take them off the premises. Yet a bartender may over-pour liquor in an effort to make the glass look as though it has a sufficient amount of spirits.

Selection of Glassware

Most restaurant operators purchase glassware that is mass produced and consequently is lower priced than blown or custom-made crystal. Yet there is brown crystal on the market, which some consider to be a cut above the mass-produced variety. Costs for the mass-produced product run from thirty-five cents to two dollars for a particular piece, while the blown glass may run to three dollars or so for the same piece.

The mass-produced glassware is usually thicker glass, which upon close inspection, will reveal some lines and bubbles in and around the glass. A check should be made to see if all parts are well fused. The edges and brims are usually rolled, and this makes the glass more resistant to chipping. The blown glass may also have either a rolled or a straight brim (hand beveled or ground down). The straight (sharp) brim is not recommended for commercial use as breakage due to chipping may be excessive. The blown glass is usually thinner than the mass produced variety, and imperfections are noted by small air bubbles in the thicker sections of the glass.

Glasses are strengthened (to reduce breakage) by a rolled bead, a thicker glass, and a barrel or a bell shape where the brim curves back to center of the glass. Stemmed glassware is weaker than glassware without a stem, although the glass can be strengthened (reducing breakage) if a thick, short stem is used instead of a long, thin stem. Weight at the bottom of the glass increases stability, and the glasses will not tip as easily.

It is difficult to recommend one over the other as each has advantages and disadvantages. Udo Schlentrich while at Omni International in Atlanta chose inexpensive glassware "because guests do not appreciate fine crystal; and it breaks," he says. He spends more money on items that he feels are most visible to the guest, such as individual center settings and expensive linen. Certainly other operators may feel that guests do appreciate fine crystal when dining out. The individual manager must make the decision on the type of glassware he/she can afford and which best complements the ambience in the dining room.

How Much to Purchase

It is most difficult to establish glassware requirements for purchase, however two of each type glass selected per seat for use should be more than adequate as an initial purchase. This can be reduced to one-half to one glass per seat for beer, cordials, brandy snifters, and some specialty wine glasses. Water goblets, iced tea, collins, highball, cocktail, and on-the-rocks glasses are used frequently and two glasses per seat are recommended.

Silverware or Flatware

The decision to select silverware over stainless steel flatware is usually much easier than selecting glassware. The cost of silverware is much more (perhaps five to ten times the amount) than the price of stainless steel flatware. Yet a dining room could not be considered an elegant dining room if stainless flatware were used instead of silverware. Very elegant establishments may use sterling silver flatware, however the number of establishments using sterling is limited. Most elegant operations or formal dining rooms use ("hotel plate") silver plated flatware, which is considerably less expensive than sterling, but considerably more expensive than stainless. In any case, good quality stainless is preferred over poor quality silver plate flatware as the latter will chip and peel. Stainless steel flatware is being used more and more, as the metal is strong, durable, and difficult to dent, scratch, or stain. It is easy to maintain as it does not tarnish or rust and never needs replating.

A buyer may check strength by:

1. Placing a fork tine on a hard edge and putting pressure on it to bend it.
2. Bending a spoon where the bowl joins the handle.
3. Noting junctures of stainless steel blades into handles, noting whether the blade is cemented or soldered in or is solid with the handle (cemented blades loosen easily).
4. Trying to dent a spoon bowl by striking it a hard blow with a hard, sharp object.
5. Checking junctures to see if they are secure, well-plated, and well-burnished; tacking should not be permitted.[6]

6. Kotcshevar, *Quantity Food Purchasing*, p. 652.

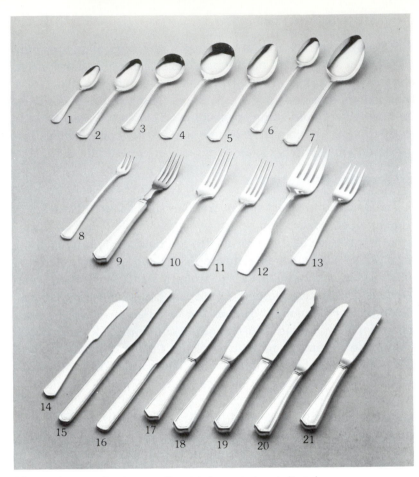

Figure 5.1 Flatware piece identification (Courtesy of Oneida, Limited)

All items shown on this sheet are silverplated except where indicated.

Spoons
1. Coffee or Demitasse
2. Teaspoon
3. Bouillon
4. Round Bowl Soup
5. Dessert/Soup Oval Bowl
6. Tall Drink/Parfait
7. Table/Serving

Forks
  8. Seafood/Oyster
□9. Fish
10. Dinner
11. Dessert
12. Serving/Cold Meat/Buffet
13. Salad

Knives
† 14. Butter Spreader
° 15. Dessert
° 16. Dinner
□17. Steak
□18. Dinner
□19. Fish
□20. Dessert
□21. Butter Spreader

□Hollow Handle   †Flat Handle   °Solid Handle

Hollow Handle—The handle of a flatware piece, usually a knife, is made from two identical halves permanently bonded together and carefully polished to give a smooth, seamless appearance. The blade is inserted between the halves and also permanently bonded for the life of the piece. Grace, balance and ease of handling are characteristic of the Hollow Handle knife.

Solid Handle—The knife (blade and handle) are made from one piece of metal stock with the handle being somewhat thicker than the blade.

Flat Handle—The knife is made from the same piece of metal stock like the solid handle knife but there is negligible difference in thickness between the blade and handle.

Figure 5.1. Continued.

1. Sauce Ladle, 4 1/2″, 1/4 oz.
2. Sauce Ladle, 6 1/2″, 1/2 oz.
3. Soup Ladle, 7 1/2″, 2 oz.
4. Punch or Soup Ladle, 11″, 4 1/2 oz.
5. Buffet Serving Fork, 13″
6. Buffet Serving Spoon, 13″
□ 7. Soup Ladle, 11 1/2″, 2 oz.
8. Punch Ladle, 15″, 4 oz.
9. Escargot Tongs, 6″
10. Lobster Cracker, Chromeplated only
11. Sugar Tongs, 4″
12. Lobster Pick, 6″

13. Escargot Fork, 6 1/4″
14. French Service Spoon, 8 1/2″
    (Tablespoon)
15. French Service Fork, 8 1/2″
    (Cold Meat Fork)
*16. Fish Fork, 7 7/8″
*17. Fish Knife, 9″
*18. Dinner Knife, 8 7/8″
*19. Steak Knife, 8 7/8″
*20. Ceremonial/Wedding Knife, 13 1/2″
*21. Pie Server, Offset Handle, 10 5/8″

*Pistol Handle   □Hollow Handle

Equipment Used in Service   **85**

The following worksheet is an invaluable aid to any restauranteur as it establishes the cost for original installation and future replacement cost as well as cost per meal.

**HOTEL AND RESTAURANT TABLEWARE
COST AND AMORTIZATION WORK SHEET**

This work sheet affords a simple and fast method to aid the food-service operator in establishing cost of flatware for original installation and future replacement cost as well as cost per meal.

PATTERN NAME _____ LINE _____

Place Setting Consists of: 2 Teaspoons, 2 Forks, 1 Soup Spoon, 1/3 Iced Teas, 1/3 Oyster Forks, 1 Knife

COST PER PLACE SETTING _____

1. Number of seats   _____

2. Number of place settings (1.5 x number of seats)   _____

3. Number of place settings x cost per place setting   _____

4. Cost for 1 years replacement @ 25% orig. install. cost   _____

*5. Total numbers 3 & 4 to get total 1st year cost   _____

6. Average number of meals served daily   _____

7. Number of annual business days   _____

8. Number of meals served per year (Multiply #6 x #7)   _____

9. Divide dollar total (#5) by yearly meals served (#8) to get cost per meal
   served for 1st year   _____

10. Cost for 1 years replacement @25% original installation cost...(Same as #4)   _____

11. Number of meals served per year...(Same as #8)   _____

12. Divide dollar total (#10) by number of meals served (#11) to get cost per meal
    served for 2nd year   _____

   Third, Fourth, Fifth and ensuing years - Same as #12

   * When using these computations, with an existing food-service operation, there
   may be a trade-in value or tax write off figure on in-use flatware. If so, simply
   subtract such value from #5 to arrive at true 1st year investment.

By courtesy of Oneida.

ONEIDA LTD. Silversmiths . Oneida, N. Y. 13421

Oneida
SILVERSMITHS
Mark of Excellence

HOTEL AND RESTAURANT TABLEWARE
COST AND AMORTIZATION WORK SHEET

This work sheet affords a simple and fast method to aid the food-service operator in establishing cost of flatware for original installation and future replacement cost as well as cost per meal.

PATTERN NAME _____ LINE _HEAVYWEIGHT PLATE_

Place Setting Consists of: 2 Teaspoons, 2 Forks, 1 Soup Spoon, 1/3 Iced Teas, 1/3 Oyster Forks, 1 Knife

COST PER PLACE SETTING _10.37_

1. Number of seats	200
2. Number of place settings (1.5 x number of seats)	300
3. Number of place settings x cost per place setting	3111.00
4. Cost for 1 years replacement @ 25% orig. install. cost	777.75
*5. <u>Total numbers 3 & 4</u> to get total 1st year cost	3888.75
6. Average number of meals served daily	800
7. Number of annual business days	360
8. Number of meals served per year (<u>Multiply #6 x #7</u>)	288000
9. <u>Divide dollar total (#5) by yearly meals served (#8)</u> to get cost per meal served for <u>1st</u> year	.014 ¢
10. Cost for 1 years replacement @25% original installation cost...(Same as #4)	777.75
11. Number of meals served per year...(Same as #8)	288000
12. <u>Divide dollar total (#10) by number of meals served (#11)</u> to get cost per meal served for <u>2nd</u> year	.0027 ¢

Third, Fourth, Fifth and ensuing years - Same as #12

* When using these computations, with an existing food-service operation, there may be a trade-in value or tax write off figure on in-use flatware. If so, simply subtract such value from #5 to arrive at true 1st year investment.

By courtesy of Oneida.

ONEIDA LTD. Silversmiths . Oneida, N. Y. 13421

Oneida
SILVERSMITHS
Mark of Excellence

The following table is based on a general operation for normal service. Quantities and items will vary according to the individual operation. To work out a proper service, consideration should be given to number of uses of the seats and rate of washing and drying, as well as quantity to be held in reserve. In most cases, reserve stock should be at least 25% of that in active service, and reorders should be placed as often as practical.

Item and Description	Multiply by Number of Seats
Spoons	
Tea	5
Dessert—Utility	2
Table or Serving	1/4
Iced Tea	1 1/2
Demitasse	2*
Bouillon	2
Forks	
Dessert—Utility	2
Dinner	4
Salad	2*
Fish	1/2*
Oyster	1 1/2*
Knives	
Dinner—Utility	3
Dessert	2
Butter	2-3
Steak, Indv.	1/2
Fish, Indv.	1/2*

*If used.

Tablecloths and Napkins (Napery)

Historically elegant restaurants and hotel dining rooms used only white linen tablecloths and napkins, and white is still considered for formal service. Yet with the advent of colorfast dyes, restaurants began to use colored tablecloths and napkins. In fact, the reason white was used in the past was because the dyed fabrics could not withstand the excessive use and subsequent cleaning that restaurant linens had to undergo. When colored linens were used, they could not be cleaned adequately lest the color would fade.

The two primary natural fibers used for tablecloths and napkins are cotton and linen. Mercerized *cotton* is relatively inexpensive, has a good sheen, and has a long life since it holds up well in soaps, detergents, and bleaches. Yet 100% cotton fabrics wrinkle or crease easily unless the cotton fabric is treated to be wrinkle free. *Linen* is relatively expensive, and does *not* have as long a life as cotton; it does not hold up as well in soaps, detergents, and bleaches. It has a moderate sheen and crisp texture (wrinkles and creases even more easily than cotton), but linen absorbs moisture quite well, sheds dirt easily, and is lint free. These characteristics make linen very suitable for napkins and towels. "All napery should be nonchlorine-retentive (chlorine weakens the fabric) and be able to be washed at 160° F with bleach."[7] Most laws require that fabrics must be treated so as to be nonflammable.

Polyester fibers (dacron) are usually combined with cotton (50:50) for tablecloths and napkins. This product resists wrinkling, but may produce an excessive amount of lint. Because of its no-press, no-iron characteristics (i.e., wash and wear fabric), some restaurants have purchased the wash-and-wear tablecloths and napkins and installed small commercial laundries *in the restaurant* for all their laundry needs. Mrs. Belle Young and Alfred Ginewsky of Avon Old Farms Inn in Avon, Connecticut, have installed a laundry for their inn (200 + seats plus a 50-room motel) and estimate that the payback period (over laundry costs for the same period) will be less than two years. Initial investment for wash-and-wear linen and washing machines and dryers for a 200-seat restaurant may range from forty to sixty thousand dollars, yet this investment can be recouped in two years. Napkins made of dacron and cotton are not as absorbent as 100% cotton or linen, and tend to spread water, wine, etc., around the guest's mouth instead of absorbing the moisture.

Service cloths or side towels should be very absorbent, lint free (so as not to spread lint on the service person's clothes or on glassware or silverware), and capable of withstanding excessive

---

7. Lendal H. Kotschevar, *Quantity Food Purchasing,* 2d ed. (New York: Wiley, 1975), p. 666.

bleaching. They are usually made from linen, cotton, rayon, or their combinations.

Some of the fabrics mentioned above dye easily while others do not. In order to check for dye that rubs off (crocking), rub a piece of dyed fabric on your hand when it is slightly moist. If the dye comes off, do not purchase the fabric. Some dyes will bleed or leach during washing, which results in fading.

Requirements for linen vary according to the individual requirements of the operation. Several factors to be considered when linen is being supplied by a linen supplier are (1) how many covers (to determine number of napkins); (2) how many tables (number of tablecloths); (3) what type of tables; (4) how long between deliveries. In any case, it is wise to *overestimate* linen requirements, since there is no way to substitute another product as would be the case with food.

Accessories and Other Equipment

There are many pieces of equipment that are used in a food service operation. Time and space do not permit a detailed description of all equipment used; however, a brief description of some of the more common pieces follows.

Salt and Pepper Shakers, Pepper Mills. Shakers should not have cut glass areas or excessive indentations as this makes them difficult to clean. Pepper mills should be decorative, but also as smooth as possible to facilitate cleaning.

Ashtrays. Ashtrays are relatively inexpensive, yet the safety ashtray is recommended over other models. The safety ashtray has two ridges and the cigarette rests on both. When the cigarette burns down to the first ridge, the cigarette falls into a trough, rather than on the table, and snuffs itself out.

Holloware. This includes pitchers, creamers, sugar bowls, ice buckets, etc., and can be made of silverplate or stainless steel. "Edges should be turned in to give extra strength and reduce chances for denting. Seams should clean easily. Handles should be separated from the unit by insulation if the container is to hold hot items. . . . insulation should be guaranteed against loosening. Points of juncture should be well soldered with silver or hard solder . . . spouts on pitchers . . . should be of the nondrip type."[8]

8. Kotcshevar, *Quantity Food Purchasing*, p. 653.

Coffee Makers. The automatic, ten-cup (glass bubble) pot coffee makers are recommended for most restaurant use. This type of equipment will reduce waste, and the coffee is usually much fresher. The large one- or two-pound automatic coffee makers are necessary when large banquets are being served; but for a la carte operations, waste can be excessive.

Espresso Machines. Espresso is a favorite after-dinner coffee drink, and cappucino can be made by combining espresso with whipped cream. Several models are available; yet the automatic, by-the-cup, vending-machine-type coffee maker is recommended over the manual machine or espresso coffee pot. The automatic vending machine is maintained quite easily and *yields a consistent product*. Some restauranteurs have mounted small espresso machines on carts. They roll the carts to the tableside and make a pot or a cup of espresso in front of the guests. This increases sales significantly.

Toasters. There are two types of toasters on the market with which service personnel should be familiar. Waiters and waitresses operate toasters as often as any other person in the kitchen, since it is one of their tasks especially in serving breakfast. One type of toaster is on a conveyor belt or rotary rack and another type is the pop-up toaster. Multiple units of pop-up toasters can increase the capacity such that, with respect to volume, one type has no advantage over the other. However, rotary or belt toasters use more energy, as they remain on during the entire serving period while the pop-up types only use energy when activated to make toast. The pop-up type of toaster is preferable to waiters and waitresses since there is no waiting to load the unit(s) to capacity.

Soft Drink Dispensing Machines. These machines are ideal to increase waiter/waitress productivity if they are self-service (i.e., the waiter/waitress selects his/her drink), and can be more profitable than single service (can or bottle) drinks. Yet many employees may take advantage of "free" drinks.

Cash Registers. This is of particular concern to the restaurant manager as this is the system for gathering management information, such as a daily sales analysis report. The electronic cash registers are designed to improve customer service (speed and accuracy), reduce costly errors (human error in tallying guest checks can sometimes run to 20%), expand the flexibility and controls available, and yield more usable management information. Machines can be programmed to the menu and reprogrammed whenever the menu changes. Programming allows for an accurate count of items sold as well as automatically pricing and tallying the menu item. Machines may have memory keys that will automatically pick up a previous balance for a particular table. Some machines even offer dual-purpose keys (i.e., the same menu item can be programmed at two prices, one for luncheon and one for dinner or one for happy hour and one for regular hours). In addition to yielding menu counts and the like, the guest check is printed in such a manner that guests can easily verify their guest checks. Some models also offer built-in digital clocks that print the time the order was placed on the requisitions (to the kitchen on a precheck machine) as well as the time payment was received. This assists management in determining turnover analysis as well as peak-period scheduling.

Tray Stands. These should be portable, but should remain stationary during the serving period if space permits. The practice of picking up folding tray stands and setting the tray down on the tray stand near the guest's table is less formal than having a tray stand in a relatively permanent position in the room. The chrome or metal tray stands that have a shelf below allow for extra storage space for such items as cups, saucers, underliners, monkey dishes, and water pitchers.

Side Stands. Stands should be centrally located in the dining room and can range from complete (i.e., coffee maker, ice maker/bins, roll warmers, water faucet, and storage space) or simple (i.e., slotted drawers for silverware and shelves for underliners, etc.). When possible, side stands should be secluded from guests' view, however doors (hinged or sliding) on side stands decrease waiter/waitress productivity by tying up one hand just to open and close the door. Doors also present a safety hazard, as sliding doors can catch fingers and hinged doors may be left open or may swing open causing one to trip over or otherwise hit the door.

Ice Machines. These can be purchased in various shapes and sizes and in several models that produce ice cubes of different sizes and shapes. The machines that produce the small ice cubes (half-inch cubes) are preferred for cocktails, since they expose maximum surface area. They are also solid, and fit well into any type of glass. Because of the fit, spirits poured into the glass fill the glass more completely than with other types of cubes. Chipped or shaved ice is not recommended except for frappes or as a base for caviar, oysters, clams, etc., since *too much* surface area is exposed causing the ice to melt rapidly. When used for cocktails, chipped or shaved ice waters down the drink too quickly, and this may be perceived by the guest as an inferior or *weak* drink. Tube ice does not fit well into glassware or goblets and is not recommended for dining room ssrvice. Half- or quarter- moon shaped ice cubes are satisfactory for ice water and wine buckets, but are not as suitable for cocktails for the aforementioned reasons.

Many other accessories must be purchased, however, and each operator must select, based on her individual needs, the equipment and accessories required.

Tables

Whether to purchase deuces, fours, sixes, rounds, squares, or rectangular tables is the decision of the individual operator in concert with his architect and food facilities designer. The mix (i.e., deuces to fours) should be determined in part by the feasibility study, in part by the menu, and by the meal to be served. Luncheon business usually requires more deuces than four tops, whereas dinner is much the reverse. When the restaurant is adjacent to areas where business entertaining may prevail, larger tables may be required. Square tables that can be converted to rounds with drop leaves offer flexibility to the operator. A thirty-six-inch square table can be configured by opening the leaves to a four-foot, five-inch diameter to seat up to seven guests (perhaps slightly crowded), six guests, or two guests comfortably by folding down the leaves to thirty-six-inch square to make the table smaller and more intimate.

Recently a franchise restaurant chain discovered that many of the seats at their four tops were unsold as a result of the customer mix during luncheon. Since they only could expect two turns (i.e., two separate groups at a table at different times) during the short luncheon service period, a considerable amount of revenue was being lost. Surprisingly, many luncheon guests were being turned away; yet, they could not increase the number of covers in this short period because of their table configurations.

Deuces are ideally 30″ × 36″ (minimum of 24″ × 30″). Round deuces should ideally be 36″ in diameter (minimum of 30″).

Fours or threes are ideally 42″ × 42″ (minimum of 36″ × 36″) or 36″ × 48″ (minimum of 30″ × 42″). It is foolish to purchase round tables for only four, as they should be large enough for six (54″ diameter), and preferably they should be convertible as mentioned previously.

Sixes are best seated at round tables (54″ in diameter desirable, 48″ in diameter as a minimum, and 60″ in diameter as a maximum), however rectangular tables for six are satisfactory (42″ × 72″ preferred, 42″ × 60″ minimum, and 84″ in length *absolute* maximum).

Eight people should be seated at round tables (66″ in diameter very comfortably, 60″ comfortably), and not at rectangular tables if at all possible.

When larger parties (i.e., twelve, fifteen, or twenty guests) frequent one's restaurant, plywood tops can be cut, curved, hinged, and otherwise fitted to rest on the operation's existing tables to accommodate any number of guests.

In all cases, a minimum of 18″ should be allowed for the chair (measured from the edge of the table) and two feet minimum as an aisle between the backs of two adjacent chairs. Total distance, therefore, from the edge of one table to the edge of another table should be (18″ + 18″ + 2′) five feet minimum.

Tables may be covered or made of wood, acrylic, vinyl, or leatherette. Depending on the formality or elegance of the restaurant, the operator should select tables that fit his decor if tablecloths will not be used.

Chairs

Restaurant chairs are terribly expensive; a single chair may cost upwards of $125-$150. It is important, therefore, to select chairs that are suitable for the operation from the decor perspective as well as for utility and durability. Depending on individual needs, the operator may choose high backs, arm rests, or upholstered chairs. Upholstered chairs add elegance to a dining room, but they may require more upkeep or maintenance, not to mention initial cost, than plain wood or metal chairs. Additionally, upholstered chairs may be more comfortable than wood or metal chairs. This raises an important point: the comfortability of the chair may help determine the amount of turnover. If chairs are very comfortable, guests may linger a while, and this may tie up a table. Coffee shop operators, especially for their counters, may sometimes design chairs so that they are slightly *uncomfortable*. Guests will spend less time at the table or counter, thereby increasing the turnover rate.

Function Room and Banquet Furniture

Folding tables can be purchased with various shaped tops, but can also be purchased quite narrow (15″ or 18″ wide) for seminars and meetings.

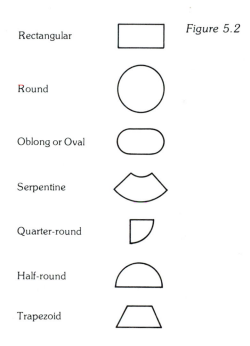

Rectangular

Round

Oblong or Oval

Serpentine

Quarter-round

Half-round

Trapezoid

Figure 5.2

Wishbone style folding legs allow for maximum seating with comfortable knee and foot room as compared to the straight or pedestal leg.

Knock-down cabaret tables with pedestal tops (center column), and bases offer considerable flexibility. Different sizes and shapes of tops may be interchanged with the same column or base, and because of styling, many of these types of tables do not require tablecloths.

Chairs that stack are beginning to replace folding chairs, as they are easier to handle, look neater, and last longer, since they have no moving parts.

Some general guidelines

1. *Strength and durability.* Be aware of the weakest link (mechanical or folding devices), safety for guests and employees (sharp edges), and ease of cleaning.
2. *Ease of handling.* Lightweight, but durable. Use of dollies for transporting furniture.
3. *Ease of storage.* Insure against nonmar stacking. Storage space is a critical concern, since this removes the amount of space that may be used for generating revenue. Storage space can limit the amount and type of function-room furniture one could purchase. A small space (smaller than is necessary) may also require improper stacking and storing, which may result in damaged furniture, or decreased life of the function-room furniture.
4. *Flexibility.* (e.g., knockdown tables with different tops).[9]

There is much additional equipment that can be and must be used in setting up function rooms and banquets; however, an extensive discussion or a listing of advantages and disadvantages would go beyond the scope of this text. A listing of the equipment would prove useful:

—Folding platforms
—Portable dance floors
—Portable bars (discussion in chapter 11)
—Folding and portable lecturns
—Trucks and dollies

Buffet Equipment

The previous discussion of china, silverware, glassware, and furniture applies directly to a discussion of buffet equipment. Yet some mention will be made about chafing dishes, portable buffet tables/units, and large shell bowls.

Chafing dishes and soup tureens may be purchased in silver plate, chrome, stainless steel, or crockery, and are priced according to the design and the material used to fabricate the particular dish. A large silver chafing dish with stand, insert, and lid may cost close to $1,000. There are many styles on the market

9. *Guide to Function-Room Furniture* (Philadelphia, Pa.: Institutional Products, Inc., 1965), p. 4.

from which an individual operator may choose. They may be heated by one of several sources: by canned gels, liquid fuel, or denatured alcohol; by bottled gas; or by electricity. Most chafing dishes use canned gels or denatured alcohol. As this heat source is only needed to maintain the heat, the heat need not be as hot as that required for tableside cookery. In order to keep food hot for any length of time (that is, buffet for a dining room, as compared to a banquet), top heat supplied by a heat lamp is necessary lest the food get cold.

Portable buffet tables come with electrically heated units and canned gel heated units. Some are designed to fit on top of a table, while others are on wheels and can be rolled into and placed in a desirable location. Recent models have wood grain finishes and can be designed to accommodate different pan size combinations. Sneeze guards will become (if not already required) mandatory, and purchase of any of these units should include sneeze guards. As with chafing dishes, it is necessary to have top heat (infrared lamp with reflectors) over each well.

Large shell bowls are quite useful for displaying seafood on ice, salad, molded gelatins or ices, hors d'oeuvres, dips, wine or beer on ice, and fresh fruits. Some are made of a molded sturdy high heat plastic, some of which resembles crystal, while others are white. The plastic is very durable and the bowls can be washed in the dish machine.

Conclusion

When purchasing equipment and supplies used in the dining room, the manager must consider each product for suitability, availability, durability, price, and overall quality. Several factors must be considered for the quantities required, and the manager must use incentives in order to reduce breakage, theft, and careless handling of the restaurant's equipment. The guidelines listed in this chapter will serve as a valuable reference for practicing managers.

Questions

1. Choose a restaurant with which you are familiar and determine the quality and amount of all equipment and supplies for that particular operation. After you have made your choices, defend your selections.
2. Would you rent linen or have your own laundry? Why?

Additional Readings

Bowden, Emily. "Managerial Considerations in the Selection of Restaurant China." *The CHRAQ*, May 1977.

Guide to Function-room Furniture. Philadelphia, Pa.: Institutional Products, Inc., 1965.

Kotcshevar, Lendal H. "Nonfood Supplies." In *Quantity Food Purchasing.* 2d ed. New York: Wiley, 1975.

Numerous catalogues and promotional material are available from manufacturers and dealers of restaurant equipment and supplies.

Chapter 6

Sanitation and Safety in Service

Sanitation in Service

Every person has been stricken with food-borne illness. Food poisoning is now almost as common as the common cold. Several million cases of food-borne illness occur each year in the United States. In spite of the effort by operators, processors, and government agencies, food poisoning continues at an alarming rate, and a majority of the incidents are *a result of poor food handling.* Yet frequently food poisoning goes undetected; for instance, people will remark, "I think I've got a little bug. I don't feel too well." They probably have food poisoning. There are many types of bacteria that cause food-borne illness. Some bacteria produce illnesses with only mild effects, while others produce more severe effects. Some are of a short duration, as the illness may last for only a few hours, and sometimes the illness may be very prolonged (i.e., salmonellosis) and severe; people may become seriously ill and even die. If the person who has become ill is otherwise healthy, perhaps the effects of the illness will disappear rapidly.

Who is responsible for the prevention of food-borne illness? The manager of an individual food service establishment is responsible for the prevention of food-borne illness because (1) it is the law and (2) the stakes are high.

Local governments are usually responsible for inspecting food service establishments for sanitary conditions and safe food handling practices. If the establishment is involved in interstate commerce, however, the federal government may have jurisdiction. The United States has proposed that specific guidelines and

uniform standards for sanitation be established for the food service industry. This document is available from the Superintendent of Documents and should prove useful, if not required,
reading for any food service operator. For example, one of the
new provisions of this document is "tableware should be set prior
to serving a meal only if glasses and cups are inverted, and
knives, forks, and spoons are wrapped and otherwise covered."
If enforced, this provision will create havoc with food service
operators.

The proposal will have a significant effect on all food service
operators, however, enforcement will more than likely remain at
the local level. Sanitation is a very important issue with government *and the consumer,* and it behooves each operator to
become a professional in his/her industry.

Violations are seldom brought before the public, and operators
are usually given ample opportunity to improve unsanitary conditions. (See Food Service Establishment Inspection Report.)
Recently in the city of New York, the local news media has
begun either publishing in newspapers or announcing over television and radio the particular food service establishments that
have violated codes for food service sanitation. Food service
operators and their employees are responsible for the health and
well-being of the public, and must insure that they are serving
wholesome food.

The most important factor is the risk an operator takes if she
does not run a sanitary operation. If a person becomes ill after
eating in your establishment and brings suit, the bad publicity
may be sufficient to eventually close the operation. Recall the incident concerning a soup canner in whose product botulism was
found. Only one person died from eating the soup, yet the particular food processing company is no longer in business. A
famous movie actor brought suit against a restaurant for supply-
ing undercooked pork from which he claims he contacted trich-
inosis. The director of in-flight services (food) for an international
airline took his own life after there was an outbreak of food-borne
illness on a flight for which his in-flight kitchen provided food.
Winning or losing the case was not material at that point. The
damage had already been done.

Guests are particularly aware of the clean appearance of a
food service establishment and have rated cleanliness very high
as a concern for selecting a restaurant. Some particular areas that

management should concentrate efforts on are the sections in the restaurant most visible to the guest. These include:

1. Clean menus.
2. Clean, unstained, and pressed linen with no holes.
3. Clean salt, pepper, ketchup, mustard, and other condiment holders.
4. Clean floor with carpet vacuumed or swept frequently.
5. Chairs, table legs, etc., clean and dusted.
6. Spotless silverware and glassware.
7. Entry, waiting area, and restrooms picked up and clean.
8. Ample trash cans and ventilation in the restrooms. An absence of odor is preferable to that of perfumed chemicals.
9. Display shelves, hanging fixtures, pictures, etc., clean and dust-free.
10. Waiter/waitress uniforms clean and pressed.
11. No smoking by any employee in guest's view.

What Can Management Do?

All food must be kept free of contaminates which means that the true food infectors, such as salmonella or hepatitis, must be checked. Bacteria capable of producing toxins that result in food poisoning are everywhere. All food, unless sterile, has stapholococcus and may have streptococcus germs, and the task for food service managers and their employees with these and other food infectors is to prevent or retard bacterial growth. This can be accomplished by reducing assembly or preparation time in the dangerous temperature zone. Food should be kept below 45° F (7° C) or above 140° F (60° C). Although bacteria may grow below 45° F, the rate is slow enough that the danger of producing enough toxins to cause disease is minimal. In every case, *bacterial food poisoning is the result of mishandling food* (i.e., leaving food in the dangerous temperature zone for too long or by allowing one who is ill to work with food).

Service managers in particular should be aware of these facts, as frequently the front-of-the-house person is responsible for keeping watch on a buffet table. Maintaining proper temperatures on buffets is not an easy task if heating equipment is inadequate.

The physical or equipment aspects are important, but so are the people aspects. A manager should be on the lookout for

DEPARTMENT OF HEALTH, EDUCATION AND WELFARE
PUBLIC HEALTH SERVICE - FOOD AND DRUG ADMINISTRATION

FOOD SERVICE ESTABLISHMENT INSPECTION REPORT

Based on an inspection this day, the items circled below identify the violation in operations or Facilities which must be corrected by the next routine inspection or such shorter period of time as may be specified in writing by the regulatory authority. Failure to comply with any time limits for corrections specified in this notice may result in cessation of your Food Service operations.

OWNER NAME

ESTABLISHMENT NAME

ADDRESS

ZIP CODE

ESTABLISHMENT I.D.					CENSUS TRACT	SANIT. CODE	DATE			INSPECT. TIME (Min.)	PURPOSE	29
COUNTY	DISTRICT	TYPE	EST. NO.				YR.	MO.	DAY			

1 2 3 4 5 6 7 8 9 10 11 12 13 14 15 16 17 18 19 20 21 22 23 24 25 26 27 28

PURPOSE

Regular 1   Complaint 3

Follow-up 2   Investigation 4

Other 5

ITEM	WT.	COL.
FOOD		
*01 SOURCE; SOUND CONDITION, NO SPOILAGE	5	30
02 ORIGINAL CONTAINER; PROPERLY LABELED	1	31
FOOD PROTECTION		
*03 POTENTIALLY HAZARDOUS FOOD MEETS TEMPERATURE REQUIREMENTS DURING STORAGE, PREPARATION, DISPLAY, SERVICE, TRANSPORTATION	5	32
*04 FACILITIES TO MAINTAIN PRODUCT TEMPERATURE	4	33
05 THERMOMETERS PROVIDED AND CONSPICUOUS	1	34
06 POTENTIALLY HAZARDOUS FOOD PROPERLY THAWED	2	35
*07 UNWRAPPED AND POTENTIALLY HAZARDOUS FOOD NOT RE-SERVED	4	36
08 FOOD PROTECTION DURING STORAGE, PREPARATION, DISPLAY, SERVICE, TRANSPORTATION	2	37
09 HANDLING OF FOOD (ICE) MINIMIZED	2	38
10 IN USE, FOOD (ICE) DISPENSING UTENSILS PROPERLY STORED	1	39
PERSONNEL		
*11 PERSONNEL WITH INFECTIONS RESTRICTED	5	40
*12 HANDS WASHED AND CLEAN, GOOD HYGIENIC PRACTICES	5	41
13 CLEAN CLOTHES, HAIR RESTRAINTS	1	42
FOOD EQUIPMENT AND UTENSILS		
14 FOOD (ICE) CONTACT SURFACES: DESIGNATED, CONSTRUCTED, MAINTAINED, INSTALLED, LOCATED	2	43
15 NON-FOOD CONTACT SURFACES: DESIGNED, CONSTRUCTED, MAINTAINED, INSTALLED, LOCATED	1	44
16 DISHWASHING FACILITIES: DESIGNED, CONSTRUCTED, MAINTAINED, INSTALLED, LOCATED, OPERATED	2	45
17 ACCURATE THERMOMETERS, CHEMICAL TEST KITS PROVIDED, GAUGE COCK (¼" IPS VALVE)	1	46

ITEM	WT.	COL.
18 PRE-FLUSHED, SCRAPED, SOAKED	1	47
19 WASH, RINSE WATER: CLEAN, PROPER TEMPERATURE	2	48
*20 SANITIZATION RINSE: CLEAN, TEMPERATURE, CONCENTRATION, EXPOSURE TIME, EQUIPMENT, UTENSILS SANITIZED	4	49
21 WIPING CLOTHS: CLEAN, STORED, RESTRICTED	1	50
22 FOOD CONTACT SURFACES OF EQUIPMENT AND UTENSILS CLEAN, FREE OF ABRASIVES, DETERGENTS	2	51
23 NON-FOOD CONTACT SURFACES OF EQUIPMENT AND UTENSILS CLEAN	1	52
24 STORAGE, HANDLING OF CLEAN EQUIPMENT/UTENSILS	1	53
25 SINGLE-SERVICE ARTICLES, STORAGE, DISPENSING, USED	1	54
26 NO RE-USE OF SINGLE SERVICE ARTICLES	2	55
WATER		
*27 WATER SOURCE, SAFE: HOT AND COLD UNDER PRESSURE	5	56
SEWAGE		
*28 SEWAGE AND WASTE WATER DISPOSAL	4	57
PLUMBING		
29 INSTALLED, MAINTAINED	1	58
*30 CROSS-CONNECTION, BACK SIPHONAGE, BACKFLOW	5	59
TOILET AND HANDWASHING FACILITIES		
*31 NUMBER, CONVENIENT, ACCESSIBLE, DESIGNED, INSTALLED	4	60
32 TOILET ROOMS ENCLOSED, SELF-CLOSING DOORS, FIXTURES, GOOD REPAIR, CLEAN: HAND CLEANSER, SANITARY TOWELS/TISSUE/HAND-DRYING DEVICES PROVIDED, PROPER WASTE RECEPTACLES	2	61

ITEM	WT.	COL.
GARBAGE AND REFUSE DISPOSAL		
33 CONTAINERS OR RECEPTACLES, COVERED: ADEQUATE NUMBER, INSECT/RODENT PROOF, FREQUENCY, CLEAN	2	62
34 OUTSIDE STORAGE AREA ENCLOSURES PROPERLY CONSTRUCTED, CLEAN; CONTROLLED INCINERATION	1	63
INSECT, RODENT, ANIMAL CONTROL		
*35 PRESENCE OF INSECT/RODENTS – OUTER OPENINGS PROTECTED, NO BIRDS, TURTLES, OTHER ANIMALS	4	64
FLOORS, WALLS AND CEILINGS		
36 FLOORS: CONSTRUCTED, DRAINED, CLEAN, GOOD REPAIR, COVERING INSTALLATION, DUSTLESS CLEANING METHODS	1	65
37 WALLS, CEILING, ATTACHED EQUIPMENT: CONSTRUCTED, GOOD REPAIR, CLEAN SURFACES, DUSTLESS CLEANING METHODS	1	66
LIGHTING		
38 LIGHTING PROVIDED AS REQUIRED, FIXTURES SHIELDED	1	67
VENTILATION		
39 ROOMS AND EQUIPMENT VENTED AS REQUIRED	1	68
DRESSING ROOMS		
40 ROOMS CLEAN, LOCKERS PROVIDED. FACILITIES CLEAN, LOCATED, USED	1	69
OTHER OPERATIONS		
*41 NECESSARY TOXIC ITEMS PROPERLY STORED, LABELED, USED	5	70
42 PREMISES MAINTAINED, FREE OF LITTER, UNNECESSARY ARTICLES, CLEANING MAINTENANCE EQUIPMENT PROPERLY STORED, AUTHORIZED PERSONNEL	1	71
43 COMPLETE SEPARATION FROM LIVING/SLEEPING QUARTERS. LAUNDRY	1	72
44 CLEAN, SOILED LINEN PROPERLY STORED	1	73

FOLLOW-UP

YES 1   74

NO 2

RATING SCORE
("100") Less Weight of Items Violated)

75 76 77

* CRITICAL ITEMS REQUIRING IMMEDIATE ACTION

RECEIVED BY (Name and Title)

INSPECTED BY (Name and Number and Title)

poor personal hygiene among the service staff and the production staff. A clean person sheds approximately two hundred bacteria per minute by just breathing, and a dirty person sheds considerably more. He or she should also be cognizant of infected food handlers. Infected food handlers transmit diseases of the respiratory tract via the nose or mouth (coughing, sneezing) and via the hands. Diseases of the intestinal tract and infectious hepatitis are transmitted when the infected person does not thoroughly wash his/her hands after using the toilet. The safe food handler must:

1. Be in good health (people who are sick or infected *must not* handle food).
2. Practice sanitary personal habits.
3. Handle food safely.

The customer is a dirty person. This is the attitude managers should take with regard to the guest's sanitary practices, as he enters your establishment wearing street clothes and may not have washed his hands after using a toilet. Although employees are examined by competent medical authorities for illness, the customer is not. He may have infections that can transmit germs, and each guest must be protected from other guests with respect to contaminating food. Self-service type buffets may soon be a thing of the past. Presently, however, it is up to the individual manager to protect one guest from the other by covering displayed food, as much as possible, from sneezes, coughs, and hands. Never serve food (butter, rolls, bread, etc.) to a table after the food has been served to another table and removed.

Service personnel do not pose a serious problem with respect to transmitting food-borne illness. The reason for this is that by the time the service person handles food, the bacteria will not have had time to grow. On the other hand, service employees who are infected with salmonella or hepatitis can transmit their disease. Practices in service are necessary because of aesthetic reasons; the guest would hardly like to see the waiter's thumb in his soup. Yet the cook's thumb in the soup can do far more damage. Service personnel can pose a problem, however, when their duties take them into the kitchen and they handle food.

The food service manager and the service manager in particular may observe much when conducting a preemployment interview with respect to sanitary habits.

—Does the prospective employee *look dirty?*
—Does he have skin infections?
—Does she display nervous habits by picking at her face?
—Does she bite her fingernails?
—Does the prospective employee cough, sneeze, wheeze, or appear to have a runny nose?

This list should not imply that the person seeking employment should not undergo a physical exam; quite the contrary. Yet a physical by a physician may mention nothing about biting fingernails or picking at one's face. A preemployment physical examination is desirable in order to screen out possible disease carriers, but this is no guarantee of the permanent health of the employee. Physical examinations are not required by most states in the United States, yet other countries may require physical examinations.

What Can the Manager Look For?

How can a manager tell if her operation is doing a good job in the sanitation area at a glance? Truthfully, she cannot. Yet there are some things she can look for as indicators.

1. Are there frequent complaints that the food served has foreign objects in it?
2. Are the guests leaving food on plates? This may indicate that portions are too large or that food is aesthetically unpleasing (e.g., off taste).
3. Is the air conditioning system working properly? Dirty filters will not remove stale odors from the dining room, and this is irritating to the guest and provides food for breeding vermine.
4. Are there frequent complaints that the food is cold?
5. Does the service staff spend an inordinate amount of time polishing glassware and silverware?
6. Do the water goblets have a fishy odor? This indicates a faulty dish machine.
7. Do the guests ask for replacements for dirty, cracked, or chipped china or glassware?
8. Are the drapes dusty; are windows streaked, grimmy, or greasy; are the walls clean and uncracked; are there cobwebs; are floor tiles loose; is the carpet stained or soiled?

What can the manager do in order to reduce the risk of hosting a food-borne illness outbreak in his establishment (designed specifically for the front-of-the-house)?

1. Provide adequate hand washing facilities that are well supplied and in all areas where hands are likely to become contaminated.
2. Provide clean and sanitary locker rooms.
3. Provide for sanitary garbage disposal—adequate number of durable trash cans with lids, and frequent collection.
4. Keep rodents and insects out or under control. Spraying with pesticides may be necessary, but the best prevention is a clean establishment.
5. Provide adequate supplies and separate ample storage for cleaning materials.
6. Provide adequate labor for proper and correct cleaning of dining room and kitchen. Check that dark, damp areas and areas where food spills (e.g., service stations, side stands, or tray stands) are cleaned frequently.
7. Provide adequate checklists and cleaning instructions for all equipment. Excellent cleaning procedures are listed in Longree and Blaker's text *Sanitary Techniques in Food Service*.
8. Provide hot and cold holding equipment that will keep food out of the danger zone of 45°F-140°F (7°C-60°C). Food should be heated to 165°F (74°C) before being placed in a steam table or chafing dish for buffet service. Are salad dressings, cream, or other condiments left on the service stands, the guest's table, or the buffet table without refrigeration?
9. Provide for adequate training of all employees preparing and handling food; suggest training films or filmstrips.
10. Impress upon each employee the importance of good sanitation habits and practices. As a supervisor, show that you appreciate the efforts of your employees to maintain a clean and sanitary restaurant.

A Checklist for Sanitary Practices for Service Personnel (Designed for the Service Employee)

1. Keep yourself in good health; report illnesses to your supervisor.
2. Bathe daily, use deodorant, wash hair at least twice a

week, and wear clean clothes; change undergarments daily.

3. Frequent, thorough, and correct hand washing (30 seconds rubbing with soap).
4. Open cuts or abrasions should be covered with antiseptic bandages and waterproof protector.
5. No smoking—contamination from hand to mouth to hand.
6. Clean uniforms donned at establishment.
7. No decorative jewelry.
8. Avoid using a handkerchief or tissues in dining room, use only if involuntary sneezing or coughing occurs. Wash hands immediately.
9. Do not touch food contact surfaces such as fork tines, spoons, knives, etc.
10. Never touch food; butter, bread, ice, etc. Use plastic gloves if touching food is unavoidable.
11. Handle glassware by the base or stem.
12. Handle cups by the handle.
13. Handle plates with the fat part of the thumb; do not place thumb on the plate.
14. Do not serve on soiled, chipped, or cracked china or glassware.
15. Any silverware or china placed on a table in which guests have been seated should never be reused.
16. Do not use anything that has dropped to the floor.
17. Do not touch head or hair or other parts of the body; wash hands if you accidentally touch your face or body.
18. Keep fingernails short and clean.
19. Never spit in the kitchen or dining room.
20. Change tablecloths when soiled, but preferably after each turnover.
21. Do not use service cloth to wipe perspiration from body or face.
22. Do not wipe hands on apron or clothes.
23. Use clean menus, not soiled ones. Requisition pads and guest check books should be clean.
24. Clean and wash chairs frequently; wash tables with warm, soapy water after each turnover and wipe dry with a clean cloth or paper towel.

25. Condiment containers should be wiped and clean for each service period.
26. Remove gum from under tables and counters (before and after service).
27. Do not invert glasses over bottles or stack cups or glasses so that the bottom of one touches where the guest's mouth would touch.
28. Use a hairnet to maintain hair above the collar.

Safety in Service

The Occupational Safety and Health Act passed in 1970 (OSHA) specifies in detail many areas with which a food service operator must comply. There are some conditions not specifically covered, and in this case a general duty clause states: "Each employer shall furnish to each of his employees employment and a place of employment which are free from recognized hazards that are causing or are likely to cause death or serious physical harm to his employees; and shall comply with occupational safety and health standards issued under the Act."

The basic management functions of planning, organizing, staffing, directing, and controlling describe the basic tasks of management. Yet the areas of safety and accident prevention really do not fit into any one of these areas. This subject and an awareness of safety is most important to management and to all employees. Accidents themselves cost untold dollars and an OSHA violation could cost the business $10,000 in fines if the violation is considered serious or willful. Criminal penalties are also provided for in the Act, which may be punishable by a fine ($10,000), imprisonment for not more than six months, or both. But this is not the only cost to business. Although all the costs could be calculated, suffice it to say that the money spent for (1) lost time, (2) Workmen's Compensation, (3) increase in insurance premiums, (4) the cost of retraining or replacing an employee, (5) time spent by other employees to aid the victim, to observe what happened, and to discuss the incident, and (6) damage to equipment or facilities is quite high. The average compensated costs (to the victim) for each accident in hotels, motels, and restaurants is $650. Averages do not tell the whole story, however. There are certainly many accidents that range into the many thousands of dollars.

A summary of illnesses and injuries recorded by a large hotel chain in one year indicate the following:[1]

Type of Injury	% of Total Injuries	Average Cost
Falls on level surfaces	16%	$750
Cuts on sharp objects (knives, broken glass, etc.)	11	100
Lifting	11	600
Struck by doors, carts, etc.	10	600
Pushing objects (carts, beds, furniture, etc.)	7	1,350
Caught in-under-between	6	200
Struck against	6	150
Foreign Particles in eyes (soaps, cleaners, dust, etc.)	5	300
Hand tools	5	90
Burns (hot objects spilled— hot water, coffee, etc.)	5	400
Falls from elevated surfaces (ladders, etc.)	4	600
Dermatitis (from soaps, cleaners, etc.)	3	140
Machine in operation	2	1,000
Inhalation, ingestion, skin, absorption of toxic chemicals	2	800
Bending, stooping	2	1,250
Miscellaneous	6	—

1. *NIOSH Health and Safety Guide for Hotels and Motels*, p. 5.

Any restaurant engaging in *ultrahazardous activity* as defined by the law is liable for the manager's behavior and the behavior of his employees. If flaming foods are on a restaurant's menu, the operator should insure that he/she is adequately covered with liability insurance. Additionally, the operator should train and make a record of training sessions in order to prove in a court of law that he/she has exercised *reasonable care* in offering tableside foods. Proof of and adherence to the procedures listed in chapter 10 of this text may help prove that an operator has exercised reasonable care in flaming foods at the table side.

What Is an Accident?

An accident is a suddenly occurring unintentional event that causes injury or property damage. An accident may be the cause of an unsafe act or an unsafe condition, and an unsafe condition may result from either poor housekeeping or poor maintenance.

To begin an accident prevention training program to help prevent unsafe acts, the manager should approach accident prevention from two lines of thought—the psychological and the physical. Low morale and a poorly trained person are ripe conditions for accidents. Over half the accidents in the food service industry are the result of new employees who have been on the job for less than two years. The emotional condition of a person under stress could present a dangerous situation, and stress conditions are very real possibilities in the service industries since the work is a high tension, rush-and-slack-period type job. Physical fatigue also creates a potentially hazardous situation. The service person who must work a double shift falls into this category.

As an industry serving the public, the hospitality industry has an additional burden of protecting the guest. Correcting sloppy housekeeping or shoddy maintenance will do much to correct hazardous situations and to protect guests and employees.

Rarely are safety efforts and accident prevention supported by a desire to anticipate, prevent, and avoid accidents. Carelessness is usually the first blame and punishment is usually the remedy. The way to protect against accidents is proper training. Although the responsibility for safety and safety awareness is everyone's responsibility, the ultimate responsibility is management's. Lip service is inadequate, and the manager must make a *concerted, planned* effort for instituting safe practices.

A standard checklist should be available to each employee, and each should be able to follow instructions.

In Case of Emergency:

— Personnel to notify in case of an emergency.
— Air raid instructions.
— Fire evacuation procedures.
— Release of kitchen CO_2 system procedures.
— Death (do not remove the remains, cover with blanket, call local authorities, call management or persons on emergency list, discourage assembly of crowd).
— Disorders (do not get involved, call management, call local authorities if situation is out of hand).
— Elevator malfunctions (find location of car; if passengers are in car, ask them to remain calm; assure them that help is on the way; call maintenance personnel; call management).
— Post a list of First Aid Instructions; make the Red Cross *Standard First Aid Guide* accessible.
— Gas, steam, or water leak procedures.
— Power failure or electrical arcing procedures.
— Policies in case of sickness or injuries in addition to first aid.

Departmental Fire Inspection Checklist

Corridors:

1. Are there obstructions to free passage in the corridors?
2. Is the wall finish in good repair so as to prevent fire extending into any concealed space?

Stairways:

1. Are stairs in good repair?
2. Is there storage of any type on or under the stairs?

Exits:

1. Is each exit indicated by EXIT signs?
2. Are the EXIT signs continuously illuminated day and night?
3. Are exits free from all obstructions?

Fire Extinguishers:

1. Is the proper type of extinguisher provided for the area?
2. Is each extinguisher in its proper place?
3. Is each extinguisher charged?
4. Are the seals intact on each extinguisher?

Stand Pipe System:
1. Is each hose station well marked?
2. Does the hose appear to be in good condition?
3. Is the nozzle attached?

Electrical:
1. Are electrical wires, conduits, panel, or junction boxes warmer than surroundings?
2. Are extension cords used where permanent wiring should be installed?
3. Are the power cords to all electrical appliances free of breaks and obvious defects?
4. Does the electrical system appear to be in otherwise good condition?

Special Areas and Hazards:
1. Is there evidence of careless smoking?
2. Are all first aid kits properly stocked?

Some Guidelines on Safety Training

—Find the problem or problem areas
—Determine why they exist
—Choose a solution to the problem or problems
—Apply the solution(s)
—Communicate the solution to others

The most important of these guidelines is finding or identifying the problem. An anecdote will highlight the need to identify the problem correctly before applying any solutions. In a high rise condominium there were frequent complaints that the elevators were too slow. A team of engineers was called in to analyze and solve the problem. Everything seemed to be normal and in accordance with design specifications, but the engineers decided to speed up the opening and closing of the doors; they also installed electric eyes in the elevator door crevices to reduce the time that the elevator doors would remain open. After a few weeks, complaints kept coming in. The engineers were called back in to again solve the problem. As much as was possible, they sped the elevators up so that they would move at a more rapid speed up and down between floors. Complaints kept coming in. Management was truly frustrated; short of buying new elevators, which would be a major expense, they did not know what to do. They called a psychologist to analyze the problem.

After considerable study and consternation, the psychologist analyzed the problem: How do we stop the flow of complaint letters? To heck with the speed of the elevators. She began studying this problem, and decided to install mirrors in the elevator lobbies or vestibules on each floor. The complaints stopped altogether!

Designing a safety training program is a major task. It is helpful to know that there are many people who can help design programs or assist managers in designing specific safety training programs. These include:

—Trade Associations (National and local or regional restaurant associations)
—Government Agencies (Health, Education, and Welfare)
—Insurance Companies—use caution as they could be looking for insurability
—Consultants

Within any particular property there are many people who could participate in or direct a safety program. A safety director or officer could be appointed to set up and administer a program, and a safety committee could be established; there could be cross-department inspections. The emphasis on safety will be felt by all, and this, in itself, will encourage everyone to be conscious of safety and safe practices. Additionally, a safety training program will give an employee an opportunity to have some additional responsibility. An individual person designated as safety director may be observed by management and used as a testing or proving ground for a possible promotion.

When an OSHA inspector arrives, the food service manager or authorized representative of the employer and a representative authorized by the employees should accompany the inspector. Be sure to:

—Check the inspector's identification
—Respect her authority—she assesses and you pay
—Cooperate with him—show him whatever he wants to see
—Learn from her by asking questions

A Checklist for Safety Practices in Service (Designed for the Service Employee)

Safety in the kitchen and in the dining room is of great importance. Safety consciousness is part of the job. With training, with the right attitude, and with alertness to hazardous situations and conditions, accidents can be reduced to a minimum and, in many cases, eliminated. Accidents cause much lost time, and lost time costs you and your employer money. Advise your employer and other employees of any safety practices you have learned. Report any accident, however slight, to your supervisor.

Dining Room

1. Stack dishes properly in bus boxes or on trays. Insure that dishes will not slide off. Do not overload.
2. Keep swinging doors and drawers to side stands shut.
3. Visually inspect food for foreign objects befors serving. Do not put hands in food; get another plate.
4. Be sure you use the correct door entering or exiting the kitchen or dining room; do not stop or backtrack.
5. Never hurry. Walk briskly, but never run. Keep to the right when rounding corners. Notify and warn guests when serving hot plates and hot beverages.
6. Remove and report any broken furnishings that may injure you or your guests (torn or loose carpets or rugs; curled carpet edges; defective or splintering chairs).
7. Remove and destroy broken or chipped glassware or china.
8. Remove knives and forks from a child's reach.
9. Keep your station clean. Clean up spills immediately and pick up everything you drop.
10. Throw nothing. Always make a positive exchange.
11. Use a dry service towel when handling hot dishes.
12. Know the location of and how to use fire extinguishers.
13. Know where the first aid equipment is and how to use it.
14. Unplug electrical equipment before cleaning.
15. Wear proper footwear—sturdy toes and nonslip soles.
16. Never scoop ice with glass.
17. Never clean broken glass with your hands—use a broom or a service towel and place in garbage or special broken glass receptacle, not in bus box!
18. Be aware of traffic flows—warn others when passing behind, and announce that you are passing through when approaching a large crowd.

19. When flaming food, keep the flame as small as possible (insure that pan is not too hot), pour from a wide-mouthed container, warn the guest when prepared to ignite, and insure that you are a safe distance from all guests and other employees.
20. Remove obstructions (handbags and briefcases) from aisles.

Kitchen

1. Use caution when opening or closing plate warmers or steam tables.
2. Remove lids from pots so the steam will exit away from your face or hands.
3. Do not operate any piece of equipment you do not know how to operate.
4. Grasp knives by the handle. If a knife is falling, do not grab for it—jump away.
5. Clean up all spills (food, drinks, and broken dishes) immediately. Use caution in wet or greasy areas (near dishwashers, stoves, ice machines).
6. Walk in the kitchen—DO NOT RUN.
7. Horseplay is dangerous—don't.
8. Do not touch electrical appliances or equipment if standing in water.
9. Make sure all traffic areas are cleared of rolling stock or other equipment. Do not block EXITS.

General

Each restaurant operator should have available the standard first aid and personal safety book published by the American Red Cross. Someone on each shift must be trained in first aid in order to handle any emergencies. (Required by law if hospital or clinic is more than ten minutes away even in heavy traffic conditions.)

General

1. Replace burned out light bulbs in your area; report all others.
2. Report frayed electric cords immediately.

ACCIDENT REPORT
Please Fill Out Completely

Check [✔]
[ ] Employee or Customer [ ]

Check [✔]

A.M.[ ]

Store-Name & Number _____ Accident Date _____ Time _____ P.M.[ ]

Name _____ Occupation _____ Age _____

Address _____ Zip Code _____ Phone # _____

Social Security # _____ Employment Date _____

What Happened? _____

_____

_____

Was First Aid Treatment Given Yes/No What? _____

Date Injured Returned to Work __ Time _____ Date _____ How Long Off? _____

Nature of Injury _____

Name and Address of Doctor _____

And/or Hospital _____

Names and Address of Witnesses _____

_____

Employees or Customers _____

_____

Check [✔]

| Permit | Full Time or Part Time | Married | Single |

Yes [ ] No [ ] [ ] [ ] [ ] [ ]

Please Give Us Your Suggestions on How This Accident Could Have Been Prevented:

_____

_____

Restaurant
Manager Signature _____ Sign _____

Injured Employee or Customer

_____   _____

Report Date
(Use Other Side for Additional Information)

HOW TO LIFT SAFELY

The factors that contribute to safe lifting are...

1. Approach the load and size it up (weight, size and shape.) Consider your physcial ability to handle the load.

2. Place the feet close to the object to be lifted 8 to 12 inches apart for good balance.

3. Bend the knees to the degree that is comfortable and get a good handhold. Then using both leg and back muscles. . .

DETERMINE IF OBJECTS CAN BE LIFTED AND CARRIED SAFELY.

Stack material in such a manner as to permit full view while carrying.

When lifting and carrying with another person—teamwork is important.

The load should be equally distributed. Movements must be coordinated so you both start and finish the lift action at the same time and perform turning movements together.

When two persons carry a long object, it should be held at the same level by both and on the same side of the body.

The following safe practices should be observed in order to avoid injury.

4. Lift the load straight up—smoothly and evenly. Pushing with your legs, keep load close to your body.

5. Lift the object into carrying position, making no turning or twisting movements until the lift is completed.

6. Turn your body with changes of foot position after looking over your path of travel making sure it is clear.

7. Setting the load down, is just as important as picking it up. Using leg and back muscles, comfortably lower load by bending your knees. When load is securely positioned, release your grip.

Avoid strain by storing heavy objects at least 12 inches above the floor.

Avoid awkward positions or twisting movements while lifting.

Over-reaching and stretching to reach overhead objects may result in strains or falls.

Use a ladder instead of chairs, boxes, etc.

NATIONAL INSTITUTE FOR OCCUPATIONAL SAFETY AND HEALTH

How You Can Save the Life of Someone Choking on Food

The Heimlich Maneuver is the newest way to dislodge food caught in one's throat.

Symptoms:

1. Violent choking—victim cannot answer if spoken to
2. Unsuccessful attempts to inhale (victim cannot breathe)
3. Cyanosis (i.e., blue lips, face, and neck)
4. Collapse
5. Unconsciousness
6. Death—imminent if not corrected

Persons Most Susceptible:

1. Children
2. Denture wearers—chewing sensation is diminished
3. Inebriated persons—chewing and swallowing sensation diminished
4. Senior citizens—difficulty in chewing

Procedures (as per diagram)

1. Sitting or standing
   A. Stand behind victim with arms around his waist.
   B. Grab fist with other hand and place fist in victim's abdomen above navel and below rib cage.
   C. Move fist quickly into abdomen with an upward direction.
   D. Procedure may be self-administered and repeated as many times as necessary.
   E. Consult physician as lung infections may result.
2. Lying down
   A. Kneel over victim straddling his hips.
   B. Place one hand atop the other with heel of hand on victim's abdomen above navel and below rib cage.
   C. Move fist quickly into abdomen towards victim's rib cage.
   D. Consult physician as lung infections may result.

Adapted from *Standard First Aid and Personal Safety Guide,* *American Red Cross.*

FIRST AID FOR CHOKING

UNIVERSAL CHOKING SIGN

If victim can cough, speak, breathe ➡ *Do not interfere*

If victim cannot
COUGH
SPEAK
BREATHE
IS BLUISH }

HAVE SOMEONE CALL FOR HELP

PHONE:_____

TAKE ACTION: FOR CONSCIOUS VICTIM•SITTING OR STANDING

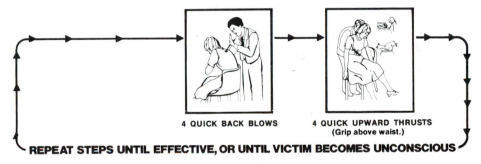

4 QUICK BACK BLOWS

4 QUICK UPWARD THRUSTS
(Grip above waist.)

REPEAT STEPS UNTIL EFFECTIVE, OR UNTIL VICTIM BECOMES UNCONSCIOUS

TAKE ACTION: FOR UNCONSCIOUS VICTIM

REPEAT STEPS UNTIL EFFECTIVE

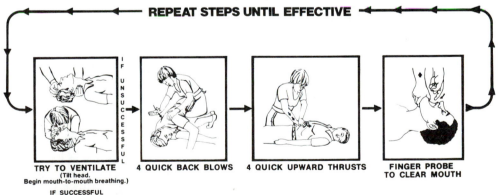

IF UNSUCCESSFUL

TRY TO VENTILATE
(Tilt head.
Begin mouth-to-mouth breathing.)

4 QUICK BACK BLOWS

4 QUICK UPWARD THRUSTS

FINGER PROBE
TO CLEAR MOUTH

IF SUCCESSFUL

CONTINUE
VENTILATION
IF PULSELESS
PERFORM C P R

Everyone should learn how to perform the first aid
steps for choking and how to give mouth-to-mouth
and cardiopulmonary resuscitation. Call your local
Red Cross chapter for information on these and other
first aid techniques.

CAUTION: Abdominal thrusts may cause injury.
Do not practice on people.

The National Research Council/National Academy
of Sciences publication—*Emergency Airway
Management 1976* is the reference for the
procedures described on this poster.

PB3851M47720M

NATIONAL RESTAURANT ASSOCIATION
One IBM Plaza, Suite 2600, Chicago, Illinois 60611
Area Code 312 / 787-2525

A person who is having a heart attack may exhibit the same behavior as a guest who is choking on food. However, a heart attack victim will usually be able to speak, and a choking victim will not be able to speak.

The following chart indicates the early warnings of a heart attack, and how to help a heart attack victim.

Early Warnings of a Heart Attack

PAIN, in one form or another, almost always accompanies a heart attack. Ranges from a mild ache to one of unbearable severity. When severe, pain is often felt as constricting, like vise on chest. Pain also often includes the burning and bloated sensations that usually accompany indigestion. Pain may be continuous and then might subside—but don't ignore if it does. Could be in any one or combination of locations shown below.

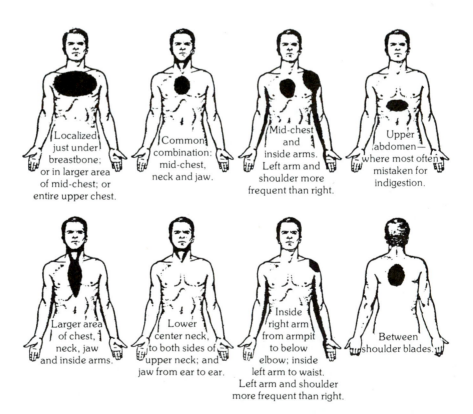

Localized just under breastbone; or in larger area of mid-chest; or entire upper chest.

Common combination: mid-chest, neck and jaw.

Mid-chest and inside arms. Left arm and shoulder more frequent than right.

Upper abdomen—where most often mistaken for indigestion.

Larger area of chest, neck, jaw and inside arms.

Lower center neck, to both sides of upper neck; and jaw from ear to ear.

Inside right arm from armpit to below elbow; inside left arm to waist. Left arm and shoulder more frequent than right.

Between shoulder blades.

Checklist of Other Heart Attack Early Warnings

None of the symptoms below is conclusive proof of a heart attack. But the more of them present, the more likely it is that the patient *is* undergoing a heart attack.

- **DIFFICULTY BREATHING**
- **PALPITATIONS**
- **NAUSEA**
- **VOMITING**
- **COLD SWEAT**
- **PALENESS**
- **WEAKNESS**
- **ANXIETY**

How to Help a Possible Heart Attack Victim

You can best help—possibly save a life—if you know in advance: (1) The nearest hospital equipped to handle heart attack emergencies. (2) How to do Cardiopulmonary Resuscitation (CPR).* (3) How quickly to call a doctor, the hospital and/or an ambulance. (4) The fastest route to the hospital. Knowing these things, you should:

1. Help victim to least painful position—usually sitting, with legs up and bent at knees. Loosen clothing around neck and midriff. Be calm, reassuring.
2. Call ambulance to get victim to hospital via your local Rescue Squad, police or whatever other method available. Speed is vital. Once the ambulance is on the way, notify family physician, if known.
3. If ambulance will arrive in a few minutes, wait, comforting victim. Otherwise, help victim to car, trying to keep victim's exertion to minimum. If possible, take another CPR-trained person with you. Victim should sit up.
4. Drive cautiously to hospital. Keep close watch on victim (or have passenger do so). If victim loses consciousness, stop car, pull victim to hard surface outside, perform CPR. Call for help. Keep up CPR until resuscitator or ambulance arrives.
5. If patient retains consciousness to hospital, make sure he is carried, not walked, to emergency room.

*Taught by local chapters of the American Heart Association and the American Red Cross.

Questions

1. Very few people actually become ill from food poisoning. Discuss.
2. Who is responsible for food-borne illness in a restaurant?
3. Why so much concern for sanitation?
4. Why is the customer a dirty person?
5. What should the manager be on the watch for
   a. with respect to his employees?
   b. with respect to the physical facilities?
6. Preemployment interviews have become a formality as very little is actually revealed. Discuss this statement as related to sanitation in service.
7. Where does money go when accidents occur?
8. What two things may cause an accident?
9. What is the first but erroneous response to an accident?
10. Who should be called on to assist in designing a safety training program?
11. How can employees be involved in an accident prevention program?
12. What should you do if you are the manager and an OSHA inspector arrives?

Additional Readings

Sanitation

Applied Food Service Sanitation. Chicago: National Institute for the Food Service Industry, 1974.

Longree, Karla, and Baker, Gertrude G. *Sanitary Techniques in Food Service.* New York: Wiley, 1971.

Rappole, Clinton L. "Sanitation in the Food Service Operation: The Implications of the Proposed Sanitation Ordinance." *The CHRAQ,* August, 1977.

A Self-inspection Program for Food Service Operators on Sanitation and Safe Food Handling. Chicago: The National Restaurant Association, 1973.

Safety

American National Red Cross. *Standard First Aid and Personal Safety.* New York: Doubleday, 1975.

Department of Health, Education, and Welfare. *NIOSH Health and Safety Guide for Hotels and Motels.* Washington: U.S. Government Printing Office, 1975.

Perkins, Charles E. "What Every Supervisor Should Know about Hotel/Motel Safety." Reprinted and available from: *The CHRAQ,* Ithaca, N.Y., 1965.

Chapter 7

Sales as a Service Function

Definition

Selling is the personal or impersonal process of assisting and persuading a prospective customer to purchase a commodity or service, or to act favorably upon an idea that has commercial significance to the seller.

The first thing that a salesman in any industry must do is sell himself. There are certain things a person can do to accomplish this. He must be interested in his job and in people, and he must have a neat, clean appearance.

—Shoes: clean, shined
—Hair: neat, clean, restrained
—Body: clean, if fragrance is used, only use a small amount
—Fingernails: clean, short, neutral or very light colored polish
—Make-up: light lipstick, no heavy eye make-up
—Jewelry: none is best, but wedding ring and simple watch are maximum acceptable
—Uniform: clean, unstained
—Smile

Recently four Army officers at West Point rated the appearance of 117 entering cadets solely on the basis of each cadet's statement of his name and home address, taking five to ten seconds per cadet. The combined ratings were positively correlated (r = .31) with the aptitude for service ratings made by peers and superiors after fourteen weeks at the Academy.

Thus people's opinions based on momentary first impressions are related to estimates of overall potential for service success. This suggests that appearance and manner, though presumably irrelevant to the job, can and do still affect ratings of job performance.

It is important, therefore, that each individual working in the front of the house have a neat, clean appearance and a pleasant manner. The guest's impression of the establishment and of his service person is determined, in part, by his first impression of the waiter/waitress.

Service personnel are sometimes referred to as sales personnel. This has both pros and cons, as it will remind service persons that their job can be improved if they are good salespersons in the dining room. On the other side, this terminology may remind the service person to be overly aware that he is a sales person and not involved with giving service.

When discussing sales with your service staff, it is important to tell them that sales in the dining room are *not* high pressure sales (i.e., using a salesman's approach), but personal, suggestive selling. The guests have already made the decision to come into the particular establishment to eat. Therefore, the job of selling is that of making suggestions to assist the person in ordering and to increase the check average.

In a recent study of waitress behavior, sociologists Suellen R. Butler and William E. Snizek found that pressure selling *does* increase the check average and hence the tip. On different occasions they subjected some diners to high pressure sales and others to no sales, and found that selling does increase the waitresses' tip which gives her a measure of control over the guest-waitress relationship. Caution should be exercised; as high pressure sales may increase the check average for the moment, will the guests return? In other words this may be a short term effort and damage the long term effectiveness of the operation. Managers should also be aware that servers operate in an independent environment since they obtain much of their reward structure (financial and psychological) from the guest, and less so from the management.

It is easy to convince service personnel that higher sales actually puts money in their pockets as well as benefiting management. In fact, the service person gets more of the sales dollar than does management.

This example will show each service person where the dollars are going. Additionally, the increase in sales should be computed on a weekly and monthly basis to make a larger impression on the service person. In the example above, "Even if you only in-

Nonselling Check	Check with Good Sales
	$1 Sherry/cocktail
	$1 Appetizer
$6 Entree	$6 Entree
	$3 Wine/person
	$1 Dessert
	$1 Cordials

$6	$13

7% × $6 = .42	15% × $6 = $1.00
7% × $13 = .91	15% × $13 = $2.00
Difference that goes to management	Additional gratuity that goes to service

creased your sales by two dollars per person, you serve twenty people in an evening. This figures out to thirty dollars extra per week, or one hundred twenty more dollars per month." In addition to making the service person happier by increasing sales, the guest will enjoy his dinner more. It is a well-known fact that wine complements the food, and an after-dinner brandy can be that final touch that distinguishes a very good meal from an absolutely superb meal—one that the guest considers incomparable to anything he has had in the past. Additionally, the customer perceives quiet, nonagressive selling as attentive service. Perhaps mention should be made here of trying to sell *too* much. If a particular establishment enjoys a very rapid and high turnover, delaying the guest by offering dessert, cordials, coffees, etc., may prevent the establishment from maximizing revenue. Additionally, this will increase the time that other guests must wait for a seat. This certainly is cause for guest frustration. Several of the newer, high-volume theme restaurants, such as The Spaghetti Factory and The Incredible Time Machine, do not take reservations and usually have at least one turn of guests waiting in the bar for seating in the dining room. A similar situation exists in a coffee shop type of operation that depends on rapid turnover. Very few coffee shops, however, offer cordials.

What Does the Service Staff Need to Know to Sell

Proper training of the service staff translates into dollars for management and staff. It is important that the service staff be competent in selling. Frequently managers are overheard in attempts to spur their service personnel to sell, "You are in partnership with management, if you do well we do well." Many, however, fail to communicate to their service personnel what they need to know in order to be good at selling.

The staff must know the basic ingredients and preparation of the menu items. They must know the quality of the raw products used. Is the fruit fresh? Is the soup homemade? What grade of beef is used—prime, choice, etc.? Is the seafood fresh, fresh frozen or convenience?

The service staff must know when to play up particular items on the menu. The franchise steak houses would not do well to advertising the source or quality of the beef they use. The term fresh frozen may be used to describe brook trout. Today's consumer is very aware of quality and value. It would not only be illegal but also foolish for either the manager or the waiter/-waitress to misrepresent the food products actually being served. Most restaurant patrons do not object to convenience foods (processed) if priced accordingly. Many are upset, however, when convenience foods are passed off as being "made in our kitchen by Alfredo our award-winning chef."

The staff must know the time required to prepare the various menu items, especially made-to-order items. Made-to-order items are just that: they are made when the guest places the order. This is not to say that menu items cannot be preprepared, but they are not cooked or finally prepared until the waiter places the specific order at the range. Such items as chicken or veal cordon bleu may be stuffed and breaded; but they are not fried until the order is placed. Roasts, stews, and certain items en casserole are prepared in advance, kept warm, and only need to be placed on the plate or platter for service. Other items must have all preparation done when the order is placed. For example, broiled chicken takes 25 to 30 minutes, whole boiled or steamed lobster is done in 20 minutes, and broiled steaks require 10 minutes preparation time.

The staff must know that ready-to-serve items are prepared in advance and what the ready-to-serve menu items are, so that if a guest is in a hurry, they may suggest such. The chef should inform the host/hostess and he in turn all of the service staff of the menu items that are ready to serve, and how long each of the menu items that are made-to-order will take.

The staff should know when to offer another cocktail. Mr. John Craver of Host Farms in Lancaster, Pennsylvania, feels that the time to offer the second cocktail is when the first cocktail is three quarters finished. The guest will then *feel* that he has the time to drink another before he is served his entree. The regular drinkers usually do not need coaxing, but the casual or social drinker can be offered and sold this second cocktail at the right time with a fair amount of success. If the waiters/waitresses present menus, they could bring the menus when asking for the next cocktail order. If waiters/waitresses do not present the menus, some other task can be accomplished (filling water, serving butter or relishes, etc.) as an excuse to approach the table.

The staff must know the various accompaniments to the various menu items. At this time, high profit a la carte (priced separately) items can be suggested. "Sir, our sauteed mushrooms are fresh and would really taste good with your steak." Other examples are chutney with curry or other highly spiced foods, mint jelly with lamb, and ketchup with fries. The staff must be instructed and made aware of the various accompaniments.

Managers must inform all service staff personnel what the accompaniments would be for each menu item (see Appendix for accompaniments to various foods).

The staff must carry through with order taking. Carrying through with order taking means that the service person must back up to the beginning of the menu, taking control of the table in a quiet way, and suggest appetizers and hors d'oeuvres. When the waiter approaches the guest for an order the guest will probably say, "I'll have the strip steak medium." It is up to the service person to say, "Would you care for a shrimp cocktail." The service person should make *specific* suggestions. "Would you like an appetizer?" does less for the guest than suggesting any specific food item. The idea here is to give the guest a visual picture of the food. "Appetizer" means little; "shrimp cocktail" means something.

Timing is also very important when suggesting appetizers. If the guest appears to be in a rush, he would be less likely to order an appetizer. If, on the other hand, the entree selected by the guest will take some time to prepare (i.e., a made-to-order item) the waiter/waitress should indicate this and offer an appetizer. "Madam, the veal cordon bleu will take about twenty minutes to prepare; may I suggest a small dish of our sauteed chicken livers, which I'll bring to you quickly?" As mentioned earlier, the guest will perceive the waiter's/waitress' behavior as attentiveness.

The staff should know menu terminology and descriptive words for the menu items. One property was noted as having a most unappetizing term, "disjointed chicken," as a description on their menu. The service person should be aware of the terminology he is using in order to describe certain dishes. (see Appendix for acceptable descriptions for food.) Managers will be well advised to furnish several canned descriptions for the various menu items so that a waiter/waitress can have this terminology at his disposal. Although the menu could have descriptions, waiters/waitresses should not just restate what is already printed on the menu.

Guest: "Well, what does the scrod taste like?"
Wrong: "It's bland."
Right: "It is a very delicately flavored fish served with an excellent sauce."

The staff must know the correct and proper service for all items. This practice may also improve relations between service and production. The chef is very concerned and proud of the appearance of the food he prepares, and the service person can destroy his work. If the waiter/waitress serves stew to the guest (assume platter service) and totally covers the plate and the rice, this is a poor presentation; the stew should cover only a portion of the rice (i.e., slightly overlapping). This brings the contrasting colors out, which makes the food more appetizing to the guest, and this is a much preferred presentation.

The staff should be able to anticipate the guest's likes and dislikes. This is a difficult thing to do, but no harm is done if the waiter/waitress misreads the guest. If a guest is overweight, the waiter may suggest a chef's salad, but this suggestion must be discrete so as not to offend the guest. If the restaurant caters to the general public, a stew or meat and potatoes may be suggested to a construction worker. Overweight men and women have a particular affinity for desserts with whipped cream topping. Each item of the menu may not appeal to a particular waiter/waitress, but *the waiter/waitress should never show distaste for a guest's selection.* Liver and onions may disgust the particular service person, but he should not react to the guest's choice.

The staff must know the proper service technique for wine. If the service person does not feel comfortable opening a bottle of wine in front of the guest, he/she will hesitate selling a bottle of wine for fear that he/she will be embarrassed. Management's responsibility is to teach the proper service procedures, as this will instill confidence in the waiter and waitress. Waiters/Waitresses who are adept at opening wine will want to sell more. Everyone, including waiters/waitresses, enjoys showing his/her better side. If he/she can put on a little show by properly and professionally handling and opening a wine bottle, this increases his tip for two reasons. First, the check is increased, and second the guest perceives this as professional, attentive service (see chapter 11 on Wine Service). If wine is served promptly, the guests may drink more, and this increases sales and gives guests more enjoyment. *Wine is a plus sale when nothing else can be sold.* The guest has already ordered his meal and all its food accompaniments. Unlike appetizers, dessert, and cordials that are served before or after the meal, the wine is served *with* the meal and greatly increases profits, since it does not increase residence time (i.e., amount of time a guest sits in a chair).

When a guest orders wine, the service person should bring a full bottle unless the guest specifically requests a half bottle. In other words, the waiter/waitress should assume that the guest wants a full bottle. He/she should *never assume a half bottle,* but if a single guest orders a bottle of wine, the waiter/waitress may *ask* if he would care *for a full bottle.* Again, never assume a half bottle. Management should stock only a limited variety of wine in half bottles. This reduces costly inventory and makes the task of taking inventory considerably easier.

When the wine bottle is empty and the guests are still eating, the service person or wine steward/stewardess should not wisk away the wine bucket, but should bring another bottle and offer it to the host/hostess at the table. If the guest rejects the bottle, the waiter/waitress should withdraw quickly, and he/she should certainly not offend the guest. Champagne is a delightful accompaniment to dessert and the service personnel should be shown this in tasting sessions.

To pick up on the idea of following through with order taking and suggestive selling, the service person may suggest a glass of cocktail sherry as an appetizer in lieu of a cocktail (i.e., martini, manhattan, high-ball, etc.). This is especially successful for luncheon, as sherry is not considered a "hard drink" and may have more acceptability during luncheon. Correspondingly, the waitress should offer a sweet sherry or other dessert wine (Port, Tokay, etc.) if any or all of the guests in the party have refused a brandy or cordial.

Many operators who have found it difficult to train their service personnel in proper wine service have found that carafe wine significantly increases their wine sales. It is quite easy for a waiter/waitress to suggest "red, white, or rose" and serve by the carafe as compared to wrestling with the terminology and the service of wine by the bottle. This suggestion does not apply to all operations; however, if wine sales are floundering, carafe service may bring the sale of wine out of the doldrums.

Mr. John Craver also feels that the waiter/waitress should give the guests a "choice of yesses." If the guest is *able* to say "no," it is easier for him to *say* "no" than if he *cannot* answer the question with a simple "no."

> *Wrong:* "Would you like an appetizer?"
> *Right:* "Would you care for shrimp cocktail?" (no, but specific request)
> *Best:* "Would you care to start with a shrimp cocktail or a fruit compote?" (a choice of yesses.)

> *Wrong:* "Would you like wine with dinner?"
> *Right:* "Would you prefer our house wine or a bottle of Pinot Chardonnay with your chicken?"
> *Best:* "I would suggest the mountain Burgundy or the Valpolicella with your steak."

> *Wrong:* "Coffee?"
> *Right:* "Would you like ice cream or our fresh baked apple pie with your coffee?"

Conclusion

Managers cannot expect their service personnel to *know* all of this information. It is the responsibility of management to train and instruct the service personnel, and the manager must insist on several important steps. There should be a menu briefing with the service personnel and the chef or his representative; service personnel must be at work in time to receive this briefing before service. The menu briefing should include all of the items mentioned above. Managers can help service personnel sell by having display racks for wine, dessert carts, and cordial carts.

Selling in a restaurant is not pressure sales. It is soft, suggestive selling, and a sale should never be forced. Managers should also insure that their service staff does not get discouraged if they do not sell well; the law of averages will take care of the "yesses" and the "nos." It is important for each waiter/waitress to keep trying to increase the check average even when it may seem that he/she is not getting sufficient response to his/her suggestions. A contest may be used to promote sales, but care must be taken so that the competition is healthy and not cutthroat. Invariably, the same person repeatedly wins the sales contest. Counting the number of people served in a given period or on a given day seems to excite restaurant operators and employees. In the classroom situation each class wants to outdo another class; while in operations the goal is to "outdo what we did on Mother's Day this year compared to what we did last year." This can result in some difficulty, since a good restaurant develops return business on quality (value) not just quantity (albeit volume is not all bad). The same holds true for each service person. "Well, we have this great waitress; she can handle fifty people at once!" The question that should follow is "how *well* can she handle them?"

Whenever a particular restaurant is having a promotion, management should first communicate this to the staff. The staff must be aware of the promotion, but additionally the personnel are consumers and can offer many useful suggestions.

Good sales techniques begin with the individual selling himself. If an individual looks good and is proud of himself, he/she has more confidence and his/her attitude and manner in turn sell the restaurant.

A Quick Reference Checklist for Increasing Sales in the Dining Room

A nice phone voice

Know menu terminology and descriptive words

Serve wine promptly

Don't let staff get discouraged; the "no's" will average out

Know how to sell wine

Smile

Know the correct and proper service for all items

Have a good appearance

Never show distaste for a guest's choice

Be accurate with the guest's orders

Leave a copy of the menu on the table

Anticipate the guest's needs

Anticipate the guest's likes and dislikes

Know the major ingredients, quality, and preparation

Don't force a sale

Know time required to prepare "made-to-order" items

Suggest cocktails/appetizers, sherry, or other aperitifs

Know "ready-to-serve" items

Carry through with order taking

Know accompaniments to the various items

Questions

1. Explain what selling oneself is.
2. How could a manager prove that good sales techniques can help the service person's salary?
3. Is it true that a higher check average can increase guest enjoyment of the dining experience? Explain.
4. What should service personnel know to be better sales persons? Embellish three of the ideas presented in the chapter.

References

Department of Health, Education, and Welfare. *Training Food Service Personnel for the Hospitality Industry.* OE-82018. Washington: U.S. Government Printing Office, 1969.

Part 2

Techniques and Procedures

Chapter 8

The Director of Service

The approach of this text so far has been directed at the upper management of a particular food service establishment. In order for service to function smoothly, the individual directly responsible for the service staff and its tasks must possess a considerable amount of knowledge. In smaller restaurants the manager may be the person directly responsible, and the manager/owner's personality pervades the establishment. In other words, this person gives the particular establishment its personality. If the host/hostess greeting guests is stuffy, the other service personnel are apt to follow his style. Correspondingly, if the host is a cordial, warm person, the other service personnel will tend to emulate him.

The larger the business becomes, the more dependent owners/managers become on their employees. Each food service establishment has certain tasks that must be accomplished. For example, if it is determined that the guest will be escorted to his table, someone must perform this task. In a formal atmosphere this task may be accomplished by a captain after receiving the guest from the host, headwaiter, or maître d'hôtel. In a less formal dining room the host would most likely escort the guest to the table, seat the guest, pass menus, and make some appropriate comment, such as, "hope you enjoy your meal." He would leave the table while the waiter or dining room attendant would take over by greeting the guests, pouring water (United States), serving butter, and perhaps serving rolls or bread. The service director must determine which tasks are appropriate for his particular establishment and assign duties accordingly. The job descriptions presented below include the tasks that should be performed and assigns them to particular individuals within the service staff. Yet, any individual may delete some of the tasks as required for that particular operation or assign them to another person within the organization. The task of presenting guests with a copy of the menu may be performed by the host, the captain, or the waiter. The descriptions presented are organized so that they may be put into operation with only minor adjustments for any particular food service establishment.

Job Description

Director of Service (Dining Room)
(Maître d'Hôtel, Host/Hostess, Headwaiter)

Job Summary:

Greets guests, supervises and directs the efforts of captains, waiters, waitresses, and bus personnel. The host must insure that gracious service is given to all guests.

Work Responsibility:

The Director is responsible for service in the dining room, coordinating the kitchen and dining room staffs, and insuring that proper service techniques are being followed.

Specific Tasks:

1. Supervises captains, waiters, waitresses, and bus personnel.
2. Assigns preopening side duties to service personnel.
3. Takes guest reservations; handles details for private functions.
4. Schedules service personnel for duty.
5. Assigns service stations to service personnel.
6. Insures that par stock items are at proper level. Requisitions or secures linen; condiments; various supplies such as sugar, salt, pepper, etc.; and requisitions additional china, silver, or glassware if required.
7. Informs management, maintenance, or housekeeping personnel of required actions: paint touch-ups, carpet cleaning, faulty electrical systems, broken furnishings, etc.
8. Supervises the set up of buffet table.

9. Greets guests and escorts them to appropriate tables (balances stations).
10. Handles guest complaints and has total responsibility to make suggestions to guests for food or beverage.
11. Insures that all closing duties are completed and that all tables are reset.
12. Dismisses service personnel.

Reports to:

Restaurant manager or his assistant.

Special Considerations:

The Director must remain cheerful and professional under the most adverse conditions or any difficult situations that occur in the dining room. The personality of the establishment rests with the Director. NOTE: Many of these functions may be assigned to the assistant manager or the manager, and this description implies that the director of service is additionally acting as host.

Although the most competent director should know every aspect of his job as well as the job of each person that works for him, a checklist should be constructed for the individual establishment, as this gives the director a guide. Proper use of the checklist does not require the host to read the checklist and then perform the particular instruction. The Director should perform his functions in the usual manner, but then refer to the checklist to insure all critical tasks prior to or during the serving period have been performed. The list should be revised or updated frequently. Pilots of large commercial airliners are required to follow checklists, yet this does not mean that the pilot could not perform these tasks without the use of a checklist.

Opening Checklist for the Director of Service

1. Record names and assign stations on Dining Room Station assignments and duties sheet.
2. Check total reservations and tables that must be set or reset. Memorize names and number in each party.
3. Check function sheets for private party settings and details.
4. Assign side duties on station assignment sheet to service personnel and check that each is properly attired and in full uniform.

5. Requisition all par stock supplies required (i.e., linen and condiments).
6. Supervise table setting check and opening side duties.
7. Check buffet table and salad bar setup progress (if applicable).
8. Specify time for menu briefing.
9. Assign reservations to tables.
10. Get menu briefing from chef or his representative. All service personnel should be present. Check menu items for shortages or excesses.
11. Check windows (blinds, drapes), lights, and air conditioning.
12. Check for proper number of clean linens and condition of menus.
13. When ready for service: open doors (assuming set service periods) and begin seating guests.
14. During service circulate dining room and function rooms. Check for courteous, prompt, and correct service: water filled; butter/bread supplied; condiments available; proper service of all items; table cleared of unused and unnecessary silver, china or glassware; table crumbed; coffee hot; check buffet for quantity of food, appearance, and heat.
15. As guests leave, insure guest checks are paid.
16. Greet guests farewell. Check with waiter or captain to insure guests have not left belongings. Assist guests with wraps.
17. Supervise closing duties and release staff as required (insure tables and function rooms are reset if required).
18. Add list of closing duties as per particular establishment.

Kitchen:

1. Ice refilled/water pitchers filled.
2. Coffee urns filled, cream dispenser filled, decaffeinated coffee and tea bag supply adequate, cups and saucers available, tea pots available.
3. Iced tea: dispenser refilled, tea made, lemon wedges available, underliners supplied.
4. Roll area prepared: baskets, napkins or cloths, fresh rolls, warmer on.

5. Soup area: cups, bowls, utensils, underliners, garnish/crackers.
6. Pantry and range pick-up areas clean.
7. Trays clean, in proper place.
8. Supply of side towels available.
9. Service bar or beverage pick-up area clean: cocktail napkins, stirrers, garnishes handy, trays wiped.
10. Butter preset: chips or pats broken out, iced.
11. Sour cream, ketchup, and other condiments available.
12. Plates, underliners, glassware, silverware restocked.

Dining Room:

1. Plates, underliners, glassware, silverware, ashtrays, matches, napkins all restocked in sidestands.
2. Linen stocked for resetting.
3. Candles, mints, condiments, doilies, sugar, salt, pepper supplied and restocked.
4. Table check: aligned, balanced (see "Laying the Tables"); proper cloth size and proper side up, spotless, pressed, lines even; proper number of settings, evenly spaced on tables; silver/glassware spotless; settings neat and correct; center settings proper, complete, and balanced.

The checklist serves an additional function. If the Director cannot be present for a particular service period, his substitute will have an excellent guide to follow. The checklist may also serve as a guide for other management personnel to evaluate the Director.

Reservations

The location of a particular property will determine whether reservations should be honored on time or not. If the property is located in a resort area, more leeway is allowed on honoring reservations. Conversely, if the property is catering to business people on a luncheon hour or catering to theatergoers, reservation times must be honored *on time*. Many restaurants realize the expense of operating a reservation system and have discontinued taking reservations. Yet, reservations have a function, and only the individual manager of an establishment can make the decision of whether a reservation system is desirable or undesirable.

If management decides to use a reservation system, several methods to record reservations should be investigated. A bound book is preferred, especially for a small property or a property where the person taking advance reservations is also on duty in the dining room. Single preprinted sheets for individual meals may be used for multiunit operations employing a full-time person to take reservations. Whether a bound book or single sheet is used, the form for recording reservations should be standardized, with spaces provided for required information (name, time, number in party, method of payment, etc.).

If reservation times are to be honored, the reservation form should have times preprinted. If these times are limited (i.e., three slots at six o'clock, three at six-fifteen, and three at six-thirty, etc.) control may be established on whether the property will have a table to seat the guest(s).

An average residence time (how long the guests stay at a table) should be calculated for each restaurant. If turnover is expected, then the preprinted times may be repeated after the average residence time has elapsed.

A countdown method may also be used for properties with single seatings (i.e., dinner theater or nightclub operations). A set of numbers with each number representing a table in the dining room may be stamped or written on the reservation form. Each number is marked when a reservation is confirmed.

222 As tables of the various configuration are
222
444 confirmed, these numbers would be crossed
444
444 off.
669

If reservations are taken, tables may be assigned one of several ways. If the operation does not take walk-in guests, tables may be assigned by name with confidence. There could be a potential problem with six stations in the dining room; six sets of reservations for eight o'clock, and six sets of reservations for eight-thirty. If tables are assigned by name, the following could result.

Mr. Kowalski with reservations at eight o'clock arrives fifteen minutes late. Mr. Barasch with reservations at eight-thirty arrives fifteen minutes early. Both have been assigned to station four. Assuming an otherwise normal evening with other reservations and other tables occupied, this system has caused one waiter to be unnecessarily busy. The guests may not get efficient service as a result of this reservation system if no adjustments are made when the guests enter.

Tables may be blocked (marked), but not specifically designated. This allows the restaurant's host the insurance of not seating guests at a table by accident. He will also always have a table that will accommodate a particular party with reservations. He then makes table assignments as he goes and is better able to balance the stations. An improved variation on this system, however, does exist. The reservations may be assigned by marking reservation times on the specific tables. As a guest enters with a reservation, the host notes the time listed for the proposed reservation, locates a table with a time and configuration identical to the guest's requests, and seats them at that table. This will allow for a bit more flexibility while seating guests and allows for a better balance of people occupying a particular station. These systems work best with a seating chart.

A representation of the tables is depicted on paper as in the example on p. 142.

Greeting and Seating Guests

Greeting and seating the guests requires a particular flair on the part of the host. Some guests feel uncomfortable when they enter a restaurant. It is up to the host/hostess to greet them cordially and smiling. He should look directly at the host of the party, making positive eye contact. This is necessary to let the guest know that you are talking to him. Since many hosts must eventually check the reservation book or begin finding a table, they forget to establish eye contact with the guest. An appropriate greeting should follow or be coincident with eye contact, "Good evening (afternoon), sir (madam)." At this point the guest(s) should be allowed to speak. The host should not assume a table for one, two, or ask for reservations. After the guest responds, "Table for two," or "Reservations for William Jones," then the host should answer, "How many in your party," or "Yes, sir/madam," or "Yes, Mr. Jones." During this brief greeting the host should be unencumbered. He should have nothing in his hand—menus or a pen or pencil. He should be standing upright, not using the host's stand as a crutch. If necessary the host should assist in removing coats that are not checked. After this the host should glance at the reservation book (if necessary), indicate that the

Seating Chart:

Time	Name	Size
6:00	Jackson	4
	Foster	7
	Holloway	3
	Slaughter	4
6:30	Cullinan	4
	Dickey	2
	Huber	3
	Allen	6
7:00	Leonard	2
	Fitzgibbon	3
7:30	Brand	2
	George	2
	Eastman	3

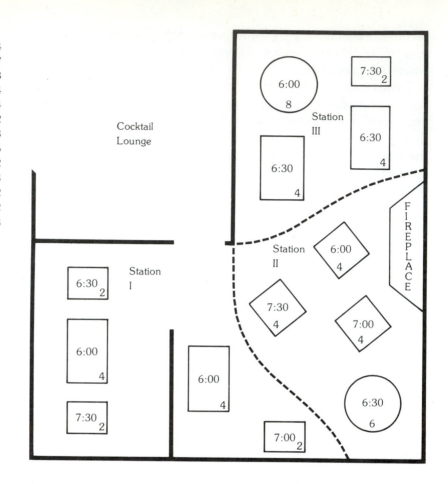

Jones party is in the house, locate a suitable table, and escort the guests to the table. If the person or group had reservations, the host should inquire if there are *still* that number in the party. Perhaps another table would be more suitable if the group had changed in size. It is very important at this point for the host to know if he does have a suitable table. If for any reason, however, the host assumes a table vacant that he finds occupied after reaching the table, he should locate a table in the dining room immediately and seat the guests. A mistake has already been made and any adjustments must be made after seating the party. At no time should the guest(s) be left standing in the dining room without escort. If there is any doubt in the host's mind, he should excuse himself before inviting the guests to follow, locate a suitable table visually, and then invite the guest(s) to be seated.

When escorting guests to a table, the restaurant's host should accomplish all administrative tasks (gathering menus, locating a suitable table, etc.) before inviting the guest to follow. When he has finished doing this he should look the guest host in the eye *again,* offer an inviting gesture with his hand and make a suitable comment, "Would you follow me please, sir." As the restaurant's host ventures into the dining room, he should walk slowly and after a few steps he should turn to see if the guest(s) are in fact following. It is very embarrassing for one to have walked the length of the dining room alone, while the guests are still standing at the entrance. After seating all guests (see Host's Greeting and Seating Guide), the host should pass the menus, attempt to establish eye contact and excuse himself, by saying, "Have an enjoyable meal," or some other suitable comment. He should check back at the table within five minutes (absolute maximum) to insure they have had service.

The host should be available throughout the duration of the meal. He should not spend time in the kitchen unless absolutely necessary. After guests have been served the main course, the host should make himself visible to the gussts by checking the table. He should not inquire about the meal unless spoken to by one of the guests, but he should make it obvious that he is available for comment. It is meaningless for the host to say, "How was your meal?" as the guest usually responds, "Oh, fine." Also, this comment could invite a negative response that may be unnecessary.

Host's Greeting and Seating Guide

1. The time spent before being seated is not as critical an interval as the time spent waiting for food after being seated. The capacity of the dining room at a given time is determined by the number and capabilities of the service personnel. It is not determined by the number of seats in the restaurant.
2. In an elegant establishment the maitre d'hotel should know how many guests in the party (reservations) and at what table he is going to seat them.
3. The host should inquire if a guest has reservations.
4. Seat well-dressed people in conspicuous places.
5. Balance the dining room so as not to overburden one station. This offers better service to the guest and an even distribution of gratuities to the staff.

6. Seat parties of more than two at larger tables; it is easier to pick up settings than to lay them. Always pick up additional place settings if no additional guests are expected. This is a nonverbal cue that alerts other service personnel as to the specific table configuration.
7. Offer the best seat (facing the dining or best view) to the lady in a party of two, or the eldest lady in a larger party. This procedure assumes normal etiquette prevails. Some guests may be offended by the preference given to women.
8. Although the restaurant's host may seat the female guests, the men in the party may, but the host should remain at the table until all guests present are seated.
9. At wall or booth tables of four, seat the women on the sofa seats facing the dining room. Pull the table out (rotate if on pedestal) so they can slide in easily.
10. Assist guest(s) with their coats, briefcases, or purses.
11. Present the menus closed from the left and assist guest with the napkin if necessary.
12. The waiter should be standing by after the host leaves the table. He should fill water glasses, take cocktail orders, serve cocktails, and place bread and butter on the table.
13. While guests are reading the menu, the waiter should occupy himself with them. He should not serve another table, however, this is most difficult to accomplish in most restaurants.

Scheduling the Service Staff

Scheduling service employees is perhaps one of the more difficult jobs for many directors, while some may not have problems scheduling service personnel. There is much variability of business in certain types of restaurants, making it very difficult to forecast covers. A manager must determine his overall staffing needs by following the rules of thumb below, and by following these basic scheduling principles: (1) know the quality and abilities of the service personnel, (2) know the reliability of your personnel, and (3) make good forecasts. Forecasts should be made by taking the following factors into consideration: (1) number of people served on the same day last year, (2) number served on same day last month, (3) number served on same day last week, (4) goings on about town, and (5) the weather.

Basically scheduling is working backwards. The number of scheduling slots is determined by the type of service, the menu, and by good forecasts. After the number of service slots has been determined, the staff is fitted to the slots. Split shifts (e.g., a waitress works from ten o'clock A.M. until three o'clock P.M. and again *the same day* from six o'clock P.M. until nine o'clock P.M. for an eight-hour shift) allow some flexibility, but labor laws as well as labor unions may place restrictions on split-shift scheduling. Operators should schedule a skeleton crew but with the opportunity to call in part-time employees as needed. Theoretically, the skeleton crew is needed to operate the restaurant if only one guest came. Many of the factors discussed for dividing the dining room into stations are extremely useful for scheduling purposes.

Number of seats in a particular station

It is appropriate to mention a few rules of thumb that may be used as a guide for scheduling and dividing the restaurant into stations.

1. *Strictly Plate Service* A waiter should be able to efficiently serve fourteen to eighteen guests *a la carte* at one time. A dining room attendant for typical plate service should be able to service four waiters efficiently.
2. *Plate Service with Some Flamed Items or Tableside Service* This should be scaled downward accordingly. If the waiter is to perform normal service and also flame items (not a recommended practice) the stations should have fewer guests. The actual number will depend on the amount of flaming.
3. *Strictly Platter Service* A waiter should be able to service eight to twelve guests efficiently a la carte.
4. *Strictly Cart Service* A waiter should be able to serve ten guests efficiently. Many establishments require their staff to serve more than ten guests per person, but this quite defeats the purpose of cart service, which is that of providing personal, attentive service. Stations for this type of service should contain approximately twenty guests, as the waiters work in pairs.

A station of thirty guests may be designated with a captain and two waiters. If the physical facilities allow, this distribution may be more efficient.

If an operator desires, he may establish scheduling guidelines based on his *dollar volume* of business. For example, if he estimates $1,650 gross revenue on Thursday night and his check (actually per cover) average is eight dollars, he expects to serve approximately two hundred and six covers. If his establishment seats approximately one hundred people, he expects two turns that night, and using the listed rules of thumb, he should have approximately six or seven waiters/waitresses on the floor assisted by two dining room attendants and a host/hostess.

Dividing the Dining Room into Stations

Several factors must be taken into consideration when dividing the dining room into stations. Some establishments have physical divisions such as walls or different sections of the restaurant. Older properties usually have one large room that must be sectioned for the most efficient service. The following factors will have a bearing for any type of food service establishment. The particular design of a restaurant may dictate the size of the service stations, and this is an important factor that is all to often overlooked during the initial planning and design phases of an operation. The director should use the rules of thumb for the number of seats in a particular station as a guideline for dividing the dining room into stations.

1. *Distance of Stations from Kitchen*. If a station requires the service person to walk a long distance, this station should be smaller than one that is closer to the kitchen. Coupled with this factor is the size of tray being used, if applicable, and the type of tables, or number of seats in the station. If the trays will accommodate six covers comfortably with all accessories, it would be best to have tables as multiples of six: a deuce and a four, a six, or two three-tops. A table of eight would be difficult to service if the table were far from the kitchen or pick-up area and the trays were small. On the other hand, if a table of eight were close to the pick-up area, the service person could make two trips without greatly affecting the flow of service.

2. *Type of Tables*. Suffice it to say that seven deuces would be a bit much to ask one to serve, but serving one six-top and two four-tops would be within the acceptable range. Therefore, the mix is very important, and the number of

seats as well as type of tables must be considered as a combined factor.

3. *Number and Distance of Sidestands/Traystands to the Stations*. Since some sidestands and traystands are portable, this factor should be of little importance, yet the specific configuration of a property may limit the portability of either a traystand or a sidestand. If a sidestand is quite far from a station, this does slightly limit the number of people a waiter can serve efficiently.

These rules of thumb must be adjusted upward to more guests per service person if there is a preset menu. It takes a considerable amount of time to take orders, record the choices, and have such plated properly and distributed correctly. A waiter/waitress should be able to serve twenty or more guests in a plate service banquet with preset appetizers, soup, and main course with vegetables, dessert, and coffee.

4. *Types of Service*. It was mentioned in the rules of thumb that the number of seats is an important factor when dividing the restaurant into stations. Along with the restaurant layout and design, the type of service should be considered as a major factor in dividing the dining room. (See chapter 4.)

5. *Quality of Staff*. Another major factor in dividing the dining room into service stations is the quality of the service staff. If one's property is located in a metropolitan area with a relatively high check average, and a low employee turnover rate among the service staff, the stations can be larger. If one's property is located in the mountains in state "A" and open only for a season, with a very high employee turnover rate from season to season, these stations should be much smaller.

6. *Location of Station*. If station one were close to the kitchen or door (i.e., a relatively unpopular station), and if station four were by the window (i.e., a popular station) station four should be slightly smaller than station one. Station four will probably turn over several tables more than station one and each service person should wait on as close to an even number of guests as possible. This division will tend to equalize the total covers for each waiter/waitress at the end of the shift.

Controlling—A Management Function

One of the functions of management is to control the operation. Although people may be controlled, the reference to controlling is usually referring to financial control. Detailing a food and beverage control system is well beyond the scope of this text, yet some mention of control should be mentioned as it relates to service. Additionally, many establishments assign the job of cashier to the host/hostess.

The purpose of sales control is to insure that all food prepared in the kitchen and served in the dining room generates revenue for the operation, and that revenue must be recorded correctly by waiters/waitresses and cashiers.

Where can the operator lose money? The customer can walk out without paying; he can sneak out undetected; he can complain that the food is unsatisfactory (taste or foreign objects); or he can claim that he did not consume four cocktails, but only three. The operator can lose when the waiters/waitresses make errors (either intentionally or unintentionally).

There are several ways that a waiter/waitress may take money from the restaurant, the guest, or a credit card company. If the waiter/waitress returns change to the guest on a tip plate, he may pocket some of the change (usually in round amounts of one, two, or five dollars) before returning it to the guest. If no receipt is given, the guest may not remember the exact amount of either the check or the amount he gave for payment. He may also simply overcharge for certain items, pocket the overcharge, and then correct the restaurant's copy of the guest check.

A crafty waiter was known to have guest checks printed on his own that were identical to the establishment's checks. He would slip one of his preprinted checks to the guest for payment, discard his "private stock" check, and pocket the full amount. A similar situation may arise when a waiter has two identical orders and presents the same check to two separate parties. He pockets payment from one party and deposits the other payment with the proper guest check to the cashier.

When the waiter/waitress collects the money and records and deposits the money in the cash drawer, the operator is leaving himself open to theft. A cashier could also use the split ring technique in which a guest presents $2.79 payment for items that are not accompanied with a guest check (i.e., coffee shop type operation); he rings "no sale" and then quickly rings $.79.

He takes a five-dollar bill, deposits $.79 in the cash drawer, gives two dollars and twenty-one cents change to the guest, deposits the five in the cash drawer, and secretly records the amount he will eventually pocket. He later pockets his overages.

Perhaps one of the slickest tricks yet involves credit card theft and/or misuse. The waitress watches for guests who appear to be in a hurry (i.e., checking the time frequently, tapping hands nervously on the table, or some mention about an engagement such as the theater, a movie, or a concert) and who pays by credit card. She returns the card, but slips it under a soiled napkin or dirty plate. If the guest leaves his card, she pockets the card and does one of two things. (1) She holds the card for several days and returns the card, reporting the lost card as found, and collects her reward. (2) She trades cards with her buddy across town (this makes tracking the theft of the card more difficult) and imprints several Record of Charges (ROCs) from the restaurant she works at with the traded card. When a guest pays for a check with cash, she pockets the cash, writes in the amount, and forges the signature on the ROC. The restaurant is none the wiser.

A more common theft technique is for the waiter/waitress to intentionally (or unintentionally) forget to write certain items (extra cocktail, appetizer, dessert, etc.) on the check for payment. This can be a "buddy discount" or he may expect the guest to notice the omission and compensate him accordingly in the form of gratuities. Guests seldom are aware of the omission and usually tip 15% of the total anyway. The waiter/waitress actually cuts himself out of a gratuity.

Another deceitful practice is for the waiter/waitress to pad (i.e., adding more items on the guest check or guest receipt) the guest's receipt and split the difference with a patron who is on an expense account.

What type of "quickie fixes" can be suggested to control revenue?

1. All checks should be totaled on a register (preferable) or on an adding machine or calculator. Some have estimated human error at 15%.
2. A dual system (i.e., precheck rung by waiter/waitress) or a duplicate check or food requisition system is essential.
3. Cash received should equal the amount totaled on the guest checks. That requisitioned on the guest checks

should equal the number of portions sold. Also, the host/hostess head count (number of covers) should equal that of the cashier's and that of the range.

4. Prenumbered guest checks are a must and if a separate means is used to requisition food from the kitchen (i.e., a requisition "req" or "dupe"), these should also be pre-numbered. Each guest check or requisition must be accounted for. It is also suggested that the checks be printed by a reputable firm *not located* in the immediate area.

5. Service personnel must be required to sign for requisitions or guest checks (if checks are used as requisitions). The requisitions must be controlled by the cashier. Many establishments assess a heavy fine (illegal in some states) to the service person if a guest check is lost. This has an advantage because the waiter is also responsible for skippers or walk-outs.

6. No erasures should be allowed on either guest checks or requisitions. Mistakes will be made, but lining through errors will suffice. It would be preferable to void the requisition and complete a new one. Additionally, each check should be rung up separately.

7. The person requisitioning for and filling out guest checks should not be allowed in the cash box.

8. Excessive "no sale" rings should be investigated.

9. The cashier should not have a key to total the cash register, and only one person per cash drawer should be allowed.

10. Exceptions to procedures must be "OK'd" by an authorized person.

11. All customers must be given receipts with the correct total.

12. Hire a spotter to test your system and your staff.

13. Review your system frequently.

Although some "quickie fixes" to employee theft can be offered, the design of an internal control system must be done by a professional. A professional will design a control system for food cost control, purchasing, and the like as well as cash receipts control. Anyone who wants to steal probably will find a way, however a professionally and properly designed control system makes theft difficult to accomplish.

There are several advantages to the new electronic cash register systems which every operator should investigate. Several of these advantages are listed below.

1. Speeds service
2. Preset keys help
    a. Reduce costly errors
    b. Expand flexibility and control
    c. Guest gets print-out of his meal (because of wide use, most guests know how to read machine-abbreviations)
3. Can be used for requisitioning (i.e., bringing inventory to par stock levels)
4. Yields more management information
    a. Employee/drawer accountability
    b. Menu item analysis
    c. Volume reports
    d. Tax summaries (sales, food, excises, etc.)
    e. Easier to isolate food and beverage items, which assists in inventory control.

Controls are essential, yet no control system should cost more than the items being controlled. Each strip steak should be accounted for; each pea should not. Additionally, controls should not be so designed that they inconvenience the guest by slowing down service. Many establishments control wine excessively, with the end result of slow wine service and perhaps a decrease in total wine sales.

Conclusion

The job of Service Director is all-encompassing, as he/she must be able to manage people and be well mannered in order to greet guests. Since the job has so many facets to it, the person designated as Service Director should use a checklist to remind him of these tasks. The particular style and flair that the host must exhibit in front of the guest can be learned. The host must have confidence in himself, and he must like people.

Accepting and assigning reservations can be accomplished haphazardly, or reservations may be standardized. The suggestions on how to handle reservations may be fitted to any establishment.

Scheduling service personnel is a difficult task. With a knowledge of the menu, the type of service, and the staff's capabilities, the rules of thumb and by maintaining good forecasts, the Director of Service should find it easier to schedule his/her service staff.

Dividing the dining room into stations is a very important function. This may determine whether the guest gets good service or poor service. It can also have a direct effect on the morale of the service personnel. Service personnel must feel they are being treated equally. If one always gets the good station, the others may feel discriminated against.

Although controlling the financial operations is the duty of the cashier, the host in many establishments does in fact perform this function.

Questions

1. Who decides what tasks should be performed and who should perform them?
2. What are the basic tasks of the Service Director as outlined in the chapter?
3. Why is a checklist helpful? List some things that the Service Director on the floor should do?
4. What is perhaps the most important thing a host should do when the guest walks in?
5. What should the host do if the table he had chosen for a particular party was occupied when he approached?
6. List five guidelines the host should follow when seating guests.
7. What are the three systems mentioned in the chapter on assigning reservations? Describe each.
8. Simulate assigning reservations at a restaurant of your choice and defend your ideas.
9. What makes scheduling the service staff such a difficult job?
10. What are the major factors that must be taken into consideration when dividing the dining room into stations?
11. What design factors determine the size of the service stations?
12. List the rules of thumb for: plate service, platter service, cart service.
13. List the major factors a dining room manager should be concerned with as related to service.

Chapter **9**

The Service Staff: Responsibilities, Procedures, and Techniques

There are countless duties that must be accomplished in any job, and it is necessary for a manager to know the specific duties within the jobs he/she is supervising. Traditionally, a manager was expected to be *the best* in a particular skill (job) before he/she was promoted to supervisor.[1] Yet a good or excellent waiter/waitress does not necessarily make a good host/hostess or dining room supervisor. And an excellent supervisor may be a lousy waitress. This does not mean that the supervisor can be ignorant of the skills required for effective job accomplishment. Quite the contrary, the manager is responsible for training and maintaining standards, if not for formulation of policy and standards. Correct and proper service is of utmost importance. Good food and the chef's art can be ruined by careless or improper service. The emphasis in this chapter is not intended to make the reader become a proficient service employee, but rather to become an *effective manager* by being aware of standards, standard service procedures, the proper method of setting tables, and serving various menu items used in first-class houses. Lest he/she be at the whims of a "trained maitre d'," it is essential for a manager to know the proper methods in order to effectively supervise.

The many tasks required of service personnel, captains, waiters/waitresses, dining room attendants, and banquet waiters/waitresses may be divided so as to obtain maximum proficiency and efficiency from service personnel both singly and collectively. Although the job descriptions that follow are com-

1. *The Waldorf-Astoria Manuals,* vol. III (Stanford, Conn.: Dahl Publishing Company, 1949), pp. 10-11.

plete and workable, individual job descriptions must be designed specifically for a particular operation. As with standardized recipes, job descriptions must be tailored to and standardized for that particular operation. The following job descriptions are expanded from the descriptions listed in *The Dictionary of Occupational Titles* (DOT), which is published by the United States Government and can be found in most major public or university libraries.

Dining Room Captain

Job Summary

Provides proper service and coordinates the tasks of two or more service personnel and one dining room attendant in the dining room.

Work Responsibility

The captain will be responsible for gracious and proper service at two or more service stations. At capacity, each station may seat thirty-five to fifty guests.

Specific Tasks

1. Greets guests.
2. Insures that waiter/waitress or dining room attendant pours water and serves butter.
3. Takes guest's order.
4. Serves guest all courses in proper sequence.
5. Insures that service personnel clear soiled dishes and silverware properly and timely, as well as performing all of their duties properly.
6. Presents check.
7. Bids guest farewell.
8. Insures that table is reset.
9. Insures that station breakdown is complete at end of shift.

Reports to

Host/Hostess or dining room manager.

Special Considerations

The captain must be a proficient waiter/waitress and capable of performing all tasks required of a waiter/waitress, teaching these tasks, and directing the efforts of waiters/waitresses.

Waiter/Waitress*

Job Summary

Sets tables; prepares dining room, counters, coffee shop, or lunch room for service; and serves meals to guests. He/she must know proper rules of etiquette in order to furnish gracious service, working in either a formal or informal setting.

Work Responsibilities

The waiter/waitress is responsible for gracious and proper service at his/her station. Each station seats approximately 10-18 guests (depending on type of service).

Specific Tasks

1. Reports to host/hostess to receive necessary instructions for the shift and for any menu changes.
2. Sets his assigned tables and insures that service area is stocked (linen, silver, glassware, and china, etc.). Sets up any special displays that may be used for that meal period.
3. Greets guests and may assist host/hostess in seating guests. Serves butter, fills water glasses, serves cocktails, answers questions about menu items, and makes suggestions about dishes and wines if customers request or desire.
4. Writes orders on check or memorizes order, and turns order to cooks with consideration to timing of preceding courses. Picks up all food and all other needed items from various stations.
5. May garnish and decorate dishes prior to serving.
6. May carve meats, bone fish or fowl, and prepare flaming dishes or desserts at guest's table.
7. May serve guests from a platter at guest's table.
8. May ladle soup, toss salads, portion pies and other desserts, brew coffee, and perform other services as determined by establishment's size and practices.

---

*This is a composite description, which includes the descriptions of waiter; waiter, buffet; waiter, formal; and waiter, informal published in the DOT. Tasks or functions may be deleted or placed under other jobs should the manager so choose.

9. Replenishes wine, water, and butter and bread supply, or has dining room attendant do it.
10. Observes guests to fulfill any additional requests and to perceive when meal has been completed.
11. After all the guests have finished each course and before the next one is served, waiter/waitress should remove all soiled dishes or insure that dining room attendant does.
12. When guests have finished meal, table should be cleared. Waiter/waitress may now present check and again inquire to see if the guest is satisfied. Waiter/waitress may receive immediate payment (in which case it is taken to the cashier). Waiter/waitress may total bills.
13. May reset table or counter at the conclusion of the meal.
14. Waiter/waitress will perform other tasks as directed by his supervisor. He/she may be asked to perform as a Captain, dining room attendant, host/hostess, or banquet waiter/waitress.

Reports to

Captain, host/hostess, or dining room manager.

Special Considerations

Waiter/waitress must be thoroughly familiar with the establishment's menu (American, some foreign dishes), and all types of alcoholic beverages. Must know how to pronounce names of foreign preparations on the menu, and what beverages complement them. Must know proper methods of serving meals of all kinds. In a meal consisting of several courses and especially when accompanied by wines, the waiter/waitress needs to learn how to regulate his/her timing so there is little or no time between courses, and he/she must know which wine goes with what course. In order to prevent the guest from feeling neglected, the waiter/waitress needs to know how long it takes to complete each course and therefore be able to regulate the service of several different tables at the same time.

Waiter/Waitress Personal Equipment

1. Bottle opener/corkscrew.
2. Ballpoint pen or two pencils (5-inch-length minimum).
3. Matches—lighter is not proper for waiter/waitress to use in dining room.
4. Service cloth (optional in some establishments).

Dining Room Attendant

Job Summary

Assists waiters and waitresses, maintains cleanliness, and keeps dining room supplied with clean utensils, china, glassware, condiments, and ice. Clears soiled dishes, removes them to kitchen, and resets tables.

Work Responsibility

The dining room attendant will be responsible for proper service, assisting from one to four waiters/waitresses.

Specific Tasks

1. Assists waiter/waitress in their tasks.
2. Removes dishes from dining room to dishwasher in kitchen.
3. Replenishes supply of clean linens, silverware, glassware, and dishes in the dining room.
4. Replenishes butter supply for guests.
5. Fills and refills water glasses for guests.
6. Resets tables. Replaces soiled table linen and sets table with silverware, china, and glassware.
7. Assists in carrying food trays to the table.
8. Makes coffee and tea and fills ice bins and fruit juice dispensers.
9. Supplies service bar with food, such as soups, salads, and desserts.
10. Dusts furniture and cleans and polishes glass shelves and doors of service bar and such equipment items as coffee urns and cream and milk dispensers.
11. May wait on and bring items to guests.
12. May transfer food and dishes between floors of establishment using dumbwaiters and be designated Dumbwaiter Operator.
13. May run errands and deliver food orders to offices and be designated a Runner.
14. Assists in breaking down service stations.

Reports to

Waiter/Waitress, Captain, and Host/Hostess.

Special Considerations

The dining room attendant must know the prescribed methods for clearing dishes, setting tables, and cleaning the dining area.

Additional job descriptions are listed in the DOT. If the preceding descriptions are insufficient or if a specific breakdown is required for union or wage administration or for the reader's needs, please refer to the DOT.

Additional job descriptions in the DOT include:

—Waiter/Waitress (water trans.)

—Waiter/Waitress Assistant (hotel and restaurant)

—Waiter/Waitress, Banquet (hotel and restaurant)

—Waiter/Waitress, Buffet (hotel and restaurant)—Serves or assists diners to serve themselves at buffet or smorgasbord table. Replenishes supplies of food and tableware. May carry trays of food to individual tables for diners.

—Waiter/Waitress, Dining Car (r.r. trans.)

—Waiter/Waitress, Entertainer (hotel and restaurant)

—Waiter/Waitress, Room Service (hotel and restaurant)

—Waiter/Waitress, Banquet, Head (hotel and restaurant)— Plans details for banquets, receptions, and other social functions. Hires extra help, directs setting up of tables and decorations, and supervises Waiters/Waitresses, Formal.

—Waiter/Waitress, Bar (hotel and restaurant)

—Waiter/Waitress, Take Out (hotel and restaurant)

—Waiter/Waitress, Outside Delivery (hotel and restaurant)

The following checklist for setting tables may be used as a guideline for banquet and à la carte operations. Realize that each individual establishment may have particular methods that do not conform to the standards listed below. This does not decrease the importance of the standard; however, the new or young manager should not try to impose the standard on an existing and prosperous operation.

Checklist for Setting a Table

Tables

1. Check table for proper position in the room—check alignment and spacing.
2. Check table balance—use cork if table is uneven, not matchbooks.
3. Use leaves as required to adjust size of table and configuration.

Tablecloth

1. Center undercloth or silencer on table—make sure it is clean.
2. Center tablecloth on table—make sure the lines are straight and that proper size is being used. The cloth should extend a minimum of ten inches beyond the edge of the table, but should not touch the floor.
   a. Be sure the tablecloth is "face up," that is, shiny or crest side up.
   b. Hems on the edge are always away from the face (hems down).
3. Some operations set two cloths, one of which will remain throughout the serving period.

China, Glassware, and Silverware

A *cover* describes an individual place setting (24 inch × 15 inch minimum).

1. Tables should be set by balancing the individual place settings and the center settings (sugar, salt/pepper, ashtray/matches, relishes, crackers, or flowers). Each center setting should match through placement and organization the center settings of like tables.
2. Do not handle silver by food contact surface; carry on a plate covered with a napkin or in a clean service cloth.
3. Handle glassware by the base or stem—never grasp by the brim.
4. Covers should face each other for an even number of settings. Odd numbers face an open space.
   a. If two places are set at a banquette, they should face the dining room.
   b. Covers are set between table legs whenever possible.
   c. Chairs should just touch the tablecloth when placed at the table.
5. Balance additional condiments if preset (i.e., butter, sour cream, dressings).
6. If a service, show, or base plate is used, insure that the crest faces the guest.
7. Place forks on left, tines up; except for informal luncheon settings when forks and spoons may be set on the right. (NOTE: Some establishments in Europe place the spoons face down and the fork tines down.)

8. Place knives and spoons to right with knife edges facing the plate, and spoons up and to the right of (outside) the knives.

9. Lay silver at right angles to the cover. Although silver may be placed following the contour of a round table, this destroys the appearance at the top of the cover.

10. Place silverware evenly 1/2 inch from edge.

11. Dinner knife and fork are placed next to plate.

12. Place individual butter plates above dinner forks—centered on and 1 inch above the forks. An acceptable alternate method is to place butter plate to side of forks (see fig. 9.6).

13. Place butter knife on right side of plate or on top edge (see fig. 9.1A).

14. Butter and/or bread plates are not used for formal service *during the meal.*

15. Carry stemmed glassware inverted in the hands with stems between fingers.

16. Place water glass centered on and 1 inch above the knife closest to the dinner plate.

17. Place other glassware as specified (see fig. 9.2).

18. Glassware should be right side up *before* guests are seated (standard etiquette). Sanitation requirements may require that glassware be placed down until after guests have been seated.

19. Place settings should not have too many pieces. As a rule of thumb, 3 forks, 2 knives, 3 spoons, and 4 glasses plus the dessert setting should be maximum. If more pieces are necessary, they should be presented just before the course being served.

20. If dessert silver (entremet setting) is laid, place parallel to cover with handle of fork left and handle of spoon right. Spoon is placed above fork.

21. Parfait or iced teaspoons and dessert knives should *not be preset.*

22. Melba toast, relishes, butter, and water should never be placed on the table before the guest(s) is seated (formal etiquette).

23. Place napkin in middle of cover—on top of showplate (hors d'oeuvre plate) in formal service. If preset menu item (i.e., for banquets), napkin should be folded on but-

ter plate, in one of the glasses, or placed behind the preset food.

24. Never place bread on a napkin.

For plate, platter, buffet and banquet service, silverware is usually preset.

For cart service, silverware is usually brought with each course.

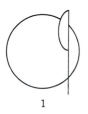

1   2   3

Figure 9.1A Three acceptable methods of placing butter knives on bread and butter plates (1) Most preferred (2) Acceptable (3) Acceptable (not recommended)

Figure 9.1B Unacceptable Methods

Correct Method for Placing Wine Glasses

The following diagrams depict the correct placement of wine glasses and the place settings for the courses or foods to be served. One should not spend time memorizing the place setting for lobster, the place setting for escargot, etc.; but he/she should have ready access to a reference in order to set the table properly for each course. On the other hand, each waiter/waitress should know the standard setting for each course on the menu of the establishment for which they are working. Correspondingly, a waiter/waitress should be able to design a place setting using the standard rules of etiquette (Checklist for Setting the Table) when given a menu. The service person must therefore know which utensil(s) is used for a particular food.

These diagrams are sketched so that any manager could duplicate the drawings in order to communicate to her service staff. For example, a banquet manager (or headwaiter/headwaitress) may sketch the desired place setting on the function sheet, and the waiter/waitress could set the table correctly from this simple line drawing.

Figure 9.2 Correct method for placing wine glasses on the table. The guide runs up and down the dinner knife (knife closest to dinner plate). The guide glass should be placed so that the edge of the base is centered on, and one inch above the dinner knife. Glasses must be removed (cleared) before the next wine is served.

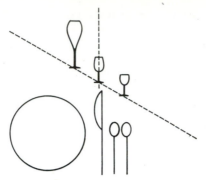

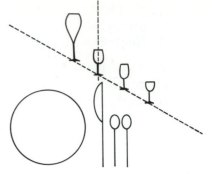

3 Wines: (From right to left in order of consumption) white wine (rhine wine glass) red wine (All-purpose wine glass) sparkling wine (tulip champagne glass)

4 Wines: (From right to left in order of consumption) white wine (rhine wine glass) light red wine (all-purpose wine glass) heavy red wine (all-purpose glass) sparkling wine (tulip champagne glass)

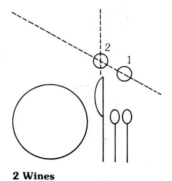

2 Wines

3 Wines

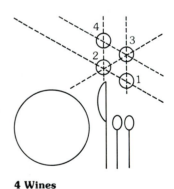

4 Wines

Table Settings

Figure 9.3 Complete breakfast

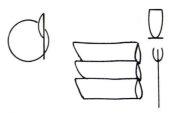

Figure 9.4 Omelette

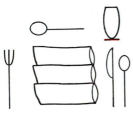

Figure 9.5 Hot cereal

Figure 9.6 Fried eggs

Figure 9.7 Standard plate service

Figure 9.8 Variation of standard plate service with added bouillon spoon

Figure 9.9 Informal luncheon. Note: No knives, forks on eight.

Figure 9.10 Standard plate with cocktail fork resting in bouillon spoon

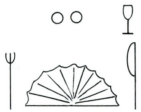

Figure 9.11 Minimum cover, also called simple or French cover

Figure 9.12 Standard plate service with entremet (dessert)

Figure 9.13 Basic a la carte (French)

Figure 9.14 Escargot

Figure 9.15 Soup, fish, meat and dessert

Figure 9.16 Hors d'oeuvres, consomme, meat and dessert

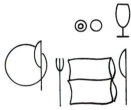

Figure 9.17 Hors d'oeuvres

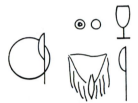

Figure 9.18 Caviar

Figure 9.19 Smoked salmon

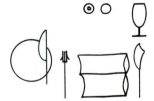

Figure 9.20 Smoked fish in general

★Note: Indicates Fish Fork; Indicates Fish Knife

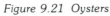

Figure 9.21 Oysters

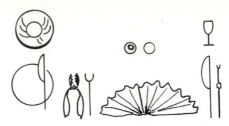

Figure 9.22 Cold lobster

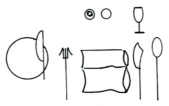

Figure 9.23 Bouillabaisse

Figure 9.24 Stew

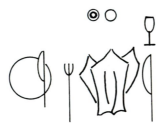

Figure 9.25 Cheese

Figure 9.26 Melon half

Figure 9.27 Melon slice

Figure 9.28 Desserts served in coupe

Figure 9.29 Grapefruit half

Figure 9.30 Peach melba served in coupe

Figure 9.31 Place setting

The following task procedures were used to train students in a four-year college[2] in the proper methods for serving a specific menu in a formal dining room. The reader should be able to duplicate these standard tasks for his/her operation and tailor the tasks to the menu in the dining room. Many of the tasks listed can be transferred to other operations, but the specific cocktails and menu presentations should reflect, more specifically, the operation in question.

The Order of Service (A Checklist for Plate Service)

1. Tables set—ready for service.
2. Host/Hostess seats guests—presents menus.
3. Greet guests with a genuine smile.
4. Pour water for each guest. Refill water glasses when less than 2/3 full. Refill all glasses to same level around the table.
5. Serve butter (if anticipate several rounds of cocktails, serve butter after "taking the food order").
6. Take cocktail order.
7. Serve cocktail from right on cocktail napkin in center of cover.
8. Take food order from host/hostess or from the left side of each guest.
9. Offer wine list and/or suggestions.
10. Remove cocktail glasses when empty.
11. Serve appetizer (center of cover).
12. Remove appetizer dish.
13. Serve soup in center of cover.
14. Remove soup dishes and *show plates* (if used).
15. Serve salad, offer rolls or bread, remove salad dishes.
16. Serve entree, place in center of cover. If side dishes are used, place on left. Offer rolls or bread again.
17. Remove main course dishes using the following order.
    a. Condiments
    b. Dinner plates
    c. Vegetable dishes
    d. Empty wine glasses
    e. Extra silver
18. Crumb table.

2. School of Hotel Administration at Cornell University, The Main Dining Room at Statler Inn, Ithaca, New York.

19. Present dessert (on cart or tray, by menu, or verbally).
20. Serve dessert course (center of cover).
21. Remove dessert course.
22. Serve coffee (if not yet served).
23. Serve brandy or cordials.
24. Present check.
25. Thank guest.
26. Help guests as they rise to leave and check that no personal articles are left behind and greet guests farewell.
27. Do not count tip.
28. Clear table and reset if necessary.

Operational Procedures

The following are step-by-step procedures for performing various tasks.

Carrying a Large Tray

1. *Carry above shoulders.*
2. *Use left hand (preferable).*
3. *Lift with palm — can use fingertips if desirable. Fingers should be at a 45° angle to front of body.*
4. Use right hand to balance until proficient.
5. Tray should be clean.
6. Place clean cloth on tray to prevent slippage.
7. Balance items on tray — heaviest towards center or in center where hand is. Glassware, etc., to edges away from the body.

Carrying a Small Tray

1. Carried waist high with left upper arm close to body. Forearm outstretched (90°) with hand under the tray.
2. Remove and serve with tray held in left hand.
3. All items removed or served with right hand.
4. Bend with knees.
5. Small trays must always remain on the left hand. They should never be set down in the dining room.

Lifting Heavy Trays

1. Bend down with knees.
2. Place tray in approximate position for carrying on shoulder.

3. Lift by straightening out your knees and move tray into place with shoulder and hand.
4. Lift with legs, not your back.

Lifting Heavy Objects (Boxes, etc.)

1. Bend down with knees.
2. Grasp with one hand close to body, other hand on opposite side of object.
3. Keep back straight.
4. Lift object with legs, not arms or back. (See chapter 6.)

Changing Linen

Figure 9.32

1. Move center setting close to edge of table nearest you.
2. Take clean cloth with double fold between thumb and index finger and single folds (2) between index and middle and middle and ring fingers.
3. Spread arms as wide as the table, if possible.
4. Drop hemmed edge (bottom of your cloth) over the back edge of table.
5. Grasp soiled cloth with butt of your palm and little finger.
6. Gradually release the double fold (between thumb and index finger) and pull to center of table while continuing to hold the soiled cloth.
7. Stop! Move center settings to opposite side of table (i.e., on clean cloth side).
8. Grasp clean cloth between thumb and index finger and soiled cloth with butt of hand and little finger.
9. Pull remaining hemmed edge toward you grasp soiled cloth *again* at edge nearest you. Center the clean cloth. Remove soiled cloth by continuing to grasp at both ends to keep crumbs from falling. Check that all folds are even.

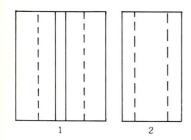

Preparing the Silver Bread Tray

1. Place properly folded white napkin in bottom of tray.
2. Place two rolls per person or assorted breads as required.

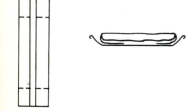

Filling Salt and Pepper Shakers

1. Remove shakers from tables.
2. Wipe all shakers clean.
3. Remove tops.

4. Use small funnel or make funnel out of paper.
5. Place several pieces of rice in salt shakers to absorb moisture.

Filling Water Pitchers

1. Determine the number of water pitchers desired for that meal (3-4 per side stand).
2. Place on rolling table (with soiled table cloth on table). Place sheet pans on top of cart and place service cloth *inside* sheet pan.
3. Place pitchers inside sheet pans (on towels).
4. *Fill* with ice.
5. Pour water from flexible hose adjacent to ice machines.

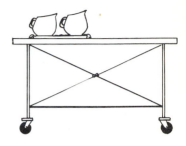

Carrying the Service Cloth

1. Select a cloth that is clean and unstained.
2. Insure that the cloth has no holes in it or that the edges are not frayed.
3. Fold cloth so that edges are not on the outside, i.e., fold edges under.
4. Place cloth on left forearm draped with edge on fat part of thumb.
5. Never place cloth under arm or in belt.

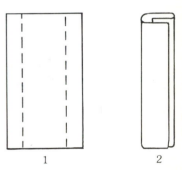

Carrying Hot Plates with Service Cloth

1. Place folded cloth *over* edge of plates and insure that edges fall down the sides and would fit under the amount of plates to be carried.
2. Lift plates close to body, but do not touch your body.
3. Do not attempt to carry too many plates.
4. Wiggle tails of cloths from underneath the plates when setting down so as to not make noise.

Figure 9.33

Using the Service Cloth to Handle a Hot Plate

1. After folding and holding cloth as specified in "carrying cloth" slide cloth over hand and fingers near one end of the cloth.
2. Grasp hot plate with cloth.
3. Hold other end of cloth with right hand so as not to drag it over guest's lap.

Figure 9.34

Polishing Silverware (Clean Water Spots)

1. Never grasp silver by any part of utensil except by the handle.
2. Insure that the cloth is *clean and sanitary*.
3. Moisten cloth slightly with clean water.
4. Wipe until polished.
5. If silver has stains or food on it, get another silver piece.

Polishing Glassware

1. Grasp glass by stem or lower to midsection of straight glass, never by the brim.
2. Polish as with silverware, i.e., slightly moisten cloth. Insert in glass.
3. Wipe clear. Insure no lint remains on glass.

NOTE: Best to use a lint-free cloth.

Figure 9.35 The proper way to handle a water goblet—by the stem or base.

Figure 9.36

Setting the Table (Standard Place Setting)

1. Place napkin (standing) in center of cover.
2. Place silverware (dinner knife and dinner fork) approximately 5 inches apart* and 1/2 inch from the table edge to establish the center of the cover.
3. Knife blade is toward the plate.
4. Place second fork parallel to first fork.
5. Place butter knife and two spoons parallel to dinner knife.
6. Place goblet in the cradle formed by the knives and spoons.**
7. If wine glasses are preset, center on the dinner knife.**

Setting the Table (Standard Center Setting)

1. Place sugar bowl facing front (entrance) to dining room so that silver is seen first.
2. Set salt and pepper shakers with salt either on host's right or closest to him, as compared to the pepper shaker.
3. Set ashtray (with closed match bookshield facing away from the salt and pepper shaker) next to salt and pepper shakers so that 1, 2, 3, are centered on the table and with each other.
4. If double setting, reverse order and center on table.

*Just touching the sides of the napkin.

**This procedure *does not* conform to standard etiquette.

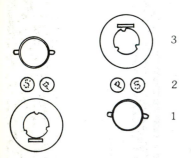

Front of Room

5. Candles and flowers are optional at the direction of the host.

NOTE: See table chart for exact settings for each table.

Greeting Your Guests (Host/Hostess)

1. Use "Sir" for gentlemen and "madam" for ladies.
2. Address yourself to the group as opposed to one person and say "Good evening, afternoon" or some appropriate salutation.
3. If you do not recognize the party (host), ask the person in whose name the reservations were made.
4. If no reservations, inquire as to how many are in the party and find an appropriate table.

Figure 9.37 (Photo courtesy of Oneida Ltd. Silversmiths.)

Greeting Your Guests (Waiter/Waitress)

1. Give some proper salutation to the group, "Good evening, afternoon," etc.
2. Introduce yourself as being their waiter/waitress for the meal as well as your name. "Good Afternoon (evening), I will be serving you this afternoon (evening)."
3. Address the hostess (on her left) and ask if she would care to order cocktails for her guests. "Would you care for a martini (sherry)?"

Seating Your Guests

1. Pull out a chair for the lady (or the eldest as the case may be) in the group.
2. Push chair in by lifting rear of chair and pushing forward with your foot on the leg and your hands on the top of the chair.
3. Face women towards the dining room.
4. If seating guests in a booth, offer buffet seat to the women.
5. Pull table away from the seats to facilitate access by the individual being seated; replace table to original position.

NOTE: See Greeting and Seating Guests in chapter 8.

Presentation of the Menu

1. Present each guest (at least those old enough to read) a menu.
2. Present the menu (closed) and from the *guests' left*

beginning with the person on the right of the host and moving counterclockwise around the table.
3. Insure that the menus are clean and not torn.
4. Present the menu with left hand.
5. Do not carry menus under your arm.

Pouring Water

1. If necessary (i.e., you cannot easily reach the glass with the pitcher) move the glass closer to you by grasping the base or stem.
2. *Do not lift the glass from the table.*
3. Pour water in glass (about 3/4-7/8 full).
4. Do not cross in front of guest, but excuse yourself when necessary (i.e., when you must cross in front of guest).

Serving Butter

1. Place two butter patties on 7 inch plate for each guest in the party.
2. Use a cocktail fork to serve the butter. Do this from sidestand.
3. Carry no more than three plates, and place from guest's left.
4. Place above and centered on the dinner fork (if possible).

Taking Cocktail Orders

1. As with all orders, ask hostess if she will order.
2. If not, ask each guest (standing on his/her left) what he would care to drink.
3. Order drinks from service bar by filling out beverage requisition.
4. Use the small tray for cocktails.
5. Use a new beverage requisition for reorders.

Serving Cocktails (General)

1. Cover cocktail tray with celery cloth.
2. Place cocktails on tray and distribute weight evenly and toward your body.
3. Obtain one cocktail napkin for each person.
4. From the *right*, place cocktail napkin in center of cover with crest facing guest.

5. Place cocktail glass on napkin and back away.
6. *Do not grasp glass by rim.*

Taking the Food Order

1. Address yourself to the host on his left if a host is apparent.
2. If no host is apparent:
   a. Address yourself to the man when a man and a woman are eating together.
   b. Address yourself to the elder if your guests are of the same sex.
   c. In large groups a host should be apparent and he decides whether he or his guests individually will give their orders.
3. In large groups begin with the person on the host's right, and on that person's left.
4. Keep sequence so as to serve guests in correct order without having to ask guests who gets what. (See Picking Up Food Order [Specific].)

Filling Out Food Requisitions

1. All food orders must be on requisition forms. Pads are available from cashier.
2. Take orders as per above—write clearly (press hard for carbon).
3. Note table number—cashier and the range files by table number.
4. White copy goes to cashier when entering kitchen.
5. Pink copy goes to range (Dinner).
6. Yellow copy is your copy (Dinner).
7. Take dessert orders on yellow form and give to cashier immediately after dessert and beverages are served.
   NOTE: Cashier *will not* prepare final check until yellow copy is received.
8. Cashier will prepare final check and hold for your call.
   NOTE: For luncheon the yellow copy should be discarded.
   If party is larger than eight, use another requisition form.

Filling Out Beverage and Wine Requisitions

1. Put all beverage (cocktails) orders and wine orders on Beverage Requisition.

2. Follow same procedure as for food checks, i.e.,
   —White copy to cashier
   —Pink copy to service bar
   —Yellow copy for your information
3. Fill out requisition completely, with table numbers and waiter/waitress initials.

Passing Requisitions to Service Bar

1. Fill out requisition.
2. Present pink slip to bartender by placing slip on counter.
3. White slip to cashier.
4. Retain the yellow slip for information.
5. Complete new requisition for each new order or another round.
6. Write "reorder" on lower portion of requisition.

Passing Requisitions to Main Range (Dinners)

1. Fill out requisition completely except for dessert.
2. Present pickup slip to expediter at main range.
3. See procedure handout for placing and picking up orders.

Order of Service for Buffet Luncheon

1. Greet the guests
2. Pour water
3. Serve butter
4. Take cocktail order
5. Place bread (1 roll per person)
6. Take food order
7. Remove cocktail glasses when empty
8. Serve appetizers—soup *or* juice
9. Invite guests to buffet
10. Serve sandwich or salad
11. Pour coffee if desired by guest
12. Remove dishes only when *all* have finished
13. Crumb table
14. Offer dessert (verbal—know your items)
15. Serve dessert—pour coffee
16. Remove dessert if discussion is obvious
17. Present check promptly

NOTE: Guests eating *luncheon* in the main dining room are usually in a hurry. *Do not wait* until they have finished cocktails before proceeding with this order.

Picking up a Food Order (General)

1. First organize all serving equipment for food and accompaniments: lemon wedges, tartar sauce, mayonnaise, horseradish, etc.
2. Cold foods are picked up and placed on tray away from where hot foods go.
3. Hot foods should be picked up last and covered.

Picking up a Food Order (Specific)

1. Diagram of placing plates on tray.
2. Stack plates thusly:

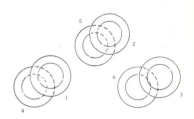

Carrying Plates

1. Place thumb over edge (not for serving) and hold plate between thumb, index finger, and middle finger.
2. Place ring finger and little finger up above rim of first plate.
3. Place second plate on thick part of thumb, and ring and middle finger, not on wrist.

Scraping Food

1. Place plates, (2) as mentioned in "Carrying Plates."
2. Scrape food gently from second plate onto first plate (out of sight of guest) and place knife and fork as indicated below.
3. Place fork prongs down and at one o'clock position.
4. Place knife under prongs of fork with the handle pointed at five o'clock position with sharp edge away from you.
5. Remove third plate and place on top of second plate. Repeat procedure.
6. Using four plates as a maximum, place first plate on top of stack.

Removing Soiled Plates

1. When *all guests* have finished eating, begin removing soiled dishes from right of the person you served first (the person on the host's right).
2. Remove the largest plates first and use the aforementioned procedures for carrying plates and scraping food.

3. Clear *all dishes* except for the water goblet and the silver required for dessert and coffee (leave coffee cup and saucer if already served).
4. *Clear dishes completely from one person before proceeding to the next.*

Figure 9.38

Stacking Plates on a Tray

1. Heaviest dishes are laid in the center of the tray or where weight would be on your shoulder.
2. Glasses and light articles to the outside.
3. Dishes with food on them should not be piled up unless covers are used.
4. Stack according to sizes of places, i.e., larger plates on bottom.
5. Cups are not placed on saucers (too much room).
6. Tray should be covered with a clean napkin.

Unloading a Tray (Soiled Dishes)

1. Place tray down on unloading rack at dishwashers station.
2. Place silverware in presoak tub.
3. Place glassware in proper racks.
4. Place cups on special cup rack.
5. If racks are full, inform DMO and then place an empty rack in its stead.
6. Wipe tray clean (top *and* bottom).

How to Crumb a Table

A. Clear all dishes except water glasses. Leave sufficient silver (if clean) for dessert course.
B. Fold dinner napkin small enough to fit comfortably in palm of hand.
C. Use folded side of napkin to sweep crumbs and debris into small dish covered with another a folded napkin.
D. Perform this function from *either side* and do not inconvenience the guest.

Serving Beverages

A. Coffee
1. Pick up empty coffee cups and saucers from side-stands and place on right side of guest with handle at 45° angle to guest's right.
2. Place all cups and saucers on table *before* pouring coffee.
3. Obtain coffee pot from hot plates on sidestands.
4. Pour coffee for guest using a saucer to shield splatter.
5. *Never* remove cups and saucer from table to pour. If necessary, slide cup and saucer closer to you for easy reach. *Always carry cup and saucer as a unit — never separately.*

B. Tea (hot — individual service)
1. Pick up empty coffee cups and saucers from sidestands and place on right side of guest with handle at 45° angle to guest's right.
2. Pick up silver teapot (short covered pot as compared to thin pot used for coffee) under coffee maker.
3. Rinse with hot water (center spigot) to warm up the pot. *Pour out water.*
4. *Refill* with hot water and place on tray with tea bag.
5. Carry into dining room and place on 7 inch under-liner with doily.
6. Before serving guest, place tea bag in hot water with string hanging out.
7. Serve guest from right and place pot to the right of the cup.

NOTE: *Cup and saucer should already be* in place on the table.

C. Sanka or Postum (individual service)
1. Pick up empty coffee cups and saucers from side-stands and place on right side of guest with handle at 45° angle to guest's right.
2. Pick up silver coffee pot from under coffee maker.
3. Rinse pot as with tea.
4. Pour contents of Sanka or Postum package into pot and refill with hot water.
5. Carry into dining room and place on 7 inch under-liner.

6. Serve on guest's right, to right of the cup and saucer.

NOTE: *Cup and saucer should already be in place on the table.*

Presenting the Check (Dinner)

1. At a reasonable time after cordials or coffee, place a handful of mints on a small glass plate.
2. Place guest checks under plate face down.
3. Present check to host by placing on table on host's left side.
4. Take guest's money to cashier.
5. Stamp check and record of charge if charge card is used.
6. Return change or card on glass plate.
7. If card, offer pen for signature.

Serving the Statler Menu

I. Cocktails (See bar garnishes as waiter/waitress will garnish cocktails)

A. Decanter Service

(NOTE: Cocktails served in decanters will be specifically designated).

1. Obtain spirit from bartender in decanter.
2. Place filled decanter on ice in supreme dish.
3. Bring empty glass and cocktail napkin. Place napkin with Statler "S" facing the guest.
4. Place cocktail glass on napkin centered in the cover.
5. Place Supreme down on table (just outside knife on right).
6. Remove water from bottom of decanter by circling the silver rim with the bottom of decanter.
7. Pour spirit into glass and replace decanter in Supreme.

B. All other cocktails:

1. Place napkin, centered in cover with Statler "S" facing the guest, down.
2. Place full glass on napkin.

NOTE: Empty cocktail glasses should be removed from the right.

II. Appetizers and Soups
  A. Fruit juices—fruit cups
    1. Place order on tray—cloth on tray.
    2. Do not place on underliner until ready to place in front of guest.
    3. Get underliner from underneath traystand.
    4. Place juice or fruit cup on 7 inch underliner with doily and place in center of cover.
    5. If garnish is required (i.e., lemon or lime wedge for tomato juice) spear wedge with cocktail fork and place on right side of underliner with handle of fork at 45° angle.

  B. Melon (honeydew, cantaloupe, casaba, etc.)
    1. Place melon in a monkey dish.
    2. Bring 7 inch underliner for each melon. Do not place on underliner until ready to serve, but serve on underliner.
    3. Spear lemon or lime wedge with cocktail fork and place on right side of underliner with handle of fork at 45° angle.
    4. Cantaloupe does not require a lemon wedge.
  C. Soup, plate service
    1. Ladle soup into heated bowl or cup in kitchen. (A pitcher may be used for larger parties)
    2. Bring sufficient amount of crackers for each order.
    3. Cover cup with saucer and bowl with 7 inch underliner (heat retention, spillage).
    4. Remove covers in dining room and *replace with clean saucers or 7 inch underliners* and serve in center of cover.
    5. Organize your tray with all required items *before* pouring soup.
  D. Soup, formal service
    1. Ladle soup into heated silver soup cup.
    2. Cover with fitted silver lid.
    3. Before service, place silver soup cup in soup bowl on an underliner.
    4. Set the three items in center of cover, remove lid and pour soup into bowl by tilting cup away from the guest.

E. Onion Soup
  1. Ladle soup (as in C). Sprinkle *one teaspoon* Parmesan cheese in soup.
  2. Bring one large cheese crouton for each order of soup and place on underliner.
  3. Cover cup with saucer and bowl with 7 inch underliner (heat retention).
  4. Remove covers in dining room and slide crouton into soup. Serve soup in center of cover with proper underliner.
  NOTE: Organize your tray with all required items before ladling soup for service.
F. Consomme
  1. Ladle soup into double handled cup (silver) cover with lid.
  2. Place on underliner with doily.
  3. Serve in center of cover. Remove lid.
  NOTE: If soup is served in cups with handles, the handles should be on the *guest's left*.
G. Shrimp Cocktail
  1. Pick up order from left side of pantry.
  2. Place on tray.
  3. Spear lemon wedge with cocktail fork and place on right side of underliner (see diagram for accepted method of spearing lemon wedge on p. 181).
  4. Place on 7 inch underliner and serve in center of cover.

III. Salad
Invite guests to buffet table for salad.

IV. Entree
  A. Specialty and tableside presentations will be briefed with student quantity class manager and will be served according to her desires.
  B. All other menu items:
    1. Pick up plated entree with vegetables (on plate) from main range (grill). Pick up steak knives for each person eating steak or chop.
    2. Cover plates with metal cover. Stack if required.
    3. Place on large tray and carry tray into dining room.

4. Place on *your traystand,* uncover and serve (from left).
5. Place plate in center of cover with meat on right side.

V. *Sauces*

1. Place "gooseneck" or sauceboat on an underliner.
2. From the left side of the guest, spoon or ladle sauce overlapping item (i.e., seafood) and carrier (i.e., rice).
3. Do not pour from a gooseneck.

Perhaps the most critical phase in any a la carte food service establishment is the point where the waiter/waitress places the order with the expediter, annunciator, or cook at the range. This writer feels that only the waiter/waitress can time the guest and the pace with which the guest wants to eat the meal or to be served. Waiter/waitress call systems somewhat defeat this idea.

A service person who argues in the kitchen makes everyone's job more difficult. Any waiter/waitress who botches the order, writes illegibly, pick up another's order, or otherwise confuses the system increases conflict, and thereby decreases everyone's productivity. Any complaints from the service staff must go through the dining room manager or host/hostess and not directly to the chef or the range. The dining room manager can then go to the chef if required.

The following procedure lists a "five-minute" warning at which time the range personnel will begin final preparation for the food or menu items to be served at a particular table. This system allows the range more time to sequence the orders and the preparation, and also insures that there is an ample supply of the particular menu item *before the waiter/waitress may return to the dining room.* Additionally, there seems to be more lead time to inform other service personnel of outages before the range is, in fact, out!

Another similar system for a la carte restaurants does away with the five-minute warning, and presenting the check or requisition at the range is synonomous with the five-minute warning. The above system requires that the waiter/waitress be *more* aware of the time it takes to prepare certain items. If boiled lobster is to be served at the same table where a filet of sole will be served, timing must reflect the span required to boil the lobster. In any case, the length of preparation time for each menu item must be communicated by the chef to all service personnel. This system also places more hardship on the range personnel, as they may have no idea about how many of this or that they must prepare until it is needed. Obviously, if many of the menu items are prepared in advance (i.e., stew, roasts, lasagne, etc.) the five-minute warning is unnecessary. Whatever system is adopted, it must be followed by all personnel. In large establishments with extensive menus, menu items must be picked up at various stations. Expediters are essential as the person to direct the flow, and they serve as a "go-between" between service and production.

Procedure for Placing and Picking Up Orders

The following procedure for placing and picking up orders will be learned by each waiter/waitress, and production person in this restaurant.

Luncheon

1. Waiters/waitresses or captains will complete the food requisitions as specified in the Operational Procedures.
2. Placing the Order
    A. *Sandwiches*
        1. Waiters or waitresses will announce *"ordering"* to the sandwich maker that he/she is placing an order.
        2. The sandwich maker will acknowledge.
        3. The waiter/waitress will transfer his/her order to the sandwich order sheet located on the main range and *present pink slip to sandwich maker.* Write on sandwich order sheet:
            a. Waiter/waitress name
            b. Type sandwich
            c. Type bread (Rye, whole wheat, white)
            d. Toasted or plain
            e. Number of sandwiches, if several of same type are ordered
        4. The waiter/waitress will read his/her order to the sandwich maker.
        5. The sandwich maker will acknowledge.

6. When the waiter/waitress comes to pick up his/her order, he/she will announce *"picking up."*
7. The sandwich maker will insure the waiter/waitress is picking up *his/her* order and will ask the waiter/waitress to *line through* his/her order.
8. The sandwich maker will file the pink requisition for the manager.

B. *Chef's Salad*
1. Waiter/waitress will announce *"ordering"* to pantry person.
2. The pantry person will acknowledge.
3. The waiter/waitress will write his/her name and how many salads he/she has requisitioned.
4. The waiter/waitress will tell the pantry person how many salads he/she needs.
5. The pantry person will acknowledge.
6. When the waiter/waitress comes to pick up his/her order, he/she will announce *"picking up."*
7. The pantry person will insure the waiter/waitress is picking up *his/her* order.
8. The waiter/waitress will line through his/her order and the pantry person should insure he/she does so.

Dinner

1. Waiter/Waitress will complete the food requisition.

Ordering

2. Insure that requisition is filled out completely to include:
   A. Table number
   B. Name of waiter/waitress
   C. Number in party
   D. All items properly circled
   E. Date
3. Waiter/waitress will present pink requisition to the annunciator and *wait* until he/she indicates that it is legible, understandable, and complete, and that the menu items ordered are available.
4. The waiter/waitress will insure that he has included vegetables, potato, entree, and the degree of doneness or characteristic for each of the menu items.

5. The expediter will announce to the range personnel *"ordering"* and place the order by verbalizing the order.
6. The back of the requisition will include (filled in by expediter):
   A. Sequential order for the evening
   B. Time the order was presented by the waiter/waitress
   C. The items on the order for easy reading by range personnel
7. The requisition will be clipped to the slide line (or circular file).
   A. Requisition number one (1) will be on the extreme right (next to post) with number two (2) on number one's (1) left, etc.

Picking Up

1. Five minutes before physical pickup waiter/waitress will alert the expediter that he/she will pick up a *particular order (designated by table number)* in five minutes:

   "Picking up table number 21 in five minutes."

2. Waiter/waitress will appear at range five minutes after he has alerted the expediter with his *tray and all other items of equipment and food* (i.e., steak knives, serving spoons, condiments, etc.) *for this service.*
3. Expediter will check with waiter/waitress the makeup of *each plate* prior to leaving range area. NOTE: A proper check at this time avoids delays in the dining room.
4. Special conditions that may apply to a particular evening or dish of an evening, will be explained by the manager or chef at the menu briefing.

The following description explains how various courses should be served following standard rules of etiquette. The list is somewhat incomplete, as no attempt was made to duplicate service procedures for any items previously listed under "Operational Procedures."

Serving Various Menu Items

Mixed Hors d'Oeuvres (Antipasto)

1. Roll cart to guest's table.
   Remove hors d'oeuvres plate from the guest's *right,* or fill small plate; supply of which is on cart.

Fill plate according to guest's instructions, while holding it on the cart and return plate from the left.

2. If serving guest from platter, hold platter in left hand and fill guest's plate directly in front of the guest.
3. If serving guests at a cocktail party (i.e., standing), simply offer hors d'oeuvres to the guests.

Steak Tartare

Served with Worcestershire sauce, Tabasco, salt, pepper, party rye, cooked, sieved egg yolk, minced onion and capers.

1. Roll cart to guest's table.
2. Present ingredients (not mixed) to guest.
3. Combine ground meat with Worcestershire sauce, Tabasco, salt and pepper in a mixing bowl.
4. Portion mixture onto plates and garnish plate with party rye slices (or other crackers); cooked, sieved egg yolks; fresh, minced onions; capers and fresh, minced parsley.
5. Serve an extra knife (butter) when serving Steak Tartare.

Caviar

1. Serve in original tin buried in crushed ice in a silver glass or bowl.
2. Serve with tongue depressor (preferrable) or dessert spoon on the hors d'oeuvres plate or fish plate.
   Accompaniments to Caviar
   a. Thin pancakes (blintzes) or hot toasts and thin slices of crustless brown bread, lemon, and chopped egg are offered.
   b. Pepper mill is optional.
3. Place a small butter knife to the right of the plate.
4. Place finger bowl to left and above the cover.

Raw Oysters or Clams

1. Serve in individual dishes (6 or 12 per order), which are placed in crushed ice.
2. Place oyster fork on the extreme right of the silverware on the right.
   Accompaniments to Oyster Service
   a. Crackers, vinegars, cocktail sauce, and horseradish.
   b. Pepper mill.

Smoked Salmon or Lox

1. Thin slices of salmon are served on bread (usually dark or rye).
2. Offer pepper mill.

Snails (Escargot)

1. Served in fitted dishes with snail clamps on the left of the cover, and a cream soup spoon and an escargot fork on the underliner 45° to guest's right or preset at right of spoon—see Place Setting 9.14 (p. 164).
   NOTE: Sanitation laws may prohibit the use of the actual snail shell. Alternatives are to place meat only in the fitted dish or use ceramic (china) cups that are made to look like shells.

Melon

1. Place silverware for melon on table.
2. Serve melon on underliner (1) (bottom of melon should be sliced so that melon does not rock on the plate) on service or show plate.
3. For formal service, the waiter/waitress or pantry worker should cut the melon at the rind from tip to tip (2), slicing the meat away from the rind. Then cut from tip to tip (3) with the knife perpendicular to the first cut. Then cut across the second cut (4) (resembles a checkerboard) and alternate cubes of melon (see fig. 9.39).
4. Offer pour-type salt shaker.

Figure 9.39 How to cut a melon slice. Cut along dotted lines in order listed.

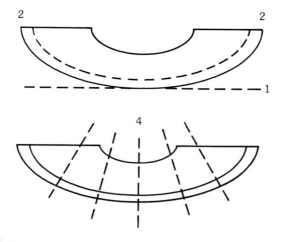
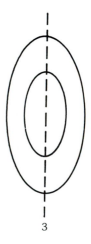

Grapefruit

1. Serve in monkey dish on underliner with grapefruit teaspoon along right side.
2. Individual grapefruit sections should be cut. Do not cut *around the* grapefruit, as this severs the section membrane from the rind and makes it most difficult to take the meat out.
3. Pour-type salt shaker recommended.

Salads

Should be served on china or glass plates. They should not be served (formally) in salad bowls. In a classical setting, salad is served in the center of the cover after the main course. *Chilled salad forks may be offered with the salad course.*

Desserts

1. Bring down the spoon and fork if they have been placed above the cover (entremet setting).
2. Roll dessert cart to guest's table, or present dessert on (silver) tray.
3. Plate the dessert in front of the guest as per guest's instructions.
4. Dessert knives should not be preset, but should be placed when serving dessert.

Cheese

1. Clear the table except for wine and wine glasses (red wine).
2. Place a small clean plate and a small clean knife and fork at the guest's cover.
3. Bring fresh bread if required.
4. Present the cheese on a platter, cheeseboard or cart to each guest.
5. Cut the pieces the guest desires using a cheese knife (tipped with two prongs) for cutting and placing the cheese on the plate.
6. A flat cheese slicer may be used if guests are serving themselves.

Fresh Fruit

1. Place a small plate in front of the guest.
2. Place a fruit knife (steak knife) and fruit fork (dinner fork) crossed at the top of the plate with the tip of the knife in the prongs of the fork, both handles 45° to the guest's right.
3. Work from the left side of the guest.
4. Present the fruit (in a basket or silver platter) from the left and guest serves himself the fruit he desires.
5. Cut grapes with scissors and place the small bunches on the guest's plate by regripping small bunches with scissor blades.
6. A finger bowl (with warm water and a lemon slice) should be placed to the left, slightly above the cover as this is a necessary accompaniment when fruit is served.

Coffee (Formal Service)

1. Clear and crumb before serving coffee, especially when serving coffee after dessert.
2. Place a coffee cup with saucer on a larger plate directly in front of the guest. Angle the handle 45° to the guest's right.
3. Place a spoon on the underliner (not saucer).
4. Offer each guest coffee inquiring how he would like it.
5. On a tray have sufficient coffee, cream, sugar cubes, and sugar tongs.
6. To fill the coffee cup serving from right with service on left arm:
   a. Lower the whole service to the level of the table.
   b. Lower the coffee pot above the cup.
   c. Tilt the coffee pot without lifting it off the silver tray.
   d. Do likewise with the cream pitcher.
   e. Serve sugar as per guest's request.

In addition to knowing the proper service for specific foods, the manager must know what constitutes proper behavior for the dining room staff. The recommendations listed are for an elegant dining room, and the individual manager may delete some of the rules if her establishment is less formal. Yet certain practices should be followed, as they relate to sanitation, safety, and etiquette, rather than formal versus informal service.

Tips for Good Service

1. Never stand around in groups—stay at your station.
2. Always greet your guests—smile!
3. Avoid conversations with other employees.
4. Do not give loud orders.
5. Never argue with anyone—especially a guest.
6. Service cloth rules:
   a. Don't mop your face
   b. Never carry under your arm
   c. Take a clean one once in a while
   d. Never wipe silverware or glassware with towel in front of guest
   e. Use a clean, sanitary towel to polish silver or glassware before opening
   f. Never put towel in your pocket
7. Don't lean on chairs, put your foot on a chair rung, or bend your knees to hear a guest. Stand erect or bend down *from* the waist to hear.
8. If you spill something on a guest, apologize, clean up the spill, and advise your supervisor.
9. Talk only as necessary for politeness.
10. Don't smoke in areas where not allowed and never during the serving period or in guest's view.
11. Don't holler in the kitchen.
12. Never use bad language.
13. Take guest complaints to your supervisor.
14. Say "thank you" when tipped, regardless of the amount tendered.
15. Don't count money or jingle coins in pockets.
16. Never hurry your guests.
17. Never eat during service.
18. Don't carry pencils, books, etc., where visible, i.e., in pockets, behind ears, etc.
19. Carry menus in your hands—not under arms or in pants, shirt, or jacket.
20. Don't lean on walls or sidestands.
21. Don't put hands in pockets or on hips.
22. Don't cross arms in front of chest.
23. Don't add or write out checks in view of any guests.
24. Don't complain about food to kitchen—tell your supervisor.

25. Don't point in the dining room or gesture at a table.
26. Always be courteous.
27. Walk briskly, but never run.
28. Don't walk briskly when leading groups to their seats.

Conclusion

A good waiter/waitress and in turn a good manager should look for certain things in order to give good service. The following checklist can serve as a recapitulation of this chapter and includes portions of other important chapters related to serving the guest.

Checklist for Waiters and Waitresses

In Order to Give Good Service
—Follow side duty assignments (opening and closing duties as assigned by host/hostess).
—Follow the order of service.
—Follow operational procedures.
—Condiments to accompany items before guest needs to ask.
—Water glasses full.
—Bread and butter supply adequate.
—Trays with soiled dishes cleared frequently.
—Serve food the way each guest ordered it (i.e., get the order right).
—Help the guest(s) order if he/she needs assistance with menu selection.
—All unnecessary silverware, glassware, dishes removed.
—Refill wine glasses frequently (half full for red and 3/4 full for white).
—Order more cocktails or wine if guest desires (i.e., ask if guest needs a refill).
—Check buffet table for food, appearance, and heat.
—Continue to follow up with service, but do not "bug" the guest.
—Smile.

Questions

1. List several important functions of the waiter/waitress, the dining room attendant, and the captain.
2. Where would one find a listing of additional job descriptions not covered in this text?

3. What is the preferred method of setting the butter knife on the butter plate?
4. Draw two ways to preset three wine glasses and two ways to preset four wine glasses at a table.
5. List ten (only) entries in the order of service in proper *sequence.*
6. Explain how to
   a. Carry hot plates with a service cloth.
   b. Change a table linen properly.
   c. Stack six plates (with covers) on a large tray for serving in the dining room.
   d. Load a tray with soiled china, glassware, and silverware.
7. What is the advantage(s) of a five-minute warning system for an a la carte restaurant? What is the disadvantage of a waiter/waitress call system?
8. How should the following menu items be served?
   a. Hors d'oeuvres
   b. Melon (include method for cutting a slice of melon)
   c. Snails (escargot)
9. List ten "Tips for Good Service."
10. The local chapter of Les Amis d'Escoffier (a national gourmet club) is having their annual Christmas dinner in your hotel. Since you have been trained in service, the General Manager has asked you to be the service coordinator/director for this very special event. The function sheet has called for a head table to seat 14 honor guests and ten rounds with ten covers each. The menu is as follows:

Lillet	Poached Eggs in Wine-Aspic, Mayonnaise Sauce
	Beef Consomme "Carmen"
Pinot Chardonnay	Small Rock Lobster Tails, Lemon Butter
	Champagne Sherbet
Santenay 1961 Burgundy	Medallions of Veal with Madeira Sauce
	Braised Leeks-Tangerine Rice
	Artichoke Hearts Vinaigrette
	Brie and Fruit
Moet et Chandon	Patisserie
	Cafe
Napoleon V.S.O.P.	

A. *Per place setting,* how many of the following silverware utensils would you requisition from the steward? Use zeros if you do not need an item. Blanks will not be considered correct.

_____ dinner knife

_____ forks, dinner

_____ forks, salad

_____ teaspoons

_____ steak knives

_____ butter knives

_____ cocktail or seafood forks

_____ dessert forks

_____ lobster pliers

_____ escargot pliers

_____ soup spoons

_____ lobster pick

B. Using the bottom line as the table's edge, draw *(silverware only) one place setting* according to the standards of etiquette for the Les Amis Dinner.

_____

C. Should you bring refrigerated forks for the artichoke hearts?
a. Yes
b. No

D. Which soup spoon should you set?

A.   B.

E. Which wine glasses should you set? Group A, B, C, or D?

1   2   3   4   5

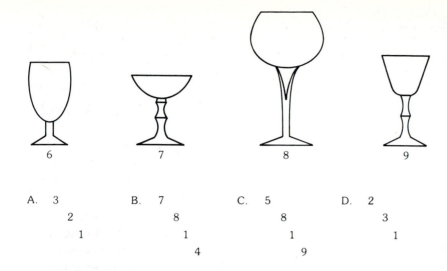

A.	3	B.	7	C.	5	D.	2
	2		8		8		3
	1		1		1		1
			4		9		

Additional Readings

Axler, Bruce H. *Focus On . . . Tableservice Techniques.* New York: Howard W. Sams & Co., 1974.

Bickel, Walter, trans. *Hering's Dictionary of Classical and Modern Cookery.* Giessen, Germany: Fachbuchverlag Dr. Pfanneberg & Co., 1974.

The Essentials of Good Table Service. Ithaca, N.Y.: The Cornell Hotel and Restaurant Administration Quarterly, 1975.

Huebener, Paul O. *Gourmet Table Service.* New York: Ahrens Publishing Co., 1968.

Lehrman, Lewis. *Dining Room Service.* New York: ITT Educational Services, 1971.

Tuor, Conrad. *Aide-Memoire du Sommelier.* Ecole Hoteliere Lausanne, 1970.

The Waldorf-Astoria Manuals, vol. III. Stanford, Conn.: Dahl Publishing Company, 1949, pp. 10-11.

Chapter 10

Tableside
Service

This chapter expands the previous discussion in which the types of service were explored from the managerial perspective. A discussion of the modern approach to tableside cookery and service follows with explanations of the staffing requirements and the equipment and utensils used in the preparation of food at the tableside. Several tested, standardized recipes appear at the end of the chapter, but their inclusion is not intended to make this text a cookbook. Rather, the simplified method is presented as proof that tableside cookery need not entail a slow service complete with elaborate tableside presentations that have been a part of the classical approach to cart service. This is not a contradiction to the previous chapter as the other was an academic treatment of the subject, and this is a modern, practical approach to the same problem. Classically, formal waiters were expected to spend at least a year in the kitchen of a first-class hotel or restaurant, and even more time as a commis de rang (classical term for a busboy) in the dining room.

The singular feature that distinguishes this style of service is some form of preparation in the presence of the guests before service. Historically, only restaurants with high-priced menus, working off higher profit margins, could absorb the costs involved with tableside cookery, such as low turnover, poor portion, and quality control, more space per guest, and excessive training time for the service staff.

The simplified approach allows waiters/waitresses with very little knowledge of tableside cookery to prepare foods in the presence of guests with complete confidence. The method is simplified because

1. ingredients are preprepared and preportioned in the kitchen.
2. recipes are standardized for the particular operation.
3. the method section in each recipe describes procedures in simplified terminology.

There are several advantages to this approach as compared to the classical. Since menu items are prepared as much as possible in advance, the residence time per guest is decreased, which increases the turnover rate. Since all ingredients are preportioned, quality and portion control are enhanced. Recipes are not left to the individual whims of the service personnel. Most important, however, is that waiters/waitresses need not spend excessive time in training. The checklists for dining room set-up *(mise-en-place),* cart set-up, and simplified procedure at the tableside make their job as easy as possible.

The most difficult aspect to accomplishing tableside service, especially with a combination of service styles, is the coordination required between the service personnel and the range, and between the service personnel working together in teams. If all service were from the cart, little coordination is required from service to production. With a combination of styles, however, vegetables or nontableside prepared entrees must come from the kitchen as the team member finishes his preparation at tableside.

The manager must be fully aware of the staffing considerations for this modern method of tableside cookery and service.

Staffing Requirements

In any staffing situation, each operator must determine his staffing requirements based on the individual need of the particular establishment. Yet the duties or tasks that need to be accomplished are somewhat similar from property to property. For example, it is necessary to prepare the dining area for service (mis-en-place), whether in an elegant restaurant or in a coffee shop. Doubtless some of the specific tasks themselves may differ, but the overall job of setting up the room needs to be done. In addition to setting up the dining room, the kitchen must also be prepared for service. Guests must be greeted and seated, and orders must be taken, placed at the range, picked up, and served to guest or picked up and prepared for the guest at the tableside.

It is essential for management to detail and to define all the tasks that need to be accomplished from the time the first

employee arrives for his/her shift until the last employee leaves. The standard tasks in the *Dictionary of Occupational Titles* for the following positions are listed in chapter 9:

Headwaiter/waitress; host/hostess; captain; waiter/waitress, formal, informal, and buffet.

It becomes obvious that the many tasks in the kitchen and dining room of a food service operation are divided among the various employees and supervisors. Almost all of these duties must be accomplished, yet the person who is designated by management to accomplish these tasks may vary from location to location. For example, the captains usually prepare foods at the tableside and serve the wines (in the absence of a wine steward/ess) in most restaurants. Serving wine, however, can be accomplished by any of the employees in the dining room—the headwaiter/waitress, the host/hostess, the captain, or a waiter/waitress. It is incumbent upon the manager to designate tasks to the various employees in his/her operation.

A restaurant operator who decides to use tableside cookery in his property should look at several factors with reference to staffing and scheduling. In a normal plate-service-style operation a waiter/waitress should be able to efficiently wait on fourteen to eighteen guests at one time. The fourteen to eighteen guests would be seated in rotation (e.g., they would not be seated simultaneously). However, if tableside cookery and service is being used, the waiter/waitress cannot *efficiently* serve the same fourteen to eighteen guests. The recommended rule of thumb for tableside service is approximately ten to twelve guests for one waiter/waitress working alone. The station division can be made several ways:

1. Two stations of fifteen or seventeen with one flamer for two stations; or,
2. Three separate stations with each waiter/waitress serving and preparing food at the tableside;
3. One waiter/waitress per station of thirteen to fifteen guests with one dining room attendant for each of two waiter/waitresses.

It is strongly recommended that a flamer be designated for each of two stations as the second method listed above may tie up a waiter/waitress at one table and force him/her to neglect his/her other guests. Additionally, when tableside cookery menu items are served at the same table where items prepared in the kitchen will also be served, the team system allows one waiter/waitress to be working at the tableside while the other picks up food in kitchen. The guests in one party will then be served simultaneously as much as is possible.

Managers must determine which pay scale is beneficial, as dining room attendants receive more in wages *from the establishment* than waiters/waitresses. It would behoove management, if this is the case, to dispense with the dining room attendant designation and call *everyone* a waiter/waitress.

The number of tableside items and the popularity of these items should also be taken into consideration when staffing or scheduling. If the restaurant offers Fresh Spinach Salad Helen and Steak Diane as the only two tableside preparations, perhaps the stations need only be decreased by two or three diners per station, and the waiter/waitress serving the station may also perform the tableside cookery. However, if only these two tableside items are offered and they prove to be very popular, the number of guests in each station should be decreased as is necessary to provide efficient service.

The configuration of the dining room and of the stations will also be a factor in staffing and scheduling. For example, one restaurant with approximately twenty-five to thirty seats in a rather small room could not accommodate more than two service personnel serving in this room. If an additional service person were placed in this small room, the room would be too crowded and they would actually be bumping into each other while trying to serve. This restaurant, however, offers many items that are prepared at tableside. The purpose of offering tableside service is to give personalized attention to the guest and increasing the size of the stations significantly somewhat defeats the purpose of offering tableside service. Yet the restaurant would lose some valuable revenue producing seats if they were to decrease the number of covers in this room. This decision can only be made by a manager who is fully aware of the guests' desires, the service they are receiving, and the operation's income statement.

Timing the Order

Recipes should have a time listed that measure the time from lighting the rechauds to serving the guest. Two and one-half minutes should be allowed on both ends of this figure (i.e., setting up the cart and cleaning the used cart) for a total time factor. It should take no more than five minutes total for set up and clean up (i.e., two and one-half for set-up and two and one-half for clean-up).

However, it is difficult to determine when the tableside item will be ready in order that all guests at the table will be served simultaneously. The difficulty arises when there is a line at the range for pick-up, and the waitress "needs her order because the food is ready at the tableside." The recommended procedure here is to give preference (i.e., "go to the head of the line") when tableside items are being served at one of his/her tables. Another method that may be used for coordinating this effort: When the waiter/waitress picks up his semiprepared tableside cookery item, the range crew can plate the corresponding vegetables, cover and hold (in a warmer) for the waiter/waitresses' call.

The timing of food coming off the range and off the tableside is much more difficult than the actual preparation at tableside due mainly to mixing the styles of service. Exactly when does the waiter inform the range to "final prep" the menu items that will be served simultaneously with tableside items? When does the waitress preparing food at the tableside inform his/her partner to pick up at the range the other main items or side dishes to accompany the tableside items? If everything were cooked at the tableside, then the style of service would be more simple. Difficulty will arise when styles of service are mixed. Yet an attempt should be made to speed the laborious process of classical tableside cookery without sacrificing flair and flamboyance.

A description of the proper sequence follows, but each person should practice in order to master it in the operational environment.

General Procedure for Flamed Items

Salads/Entrees/Desserts

1. Waiter/waitress informs captain that he/she is picking up the required items for flaming. (Place five-minute call for nonflamed items at this time, which indicates to range

that they should perform final prep and plating of nonflame items and hold for service.)

2. Captain will prepare his cart and then wheel to guests' table.
3. Captain will wait for waiter/waitress to bring ingredients for preparation.
4. After waiter/waitress brings ingredients for flaming, he/she will return to kitchen to pick up nonflamed items.
5. Captain begins preparing flamed items at the tableside as per recipe.
6. Waiter/waitress should return to dining room, serve guests eating nonflamed entree, and assist captain as necessary.
7. When captain has finished preparation, waiter/waitress will serve.

Specific Procedure for Steak au Poivre Flambe

1. Waiter/waitress will take order from guests, including desired degree of cooking (well, medium, etc.).
2. Orders will be turned in to the range, who will prepare all nonflamed items as normal. At the same time he will perform all kitchen preparation (e.g., portioning brown sauce into gravy boats, portioning clarified butter into pitcher, browning steaks) on a tray with specific ingredients needed for that waiter's tableside items. This will include the garnished steaks, butter, scallions and brown sauce (from the steam table). Should the order require a well-done steak, preparation of cooking will be done in the kitchen so that steak only has to be finished on the cart.
3. Waiter informs captain he is picking up items needed for flaming. When he picks up these items, he will place five-minute call for nonflamed items. Captain will prepare his cart with the other ingredients needed for tableside preparation (Worcestershire sauce, Madeira, brandy) and wheel to guests' table and wait for ingredients from waiter.
4. After giving the captain the ingredients, the waiter will return to the kitchen for nonflamed items along with plates, for the Steak au Poivre, which will have vegetable and potato already on it. Captain will prepare flamed item.

5. Waiter will return to dining room, serve guests eating nonflamed entrees, and assist captain as necessary.
6. When captain has finished preparation, waiter will serve the Steak au Poivre, making sure "medium steak goes on plate with baked potato and zucchini," etc.

Equipment

The equipment used in the dining room for preparing tableside items must be analyzed as to its advantages and disadvantages. The total investment for the equipment necessary for tableside cookery is less than might be anticipated. For example, a 100-seat restaurant could invest $1,000 to $1,500 in equipment, offer two items to be prepared before the guest, and provide tableside exposure to upwards of sixty patrons over a two-hour meal period.

Enumerated below are the pieces of equipment required for tableside cookery.

Carts

While functional considerations are the most important when choosing a serving cart, the basic features of the cart must complement the decor of the dining room. Having selected a cart that blends with the ambience of the dining room, the restaurateur should verify the equipment's practicality in light of several factors. It is essential that carts be structured for versatility, permitting the use of a single cart for the service of appetizers, entrees, salads, desserts, and cordials. Hinged side leaves provide maximum work surface when required, but allow the cart to be folded into a more compact unit for storage. A low ridge around the perimeter of the cart's work surface prevents items from falling off easily, but requires special attention when cleaning.

Carts should be easily maneuvered through the aisles and must, of course, fit through doors in the dining area and kitchen. If there is tiering in the dining room, it is advisable to provide carts for each level. Large diameter caster wheels, each swiveling independently, should be made of rubber to reduce noise if portions of the dining room are uncarpeted. All parts of the cart should be tight-fitting, both to facilitate the preparation of food at tableside and to reduce noise.

Several companies manufacture carts for tableside cookery or tableside or dining room display. Some carts, although conform-

Figure 10.1 Flambe cart (2 burners) (Photo courtesy of Aris Manufacturing Company. Cart Design © A. Fafoutis, 1977)

Figure 10.2 Service cart with dropleaf (Photo courtesy of Aris Manufacturing Company. Cart Design © A. Fafoutis, 1977)

Figure 10.3 Flaming carts equipped with Rechauds

Tableside Service   203

ing to the above-mentioned criteria, are not well-balanced (i.e., center of gravity is too high on the cart and this may cause the cart to tip over easily). A simple test will determine whether the cart is well-balanced and has the proper casters. Roll the cart around a room that has no carpets and a few cracks in the floor. If the cart chatters, the casters are poor. Similarly if fixtures on the cart are loose fitting the cart will rattle and be quite noisy. Secondly, clear the cart of all equipment, provide ample space in the room, and spin the cart around. If it tips over, the cart is not balanced and could cause problems in the dining room when loaded with flaming lamps, food, and bottles of spirits.

The weakest link in most carts is the brace(s) that suspend the drop leaves. Is this equipment sturdy? Is it easy to operate? Is it sharp? Can someone pinch his hand on it? Does it fasten the leaf firmly to the other portion of the cart when extended? If the answer to any of these questions is yes, the purchaser is compromising something, and therefore the purchase price should also be compromised. It is strongly recommended to purchase carts with leaves, since the cart will be easier to store as well as more versatile in the dining room. Another weak link in the cart is how the tiers or shelves and the top fasten to the supporting posts. If glue is the only thing holding the posts to the horizontal shelves, do not purchase the cart. They should be fastened with screws that *pass through* the shelves.

One safety factor that should be considered is the type corners used on the cart. If they are at ninety degrees, someone may catch a corner in his/her thigh. It is recommended that the corners be rounded at approximately three-quarters to one-inch radius. Additionally rounded corners improve the appearance of the cart by giving smooth lines versus sharp points. Sharp corners are more easily damaged, as well as causing damage, because they impact directly as opposed to glancing blows. The plastic coverings on some sharp cornered carts have been known to chip because they are formica-covered and butted rather than molded.

All-purpose, plain carts range anywhere from $100 to $350. If the cart costs more than that, you are probably paying for many things you do not need. Carts with built in rèchauds are considerably more expensive and offer little flexibility. Yet, a simple hole can be cut in the top of an all-purpose cart and a rèchaud may be dropped in. The hole can otherwise be covered for dessert or cordial display.

The restauranteur must be aware of storage space for the carts. It looks very poor to have rolling stock strewn all over the dining room, and the equipment can be damaged if not stored properly. As previously mentioned, drop leaves make carts easier to store. Additionally, poorly stored carts present a safety hazard since they may block aisles. Purchase *only* the number of carts needed even though the total investment in carts alone is minimal.

Flaming Lamps (Rèchauds)

Flaming lamps, or rèchauds, should fit the style of tableside service, complementing the carts selected for the operation. For example, a tall flaming lamp placed atop one of the higher carts available would bring the cooking vessel to a level that would make the server's work difficult. Further, it would defeat the purpose of tableside cookery, making it difficult for the patron to see the food being prepared.

Of the numerous models available from different companies, each rèchaud has its own advantages and disadvantages. Some flaming units use clean burning fuel (canned gels), while others utilize denatured alcohol. The clean burning fuels leave no carbon deposits on cooking utensils and are especially desirable when producing flaming coffees. The butane or propane burners (either in cans or refillable tanks) are becoming more popular and have their distinct advantages and disadvantages.

Alcohol Burners

The small double burner, denatured alcohol, (one-inch diameter with holes 1/2 inch away from center circling the center opening) rèchaud, figure 10.4, has a distinct advantage: it produces a very large flame after the unit heats up, but does not produce an excessive amount of heat. Recharging the unit is very simple, taking almost no time to recharge and hence refuelling can be accomplished after one or two tableside preparations. The amount of fuel that each heating unit takes is minimal and therefore there is little wasted fuel. The large flame is quiet and romantic as the flame curls around the pan, but it seldom overcooks the product. Incidentally, the large flame makes it easier to ignite the spirit, as the spirit need not be diluted in any sauce, and the flame curling around the pan will ignite the spirit when it is at the proper temperature. Correspondingly, if volume cookery is in order, this unit does require more time at the tableside. I recommend using a preheated pan for all tableside cookery for all rèchauds, but more importantly for alcohol burners as this shortens the time at tableside, but does not decrease the show for the guest. The alcohol burners produce large deposits of carbon, which typically collect on the bottom surface of the pan. This carbon is difficult to clean and makes an unsightly pan.

Another disadvantage to the alcohol burner rèchauds is that the flame is difficult to control or adjust. The only adjustment is the opening or closing of the smaller holes that encircle the major opening. This in and of itself is not a major disadvantage, as the heat produced (as previously mentioned) by the flame is minimal for the size flame. However, unless the following procedure is adhered to when the unit is hot, the flame is very difficult to extinguish. After the major cooking (flaming) has been accomplished, the flame should be lowered immediately. Although it does not respond immediately, the flame will subside, and only then can the flame be extinguished. Several unsuccessful attempts to extinguish the flame have been made when it is billowing away.

Another type of alcohol burner that offers more heat and a greater ability to adjust the flame is depicted in figure 10.5. This unit has a major opening of slightly greater than two inches with holes around the edge. The flame control adjustment on other similar models not only has rotary control (i.e., opening or closing the small holes around the major opening), but it has a push-pull mechanism, which opens or closes the opening of the center hole. Yet an extreme disadvantage here is that the *unit sometimes cannot be extinguished.* As the flame heats the unit up it becomes increasingly difficult to extinguish; however, the size of the flame can be reduced significantly. Loose fitting parts allow the alcohol to vaporize, where well-constructed units will not leak and can be extinguished more easily. Another disadvantage is that the unit requires at least one pint of fuel (alcohol) before it will work satisfactorily. For an establishment with a limited tableside menu, this unit may, through evaporation, waste fuel. Denatured alcohol solvent has a very distinctive, strong odor that can be objectionable. The person preparing foods at the tableside may frequently experience tearing, as the eyes are particularly sensitive to fumes of the burning alcohol. Yet, experimentation with several fuel sources revealed that, although considerably more expensive, the burning of Sterno liquid fuel diminished the odor significantly. Isopropyl alcohol is absolutely pungent and should not be used in the dining room. Neutral spirits (ethyl alcohol from petroleum or grain source) also produced a putrid odor, but it was not as predominant as the isopropyl alcohol.

Figure 10.5 Heavy duty Rechaud (Photo courtesy of Spring Brothers)

Solid Fuel (Gel) Burners. The solid fuel burners have two distinct advantages. There is no odor while the fuel burns, and it leaves a very small amount of carbon residue on the cooking vessels. Yet the heat source is insufficient unless the fuel is spread over a wide area. Simply opening the cans and burning from the can (with the small opening) does not produce adequate heat and the time spent in preparation is excessive. Additionally, the quality of the food products may be less desirable because saute items may not brown. However, heat intensifiers (available from suppliers) using the gel in bulk helps eliminate the low-heat problem.

The best use for the canned fuels (gel) that was found was for flaming beverages in the glasses. The can of fuel can be shrouded in a silver bowl or supreme dish and placed on a cart as is. The heat is quite adequate since undiluted spirits are being ignited, and it is a clean burning fuel. Another use for the canned fuels is for chafing dishes on buffet lines, or for hot plate warmers, which can be used in tableside cookery and service.

Gas Fuels (Propane/Butane)

Rèchauds using canned gas or refillable bottled gas have several distinct advantages. The fuel burns cleaner than the alcohol, but not quite as clean as the gel. The size of the flame can be low or sometimes high (depends on the element), but the amount of heat in each case is relatively high as compared to the gel or the alcohol. This may present some problems, as the food may cook quite rapidly and does not allow the normal time sequence for the service team member to pick up the nontableside items. Although this does not pose a major problem, this limitation does exist. This type unit (i.e., high heat) is useful when blinis, crepes (the pancake itself), or omelettes are to be prepared at tableside.

Figure 10.6 Rèchaud stove with grill top— Premierware (Courtesy of Oneida Limited)

The small flame gas rechauds are not recommended for two reasons. First, they hiss rather loudly, which is disturbing in a quiet room. Second, although the heat (BTU output) is high when the flame is small, it is more difficult to get the spirit in the pan to ignite. Usually the pan must be tilted to the flame, which results in inevitable spills; or if the spirit mixes with any sauce in the pan as a result of tipping the pan, the diluted spirit may not ignite. Additionally, the flame is not as theatrical or romantic as the large billowing flame produced by the alcohol.

If a decision is made, however, to purchase propane or butane fired rechauds, the unit must have a spreader mechanism at the flame source in order to more evenly distribute the heat. If a spreader is unavailable, do not purchase the unit, as the heat will concentrate on one section of the pan, scorch the pan, and cook the product unevenly.

Sautè Pans, Crèpe Pans, and Sauce Pans

The selection and purchase of the pans to be used for preparing the various menu items at tableside deserve careful consideration. Of utmost importance is the fact that the pan must be copper, heavy gauge aluminum, or stainless steel and never a thin aluminum or stainless steel pan. The heat sources (previously discussed) are quite variable and tend to concentrate in sections of the pans. A light, flimsy, thin-bottomed pan will not distribute the heat adequately, and the food products will be inferior. Similarly, the pan will not sustain the rough treatment usually found in commercial operations. Copper is preferable to stainless, as it makes a good presentation and distributes the heat more evenly. Yet copper is difficult to clean, since it must be washed, scoured, and polished. The lining of copper pans should be stainless steel. The steel wears considerably better than tin and most likely will last *for the life of the pan*. Additionally, stainless steel is much easier to clean.

Figure 10.7 *Oval saute pan (Photo courtesy of Adriana L. Hart)*

Figure 10.8 Oblong pan (Photo courtesy of Spring Brothers)

Copper pans with tin linings produce a superior food product, as tin does not react with the food products to cause discoloration or any off flavors. Yet the tin wears off very rapidly and needs to be resurfaced frequently. Acidic (low pH) food products react with the copper, which produces toxic food. If there is a person in the local area who can retin the pan, then purchase of these pans is advisable. However, this added task for a busy operator is uncalled for, and stainless steel pans are recommended.

Several shapes and sizes are available, and the size and shape should be compatible with the rèchauds. Although it is not a poor practice to use a rectangularly shaped pan on a round rèchaud, it is preferable to use the rectangular or oval shaped pan on a rectangular rèchaud (fig. 10.4). The heat is utilized more efficiently and is less likely to concentrate on specific areas of the pan.

For most entrée-type foods, the rectangular- or oval-shaped pans are preferable. There is more usable space in the pan, and this area can be used to separate items (meat and vegetables or sauce and spirit) in the pan while cooking. The size pan should be determined by the operator based on the menu items and the size of the portions he is going to offer. Standard sizes can be obtained from the various companies and the recommended size for all-purpose use is the 8-inch by 13-inch size. Do not purchase oval or rectangular pans without long handles, and never attempt tableside cookery from a pan *without* a long handle. It is foolish and dangerous to grasp the sides of the pan with a side towel.

The round open skillets come in diameters ranging from six to twelve inches. The eight- and ten-inch pans are recommended over the smaller or larger pans. The large pans (larger than 10 inches or 11 inches) are too cumbersome to use at the tableside, while the small skillets are not practical for preparing entrées at the tableside. The small skillets may be used to ignite undiluted spirits for pouring over Cherries Jubilee. Small sauce pans (1 quart) may also be used for igniting undiluted spirits, while larger sauce pans should be used for flaming beverages such as Cafe Diable.

Crêpe Pans (Fig. 10.9)

These should be used primarily for Crêpes Suzette, however, they are useful for cooking other desserts at the tableside (i.e., Bananas Flambè, Peaches Flambè, or Cherries Jubilee). Crêpe pans should be rather large (11 inches to 12 inches in diameter), as compared to skillets, and the ridge should be near vertical (i.e., perpendicular) short (3/4 inch or less), and made of heavy gauge metal. The large surface area is used to thinly distribute the sauce around the pan or to separate the sauce from the spirit so the spirit will ignite. It is difficult, if not impossible, for example, to flame Crêpes Suzette when the spirit has been mixed with the butter, sugar, and citrus juices.

There are several models of all stainless steel crêpe pans, which are as eye appealing as the copper-coated models. From the aesthetic viewpoint, the copper on the crêpe pans is not as essential as on the sauce pans, saute pans, or skillets, as the small ridge is hardly visible.

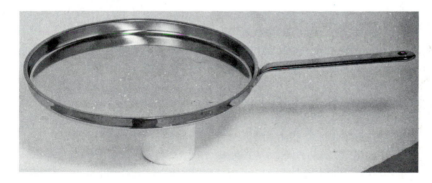

Figure 10.9 Round crêpe pan (Photo courtesy of Spring Brothers)

Carving Tools and Equipment

The basic tools required for carving at the tableside are knives, forks, and a steel. There are several different types of knives available, as well as different types of forks and steels.

Although a chef's or French knife is used in the kitchen for cutting vegetables, it becomes a useful tool for cutting some meats at the tableside. The wide blade is most effective when removing the chicken breast from the bone of a roasted chicken, as it keeps the meat in large pieces. A boning knife, although most desirable for boning raw chicken, is not as useful as the chef's knife for carving the cooked product. I recommend a small chef's knife; the large knives (greater than 8-inch blades) are unnecessary and obtrusive when used at the tableside. The blade should be stainless steel or nonstain, high-polished carbon, since carbon tool steel blades stain and may look dirty or unsanitary. Stainless blades do not hold edges as well as carbon blades and therefore I recommend the nonstain, high-polished carbon.

The standard bone or wood *handle* will soon be phased out as it is becoming illegal (for sanitary reasons) to use this type in commercial restaurants. The plastic, single-mold handles are recommended for several reasons: (1) sanitation; (2) ease of washing (they can be washed in a dish machine); and (3) safety (the rough surface and contoured shape of the handle provide minimum slipping).

There are several models of *forks* available which may be used at the tableside. The small cook's fork, with a short handle is acceptable for carving roasts—rack of lamb and chateaubriand—and recommended for carving whole roasted chicken. Of concern to the person carving at the tableside is the distance between the tines of a two pronged fork. If the tines are separated by an inch or so, the fork is of little use in attempting to carve a whole baked chicken. The bones of the chicken are so small that the tines straddle the food rather than holding it steady. Large forks are cumbersome and gaudy for tableside use. A standard dinner fork is a suitable tool for carving at the tableside, especially for baked chicken. The metal of a carving fork should be compatible with the metal selected for the knife unless the decision is made to use the standard dinner fork.

The steel is a useful and necessary piece of equipment, which is *used for finishing the edges of a sharp* knife as well as removing tiny metal burrs that appear as a result of sharpening on a stone. Many people use the steel in lieu of a stone for sharpening the knife, but this practice is not recommended. Several steels on the market are poorly designed and will be explained. One steel is flat (top view) or oblong (cut-away view), with the guards (around the handle) protecting the user *only if* he/she were using the narrow edge to hone the knife. Many users would choose the flat or larger surface and hands would not be protected from the blade of the knife were taken beyond the handle/steel juncture. Additionally, if used correctly, the steel would wear very quickly, as the narrow edge exposes little surface. This model is *not recommended.*

Another model has only two guards extending from the handle/steel juncture. The steel itself, however, is round. This limits the safe use of the tool, as again only two areas may be used.

The best steel has three guards extending from the handle, and this provides maximum protecion from injury. Additionally, all of the round steel surface can be used safely for honing the edge. The size steel used should complement the knife, especially for use at tableside. Using a fourteen-inch steel for a small knife looks foolish, while using a small steel eight to ten inches with a roast beef slicer with a fourteen-inch blade is dangerous as well as foolish.

The composition of the blade may be either ceramic stainless or nonstain, high carbon. Carbon tool steel is not recommended, as these will tarnish and look unsanitary.

If absolutely necessary, knives may be honed in the presence of guests, but it is preferable to have the knives sharpened, honed, and ready for use *before* serving the guests. Obviously the steel is necessary on buffet lines. *Proper use of the steel* requires the heel of the knife blade and the tip of the steel to meet with an angle of the blade on the steel of about twenty-five degrees. The knife is moved toward the heel of the steel with the tip of the knife ultimately reaching the heel of the steel simultaneously. The knife should be removed from the steel and the process repeated on the opposite side of the knife. The steel should be held rigid.

Many run the knife blade back and forth on the steel, but this method is improper. The minute particles which make up the blade edge of the knife should all be aligned the same way, and this can only be accomplished by using the above mentioned procedure. After the knife has been honed, the blade should be wiped clean with a cloth with the sharp edge facing away from the individual's hands or fingers.

Spoons used in tableside service should be the same design as well as complement the dinner forks in size. A standard serving spoon should be used, as soup spoons are too small and do not fit properly with the dinner fork. Ladles may be used for spirits or gravies and sauces, but should not be used in lieu of using a fork and spoon properly.

Boards and Platters

When selecting boards for carving at the tableside, consideration must be given to the platter that must be used under the board. Liquid invariably runs from the product and must be trapped so that it does not spill on the cart or on the floor. Sanitary laws will soon require commercial establishments to use the nonscore type (composition) cutting boards. The operator should investigate the state laws in his/her state before purchasing any natural wood product.

Boards with carved out portions for collecting the juices (well and tree design) are not recommended for commercial use as they are difficult to clean. Additionally, the carved out portions create a void when one attempts to cut through a product. Effectively there is no surface on which to carve. The size board should complement the product being carved. It would be foolish to place a small trout on a board designed for a steamship round.

Any product that is brought on a board for presentation to the guest should be garnished. Even a large product on a small board needs some type of garniture. The garnitures may be reused (i.e., a suet carving), as they are never served nor should they come in direct contact with the food.

Several platters are available for presenting the raw or partially prepared product to the guest. Oval platters, rectangular platters, round platters, and special design platters are available from several suppliers. Perhaps the most important consideration in platter selection is the size relative to the product being prepared. Shrimp Scampi would look foolish on a ten- or eleven-inch platter unless there is a considerable amount of garniture to fill in the voids. This decision should be made by the operator after he has selected the menu items he will feature for tableside preparation and after he has designed a standardized presentation platter for his operation.

The composition of the platters, whether silver, china, stainless steel, or polished pewter should complement the decor of the dining room. In an elegant room a stainless steel platter would be out of character, as would a silver platter in a restaurant with English Pub decor. Again, the final decision as to shape, size, and composition must be made by the operator.

Vegetable platters may be presented separately from the entree or may be displayed on the same platter. With a small cart, however, it is difficult to heat the entree and the vegetables in the same pan or even on the same rechaud. It is perhaps preferable to present the entree on one platter, prepare the entree at tableside, and while one is finishing his/her preparation, the other may fetch the hot vegetables from the range. The vegetables may be transferred to the guest's plate on the cart; or by using a combination of types of service, the guest may be served the entree on a properly garnished plate and then transfer the vegetables from the platter to the plate in front of the guest. Vegetables may also be served properly in separate dishes simultaneously with the entree.

The *condiment holders,* such as the small dishes referred to in the recipes, may either be made of china, stainless steel, pewter, or silver. These dishes should complement the platters used for presentation of the entree. If china dishes (monkey dishes) are used, it is essential that they have underliners (saucers). Metal is preferred to the china for appearance and breakage purposes. It is not necessary, however, to have underliners for such items as Worcestershire sauce, pepper mills, etc., as this would unnecessarily clutter the cart.

The *equipment and utensils used for preparing salads* at the tableside is the same equipment used in preparing other tableside items, with the exception of the salad bowls. The fork and spoon should be the same utensils used for preparation of other entrees, and the condiment holders should also conform to the aforementioned criteria.

The *salad bowls,* however, should conform to the sanitary standards established by the operator's state. Wooden salad bowls have more eye appeal than other models; however, the simulated ceramic models or simulated wooden models may serve as suitable substitutes. The important aspect for managerial consideration is the case of cleaning and sanitizing the soiled salad bowl, and they should be able to stand dish machine temperatures. Salad should be served appropriately on eight- or nine-inch plates. Salad should not be served in salad bowls or with the large wooden fork and spoon commonly used in the home.

Recipes

FRESH SPINACH SALAD HELEN			

Yield: 2		Temp.:	
Portion: Fills a 9″ plate		Time:	

Ingredients	Weights	Measures	Method
Spinach	5 oz. A.P.		Wash spinach well. Remove large stems and dry well.
Mushrooms, fresh medallions		6 medium	Tear into bite size pieces.
			Partially pan fry bacon, reserving the fat.
Bacon, thin slices chopped	2 oz.		Add onions to bacon when bacon is clear and saute until onions are transluscent and bacon is crisp.
Onion, 1/4 diced		1/4 c.	Reserve bacon, onions, and fat. Do not pour off fat. Keep bacon and onions warm. Bacon fat must remain liquid.
Vinegar, wine, or cider		1 tsp.	
Pepper, freshly ground		TT	Place spinach leaves in salad bowl. Add mushrooms to spinach and toss. Add bacon and onion mixture to spinach and toss. If required, add salad oil as needed and toss. Add vinegar and toss. Plate, sprinkle with fresh pepper, and serve.

STEAK DIANE

Yield: 2		Temp.:	
Portion: 3 2 oz. filet		Time:	

Ingredients	Weights	Measures	Method
Beef, tenderloin steaks, 2 oz.	12 oz.		Ignite burners of rechaud at tableside.
Shallots, minced		2 tbsp.	Place clarified butter in heated pan.
Mushrooms, medallions	1 oz.		Add Worcestershire sauce to butter.
Lemon		1/4	Place filets, shallots, and mushrooms in pan, keeping filets separate from shallots and mushrooms.
Butter, clarified	1 1/2 oz.		
Garlic, powdered		1/4 tsp.	Place lemon in cheesecloth and sprinkle steaks with juice. Season steaks with salt and pepper.
Mustard, dry		1 tsp.	
Thyme		1 tsp.	Season "vegetables" with mustard and thyme.
Cream, heavy		2 oz.	Turn steaks when browned on bottom. Continue to cook to desired degree of doneness.
Parsley, chopped		1 tbsp.	Add cream to vegetables, stirring until hot and thick.
Parsley sprig		2 sprigs	
Brandy		1 oz.	Pour brandy in pan and flame.
			Lower flame.
			Serve.
			Extinguish flame.

DESSERT CRÊPE BATTER

Yield: serves 8
Portion:

Temp.:
Time:

Ingredients	Weights	Measures	Method
Flour		1 1/4 c.	Stir in flour, sugar, and eggs into mixing bowl.
Sugar		3 tbsp.	
Eggs		4	Gradually stir in milk and liqueur.
Milk		1 3/4 c.	Beat with wire whisk until flour lumps disappear.
Grand Marnier or Cointreau		1/4 c.	Rub through a fine sieve in another bowl and stir in the oil.
Oil (Wesson or other)		2/3 c.	Cover and refrigerate batter for at least two hours before using.
Butter (clarified)		as needed for pan	To fry crêpes:
			Warm 4-5″ crêpe pan or skillet over high heat until drop of water evaporates instantly.
			Lightly grease bottom and sides of pan with oil.
			Stir batter lightly and pour about 2 tbsp. of batter into pan.
			Roll batter around pan so it quickly covers bottom.
			When batter firms up, pour off excess by tilting pan.
			Cook crêpe until light brown rim shows on edge. Turn over and cook for one minute on that side and then slide crêpe onto a plate.

CRÊPES SUZETTE FLAMBÈ

Yield: One serving for 2	Temp.:
Portion: 3 crêpes per person	Time: 6 min.

Ingredients	Weights	Measures	Method
Sugar, granulated		1/2 c.	Light burners of rèchaud at tableside.
Butter		12 pats	Put butter into pan and allow to melt.
Orange, fresh		1/2	Add the sugar to the melted butter, stir and allow to dissolve.
Lemon, fresh		1/2	Add the rind of the orange and the lemon.
Orange, grated peels		1 tsp. (optional)	Wrap the orange in the celery cloth, hold above the pan and squeeze juice into the pan. Repeat the procedure with the lemon.
Lemon, grated peels		1 tsp. (optional)	Stir mixture until it begins to bubble (avoid carmelization) and add crêpes, one at a time. Turn crêpe in the sauce using fork and spoon, being very careful not to tear or rip crêpe. Then fold it into quarters and place to one side in the pan. Repeat the above procedure with the rest of the crêpes. When all are folded in the sauce, move them toward the center of the pan, add the Grand Marnier and stir gently. Then add the brandy to flame.
Grand Marnier		1 oz.	
Brandy		1 oz.	
Crêpes		6	
			Spoon sauce over the crêpes. Use fork and spoon to dish crêpes on to 9″ plate (3 per plate) and spoon the sauce over them. Serve.
			Extinguish flame.

THE FLAMING ISLE OF SKYE

Yield: 2
Portion: 6 oz. coffee and cream

Temp.:
Time:

Ingredients	Weights	Measures	Methods
Lemon, wedge		1/4	*Rim the brims of each 8-oz. wine glass with lemon juice from the wedge; dip the brims into the sugar to coat.*
Whipped cream		6 tbsp.	
Sugar, granulated		1/4 c.	*Light flame.*
			Warm glasses over flame by rotating glasses.
Drambuie		1 1/2 oz.	*Pour 3/4 oz. Drambuie into each glass.*
Scotch		1 1/2 oz.	
Coffee		9 oz.	*Ignite spirit in glasses and continue rotating.*
			Add Scotch (3/4 oz. each) to glasses, ignite and rotate.
			Pour in hot coffee and top with whipped cream.

Notes

Igniting a nondiluted spirit produces a large flame. Insure that it is not too hot or you will get an explosion, not a flame.

Tea may be substituted for coffee for an unusual flaming beverage.

CAFE DIABLE

Yield: 4 cups (demitasse)
Portion: 2 cups (demitasse)

Temp.:
Time:

Ingredients	Weights	Measures	Method
Lemon peel		1 whole	Cut the peel from the meat of the orange and the lemon so the whole peel is intact and resembling a corkscrew worm.
Orange peel		1 whole	
Coffee, strong		10 oz.	
Cloves, whole		as required	Insert whole cloves into the peels on the outside surface. Attach both peels to the fork.
Brandy		1 oz.	Portion coffee into coffee pot.
Triple sec		1 oz.	Light rèchaud.
Brown sugar		1 tbsp., 1 tsp.	Place brandy and Triple Sec into small saucepan over flame.
Cinnamon, stick (broken lengthwise)		1/2 stick	Add cinnamon stick to spirits.
			Add peels to spirits, but keep attached to fork.
Lemon zests		2	When spirits are warm (not hot), remove spirits with ladle to flame and ignite.
			Take flame to spirits in saucepan and ignite.
			Stir with peels and ladle flaming spirits over peels while holding peels over and above saucepan.
			Add coffee into suacepan, add brown sugar, and stir.
			When sugar is diluted, fill cups and garnish with zest of lemon.

CAUTION!
Igniting a nondiluted spirit produces a large flame. Insure that it is not too hot or you will get an explosion, not a flame.

Chapter **11**

Wine and Beverage Service

The study of wines has begun to interest many people, and the consumption of wine has increased considerably in the last decade. This trend is especially delightful for the restauranteur or hotelier, as wine sales can add immensely to an operation's profit picture. As discussed in chapter 7, "Sales as a Service Function," wine is a plus sale when nothing else can be sold at that particular time. It is no wonder that a food service operator enjoys the trend for increased wine consumption, yet there is a disadvantage to the increased wine sales—a decrease in hard spirit sales. "Americans have moved away from this traditional pattern of hard, purposeful drinking to a style at once more moderate and more varied. More people are drinking, and they are drinking a greater variety of alcoholic beverages, particularly wines and . . . 'white goods'—i.e., vodkas, rums, gins, and tequilas."[1] The sale of hard spirits appears, and perhaps may be, more profitable for the restaurant operator. Beverage (hard liquor) costs run between twenty and thirty percent, whereas wine may run in the fifty percent cost range. Since wine is much easier to handle and to dispense, an operator should look at his *dollar profit* rather than simply percentages in order to determine his/her profit.

Wine and Wine Service

The study of wines is complex and even the study of wines within one country is quite complex. The restaurant operator should know something about wines in general, and he/she

1. Charles G. Burck. "The Whiskey Distillers Put Up Their Dukes," *Fortune* (September 1977):155-56.

should know about wines from many of the countries that are producing more and more wine. An excellent book, *Signet Book of Wine* by Alexis Bespaloff, would definitely increase one's knowledge of wines not from one country alone, but from many of the countries that produce wines for export. It is beyond the scope of this text to present a course in the study of wines, but some mention of the product is interesting, useful, and essential for the operator and for service personnel.

What Is Wine?

Classically speaking, *wine is fermented grape juice*. Recently, however, pop wines are being produced from many different types of fermented fruit juices, such as strawberry juice, pineapple juice, and apple juice. These pop wines, however, are seldom seen in food service establishments.

The Classification of Wines

Wine is classified by (1) the country from which the wine was produced, (2) its intended use, and (3) general category. There are several major wine-producing countries, and many other countries that produce wines that perhaps are not known in the United States as being wine producers.

By Country

The *United States* is a major wine-producing country, and the regions in the United States that produce wines for national (and some international) distribution are California and New York state. Ohio, Maryland, and some other states also produce wines that are distributed nationally, but these wines are not as well-known as the wines from California or New York. Several other states have vineyards and wineries, but the production from those wineries is usually distributed locally through retail sales at the winery store.

California has several wine-producing regions; and most California wines are considered premium wines, although there are several commercial wineries in California (Gallo, Italian Swiss Colony). Many of the commercial wineries are now producing what some consider premium wines. New York State produces several premium wines (Bully Hill, Dr. Konstantin Frank), but these wines are not readily available nationwide. New York state produces several commercial wines that are available nationally,

Figure 11.1 Standard shapes of bottles used in bottling wines

Sparkling
or Champagne

German
or Alsacian

Bordeaux
Region

Burgundy, Loire, Anjou
Cotes Du Rhone, Provence

and New York state sparkling wines enjoy a very good reputation. Grapes grown in California are of the same type as the grapes grown in Europe—Vitis Vinifera—and hence are considered premium wines. Native New York state grapes are of the Vitis Labrusca variety, and have a very definite grapy or fruity flavor.

France is generally regarded as the leading wine-producing country in the world; and although France produces a enormous variety of wine, actual production in gallons is less than production in Italy. French wine is controlled by a government agency, *Appelation Controlee,* which guarantees its authenticity if not its quality. Most of the French wine sold in the United States is appellation controlee wine; and certainly in most restaurants French appellation controlee wine predominates the market. French wine is usually named for the producing region (Burgundy, Loire, Bordeaux, Champagne, etc.), which is the *Generic name.* Recently the French have been naming wines from the grape variety (Pinot Chardonnay, Pinot Noir, Cabernet Savignon, etc.), which is the *varietal name.* The wines from France are produced in the regions of Bordeaux, Burgundy, Champagne, Cognac, Alsace, Loire Valley, Rhone Valley, Armagnac, and Provence. Each of these regions is further broken down into the various districts (Graves, Beaujolais, etc.) and even further into communes, villages (Chablis, etc.), and then the vineyard proper. Generally the more specific the naming (i.e., "Les Saint-Georges, from Nuit Saint Georges in

Burgundy" as compared to just "Burgundy") the better the wine. When the region appears between the words *appellation* and *controlee,* the production of the wine has been controlled more closely and therefore the wine is apt to be of a higher quality. Usually the more specific the area designated between the two words (i.e., a village versus a district such as Medoc versus Bordeaux), the better the wine.

Italy produces more wine (in gallons) than any other country in the world, and the United States imports more wine from Italy than from any other country. Yet the typical American knows very little about Italian wines. The Italian government recently strengthened the controlling agency, Denominazione Di Origin Controllata (DOC), and this has increased the popularity of Italian wine, since quality is more consistent with price. Italian importers are marketing their product more vigorously, and excellent values are available in the Italian wine market. Lambrusco surpassed Chianti as the greatest seller in the United States, and this is proof of success for recent marketing efforts.

The Italian wines are also divided into wine producing regions, which are not well-known in the United States. Italian wine is more easily recognized by the names of the wines rather than by the regions. Popular Italian white wines include Soave, Est Est Est, and Verdicchio. Popular Italian red wines include Chianti, Barolo, Gattinara, Bardolino, Barbera, and Valpolicella. Italy produces two wines worthy of noting—Marsala, which is sweet, fortified (greater than 14% alcohol by volume) wine similar in taste to a cream sherry, and Asti Spumante, a sparkling wine that is similar to champagne, although slightly more bittersweet than champagne.

The *Wines of Germany* are delightful as a sipping wine; and since they are generally mild and some very slightly sweet, they appeal to the American palate. German wines can be sold easily in many food service establishments. Since they are relatively low priced, as compared to the French, they therefore may find great popularity in commercial and family-type restaurants.

German wines are divided into two major areas: the Rhine and the Mosel. Rhine wines are bottled in brown or dark amber bottles, which are taller and thinner than the standard French wines, but identical in shape to those from the Alsace region in France. Some wine experts feel that the wines from the Rhine (i.e., liebfraumilch) are good wines to complement food, but they do not feel that Rhine wine has the charm that is found in the Mosel wines from Germany or the white wines from France. Mosel wines are slightly fruity, very light, and are superb either with or without food. Mosel wines come in green bottles and the bottles are identical in shape and color to those from Alsace.

German wines are very closely regulated. Due to poor sugar production in the grape as a result of little sun, sugar is added to aid the fermentation process. The addition must be closely controlled so that producers may not illegally alter the wine. While French wines are graded on location (i.e., what vineyard produced the grapes), German (Qualitatswein mit Pradikat or quality wine with predicate) wines are graded on when the grapes were picked:

Auslese—select picking (picking the best grapes).

Spatlese—late picking (the longer the grower waits to pick the grape, the more desirable the wine is considered).

Beerenauslese—grape that has been attacked by the "noble rot" or *Pourriture Noble* (a fungus) that makes the wine sweet.

Trochenbeerenauslese—a select picking of grapes that have been attacked by the noble rot.

Eiswein (Ice Wine)—from grapes picked on the day of the first frost. This yields a very concentrated grape juice.

Each Qualitatswein has a coded control number on the label that tells the area the wine came from (first digit), the shipper or grower (next three digits), the cask number submitted for sample (digits five, six, and seven), and the date the particular wine was submitted for sample.

Other countries produce some very fine wines; however the general use of these wines, with the exception of Spanish and Portuguese wines, is limited. South America (Chile and Argentina primarily), South Africa, Australia, Austria, and Switzerland produce wines; but as yet, these are not widely distributed.

By Use

Although most wine is used for drinking (i.e., table wine), wine can also be used for cooking and as a marinade; for celebrating various occasions such as weddings, toasts, christening ships, communion in church; for medicinal purposes; for flavoring; as a beauty aid; and for tobacco.

By General Category

Wine is categorized by general category or what the wine is. Wine complements certain foods, and food complements certain wines. Yet a host or hostesses preference, whatever he/she chooses to drink, is the correct wine to serve:

Food	Wine
Canapes, hors d'oeuvres, cheese, crackers, relishes	Sherry (dry or cocktail), Champagne, Madeira
Soup	Sherry (dry or cocktail), Madeira
Fish	Dry white wine
Dark or fatty fish	Rose or light red
Fowl	Dry white, rose, or light red
Meat	Red or rose
Nuts, desserts, fruit, cakes . . .	Tokay, Port, sweet or cream sherry, or Muscatel, Champagne.
Cheese	Rich red wine

In order of presentation in the meal one would find:

Appetizer Wines

Aperitifs are sometimes called aromatized or fortified wines because of the additional ingredients that are added for flavoring, and the additional alcohol (18% to 22% alcohol by volume), which is added to stabilize the wine.

Drinking an *aperitif* is the proper way to begin a meal, since the product is intended to sharpen the appetite when a cocktail with hard liquor may dull the appetite. There is a higher profit in cocktails, which causes restauranteurs to play down the appetizer wines. Since aperitifs are less expensive, they could be used to sell a banquet where the guest(s) might reject an open bar.

Vermouth is a generic name, and it is the most common aperitif. The product ranges from the dry whites to the bittersweet reds. Dry or cocktail sherries are excellent appetizers, but the sweet or cream sherries should not be served as appetizers unless specifically requested by the guest. As with dessert wines and cordials, aperitif sales may be increased by rolling a cart to the tableside with the wines displayed and offered to the guests. There are many other aperitifs that are quite popular; and each has a common ingredient and characteristic—they taste bitter because of the quinnine added. Some of these are: *Dubonnet* (red or blonde), which is now being produced in California from the original recipe; *Lillet, St. Raphael,* and *Byrrh,* which are French products; and *Cynar* and *Campari* from Italy. Cynar (pronounced Chē när) is made from an artichoke base.

White table wines are usually served as accompaniments to fish and other seafood; light-meated fowl such as chicken, capon or breast of turkey; or light meat such as veal or pork cutlets. White wines should be served chilled or approximately fifty degrees Fahrenheit (50° F) or ten degrees centigrade (10° C). Some examples of white wines include generic, varietal, and proprietary names (named by the producer such as Emerald Dry). Popular white wines include Chenin Blanc, Niersteiner Oldberg, Pinot Grigio, Bernkastel, Chablis, Sauternes, Pinot Chardonnay, Pouilly Fuisse, Pinot Blanc, Zeller Schwarze Katz, Rhine, Grey and Johannisberg Reisling, Liebfraumilch, Moselblumchen, Semillon, Montrachet, Soave, Verdicchio, White Chianti, Sauvignon Blanc, Sylvaner, Aurora, and Delaware.

Red table wines also include rose wines in the general category. Very light red wines, such as the roses, Beaujolais, and Zinfandel may be served chilled, but most red wines are served cool or at cellar temperature—about sixty-five degrees (65° F) Fahrenheit or eighteen degrees Celsius (18° C). Red wines are served to accompany red meats, dark-meated fowl, Italian or tomato dishes, or cheese or nuts. Some examples of red wine are Burgundy, Bordeaux, Barbera, Bardolino, Barolo, Gattinara, Grignolino, Gamay, Beaujolais, Pinot Noir, Claret, Cabernet Sauvignon, Zinfandel, Chianti, Concord, Vino Rosso, Lambrusco, Brunello, Chateauneuf du Pape, Nemes Kadar, Petite Sirah, and Brouilly. Some roses include Lancer's, Mateus, Tavel, Chateau St. Roseline, and Grenache Rose.

Sparkling wines can be served either as an appetizer wine during the meal or for dessert and should be served *cold.* As temperature is increased the solubility of a gas in a liquid decreases which, if too warm, will produce an explosion upon opening the bottle of sparkling wine.

Sparkling wines may go through a complicated production procedure (methode champenoise or champagne method), which, when combined with a tax of twenty times that of still wine, makes their cost high. There are other processes to reduce the production costs considerably, namely the Charmat or bulk process method where the natural carbon dioxide (CO_2) is produced during the fermentation process in large vats instead of in the bottle. The sparkling wine is then bottled under pressure retaining the carbonation. Another process injects a still wine with carbon dioxide (CO_2) to make the wine sparkling.

The champagne method of producing sparkling wines is a long, slow process; however, the secret of champagne is the blending, not the method. Champagne grapes are pressed separately and blended later. Four pressings are standard (1) Vin de cuvee—finest champagnes; (2) first tailles; (3) second taille and (4) rebeche—used only for nonalcoholic beverages. The juice must be quickly separated from the skins, as the inside of the skin gives color to the wine. After the juice is placed in casks and then blended, a sugar/yeast mixture (cuvee) is added for the second fermentation where the (CO_2) gas (carbonation) is produced and the alcoholic content is increased. Capped bottles are placed in A-frame boards with the necks turned down. *Each day* the bottles are turned a quarter turn and tilted more neck down to loosen the sediment. All sediment will eventually collect at the cork, when the bottle is upside down vertically. The necks are then dipped in a cold brine solution, which freezes the sediment; the cork and with it the sediment is disgorged, and a dosage (another sugar/wine mixture) is added, which determines the relative dryness of the champagne.

Type of Champagne	Percent Sugar Added	Characteristic / Taste
Brut	.5–1.5%	Very, very dry
Extra dry or extra sec	1.5–3.0%	Fairly dry
Dry or sec	3.0–5.0%	Sweet
Demi-sec	5.0–7.0%	Quite sweet
Doux	7% or more	Very sweet

Sweet Champagnes are usually of lesser quality (sugar hides the imperfection), and are not found very often in the United

States. Vintage champagne (85% of the grapes from the same year) is not necessarily of better quality, although vintages are declared only for exceptionally good years; but it does have a distinctive character.

SIZES OF STILL WINE AND SPARKLING WINE BOTTLES

Miniature or *Miniature* (3.4 oz. or *100 ml*)

Split or *Small* (6.3 oz. or *187 ml*)

Tenth or *Medium* (12.7 oz. or *375 ml*)

Fifth or *Regular* (25.4 oz. or *750 ml*)

Quart or *Large* (33.8 oz. or *1.0 liters [1,000 ml]*)

Magnum or *Magnum* (50.7 oz. or *1.5 liters*)

Jeroboam or *Extra Large* (101.4 oz. or *3.0 liters*)

Rehoboam *4.5 liters*

Methuselah *6.0 liters*

Some examples of sparkling wines are Champagne, Pink Champagne, Cold Duck, Sparkling Burgundy, Sparkling Muscat, Asti Spumonte or Spumonte, Sekt, and Mousseaux.

Dessert wines are served for or after dessert, and the distinguishing characteristic is that they are sweet. With the exception of Sauternes, most of the dessert wines are fortified. Dessert wines are not popular among restauranteurs; as with appetizer wines, they yield less profit than after-dinner cocktails, cordials, or brandies. Dessert wines are usually served by the glass and chilled; and an excellent method of increasing dessert wine or cordial sales is to have a cart displaying the spirits rolled to the guests' table. Some examples include Port—red, tawny, or ruby; Muscatel—gold, red, and black; Black Muscat; Sherry—sweet or cream only; Angelica; Madeira; and Marsala.

Abbreviated Checklist for Service Personnel

Wines

Wine complements certain foods and food complements certain wines. Yet the host's preference, whatever he chooses to drink, is the correct wine to serve. Wine can also add to your tip.

Appetizer Wines—sometimes called aromatized or fortified wines.
Vermouth (red or white), Sherry (dry only), Cynar, Lillet, Dubonnet (red or blonde), Campari, St. Raphael, Byrrh.

White Table Wines—usually served with seafood, light-meated fowl, chicken, etc. Serve at approximately 50° F. Chablis (dry), Pinot Chardonnay, Pinot Blanc, Rhine, Liebfraumilch, Semillon, Sauvignon Blanc, White Chianti, Light Muscat, Delaware, Niersteiner Oldberg, Pinot Grigio, Bernkastel, Sauternes, Pouilly Fuisse, Zeller Schwarze Katz, Grey and Johannisberg Reisling, Moselblumchen, Montrachet, Soave, Verdicchio, Sylvaner, Aurora.

Sparkling Wines—Champagne can be served as an appetizer, during the meal, and with dessert. Serve cold. Champagne, Cold Duck, Sparkling Burgundy, Sparkling Muscat, Spumante, Asti Spumonte, Sekt, Mousseaux.

Red Table Wines—usually served for dark-meated fowl, red meats, Italian dishes, cheese, and nuts. Serve at approximately 65° F. Burgundy (dry), Barbera, Charbone, Gamay, Beaujolais, Bardolino, Barolo, Bordeaux, Brunello, Pinot Noir, Red Pinot, Claret (dry), Cabernet Savignon, Gattinara, Grignolino, Lambrusco, Zinfandel, Red Chianti (dry), Concord (sweet), Rose (dry to sweet), Vino Rosso (semi-sweet), Chateauneuf du Pape, Nemes Kadar, Petite Sirah, Brouilly.

Dessert Wines—generally served for dessert. Port (red, tawny, ruby), Muscatel (gold, red, black), Sherry (sweet or cream only), Black Muscat, Tokay, Angelica, Madeira, Marsala, Sauternes.

Glassware and Equipment Used in Wine Service

In an elegant restaurant a wine steward/ess (sommelier) and his/her assistants are responsible for the restaurant's wine cellar; this may include ordering wines, maintaining inventories, tasting new wines to accompany menu items, and insuring that the wine is being handled and stored correctly. Additionally, the wine stewardess is fully aware of the wines she has in stock, and should be most capable in discussing wines with restaurant guests. Wine in an elegant restaurant is a natural accompaniment to the meal; whereas in a medium-priced, theme restaurant, the wine list may not be extensive and those selling wines—captains and waiters/waitresses—need not be so aware of wines in general or of fine vintage wines.

The wine steward may wear a chain around his neck with a tasting cup and key attached (actual key or symbolic key to the cellar). Most tasting cups are made of silver, aluminum, or other metal. This makes it difficult to see the clarity of the wine, and some cups have an arrangement of indentations (both convex and concave) in order to reflect light through the wine. The wine stewardess, upon opening the wine, sniffing and squeezing the cork, will pour a small amount for herself, swirl the wine, nose (smell) the wine, and taste it. She should then pour a small amount for the host who may do the same. Upon the host's approval, she should then pour for all guests at the table. (See wine service procedures.)

Some guests may ask that a red wine be opened an hour or so before the wine is to be consumed. Recently *New York Magazine* conducted a blind test with several wine experts as the wine tasters with the following results. Wine that was opened and poured immediately was considered superior to wine that had been allowed to "breathe." The writers felt that the presumed improvement in the wine had little to do with the *flavor* of the wine and more to do with the fact that, by the time the wine had had an opportunity to breathe, the drinker's taste was impaired by the amount of alcohol consumed.

Corkscrews

Careful consideration must be given to selecting a corkscrew for opening wine with corks. If a corkscrew is not designed properly, the waiter/waitress, captain, or wine steward/ess will have difficulty and look clumsy in front of the guest. A "professional waiter's corkscrew" (fig. 11.2) is the only acceptable tool to use in the dining room, and *it is the easiest to use*. The corkscrew must have a knife and the knife blade should be straight, as compared to a hooked blade, to cut foil neatly below the bulge. The lever should also be designed to remove bottle caps. More importantly, the lever must be relatively rigid. It must stay wherever placed, without dangling, and at any angle. A loose lever will flap into the bottle when the stewardess is trying to screw the worm into the cork, and this makes her look unprofessional or incompetent. The worm (borer or screw) should not have sharp edges, as this may cut the cork and thus prevents a smooth withdrawal. The point of the worm should follow the contour of the worm. If it is a straight point, the corkscrew may pull *through the cork* and leave the cork in the bottle. Some screws have a

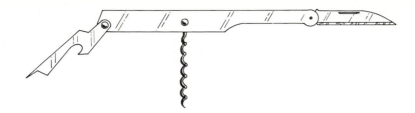

Figure 11.2 Professional corkscrew

small, smooth indentation on the outside of the screw, and this eases the task of drilling the screw into the cork. The portion of the lever that rests on the lip of the bottle should not have sharp edges. If the cork is stubborn, the glass may chip or crack before the cork can be removed. The corkscrews with wings used to apply pressure on the lip in order to remove the cork are *absolutely not recommended* for professional use. The corkscrews, which look like the professional type, but with a bottle opener on the knife end, are not recommended since there is no knife to cut the foil, and there is already a bottle cap remover on the lever. The double-screw corkscrew is minimally acceptable, but not recommended. The wooden-handle corkscrew, with an attachment that rests on the lip, is also minimally acceptable but not recommended. The two-pronged cork puller, which one wiggles down the side of the cork and then twists to pull the cork, is ideal for home use. The same tool can be used to reinsert the cork, and it does not damage the cork as the worm does. (This cork puller has been known as the *dishonest butler*.) *One caution:* The prongs exert an outward force on the bottle and have been known to shatter the glass. The two-pronged cork pullers are not recommended for professional use. Cork removers that use air pressure or carbon dioxide (CO_2) are extremely dangerous. Still wine bottles are not stressed for pressure and the bottle could explode if the cork is tight fitting.

Baskets

Although baskets are used for serving wine, this practice is foolish. The basket serves two specific functions: (1) it is used to transport the wine (at approximately a thirty degree angle) from the cellar or wine storage area to the dining room, so as not to dislodge the sediment, and (2) it is used to hold the wine bottle for decanting. After decanting, the wine basket and empty bottle may be displayed on the guests' table. Baskets are made of wicker or silver/chrome covered wicker.

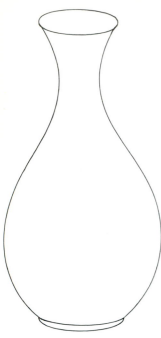

Figure 11.3 Decanter

Decanters

The standard wide-mouthed (litre or half litre) carafe is ideal for serving wines by carafe, but should not be used for decanting fine wines. Fine wines should be decanted into plain (non-colored) decanters (fig. 11.3) and the decanters should not be cut glass, as this destroys the appearance of a clear wine.

Wine Buckets/Stands

There are several different wine buckets on the market that are made of plastic, aluminum, stainless steel, and silver plate. Plastic or aluminum buckets are perhaps the least expensive, but they do not have as long a life as the stainless or silver buckets and they dent easily. Some silver wine buckets are quite heavy, especially when used with weighted silver stands. They are difficult for a strong person to carry, let alone an average or weak person. Stainless steel buckets and stands are compatible with the decor in most restaurants; perhaps only the elite, elegant theme restaurants should not use the stainless models. Whichever bucket is selected, the stand must be compatible with the bucket (i.e., it must fit).

Glassware

The companies that sell glassware produce countless varieties of glasses for *this* purpose and countless others for *that* purpose. Yet many operations need only stock an eight-ounce wine glass that will be satisfactory for all the wines served. There are special glasses for the wines of Bordeaux, for the wines of Burgundy, etc., but this specialization is not required for many modern operations in the United States. The champagne saucer, which has been used traditionally to serve sparkling wines is ill-suited for that purpose. As the surface area is increased there is an increase in the amount of effervescence lost. The champagne tulip, therefore, is much superior for serving sparkling wines, as the shape tends to retain the gas. Additionally, the tulip is an attractive glass, which will sell more product (because of appearance *and size*) than the saucer.

The operator should also realize that large bowl glassware may not be compatible with the dish machine or dish machine racks, and this may cause excessive breakage.

If a restauranteur is anxious to stock several different kinds of wine glasses, the following are recommended:

Figure 11.4

All Purpose.
Use for reds or whites.

Brandy Snifter or Inhaler.
Use for brandy and some cordials.

All Purpose Wine Glass.
Good for reds, roses
and hearty whites.

Dessert Wine Glass.
Use for Ports, Tokay
other dessert wines,
sweet sherries.

Sherry Glass.
Use for dry or
cocktail sherries

Rhine Wine Glass.
Use for light whites.

Champagne Saucer.
Not recommended
for any beverages.

Champagne Tulip.
Recommended for
all sparkling wines.

Cordial or Pony.
Use for cordials
or liqueurs.

**Brandy Up
Glass.**
Use for cordials
or brandy.

Minimum Stock should include (1) one of the all-purpose wine glasses (eight-ounce size); (2) a dessert wine glass (three- or four-ounce size); (3) a tulip chamagne glass (six- or eight-ounce); (4) a cordial or pony glass (one, one and one-half, or two ounce); (5) a brandy snifter or inhaler (twelve to fifteen ounce).

Several factors should be considered when purchasing glassware. (1) durability and compatibility—do the glasses have flimsy brims, stems, or feet? Will they fit into the dish machine easily?

(2) Are they easily replaceable—will you end up with three different types or sizes of all-purpose wine glasses? (3) Are the glasses compatible with the decor and overall ambiance of the dining room—lead crystal would be out of character for the franchise steak houses.

Wine and Champagne Service

Red Wine Service—red wines should be served at cellar temperature (65° F; 18° C). Use extreme caution when handling vintage wines, as most red wines throw a sediment. Decanting may be required (see separate procedure). Insure that you use the proper glass for the type wine being served, that is, red wine or all-purpose glass. After wine has been ordered:

1. *Present* the wine to the host. Cradle the bottle in a towel and show the bottle with the label toward the host. The bottle must be unopened.
2. *Open* the wine after the host has approved.
   a. *Cut* the foil well below the lip and *just below the bulge*. Peel off the foil on top.
   b. *Wipe* the cork and the exposed glass.
   c. *Draw* out the cork with one motion and wiggle out for last half inch. Do not allow the cork to "pop" out. Place cork to the right of the host on an underliner.
   Note: After the foil is removed and the cork wiped, pressure may be applied to the top of the cork to break the seal created in the bottle.
   d. *Wipe* the mouth of the bottle again.
   Note: The guest's table may be used to rest the bottle when opening, or the bottle may be held in one's hands.
3. *Serve* the wine by allowing the host to sample a small amount. After the host has approved:
   a. Serve the person to the host's right and move counterclockwise around the table until all guests are served. The host should be served last.
   b. Fill red wine to no more than one-half full.
   c. Place the bottle to the right of the host's wine glass.

Figure 11.5 Pouring red wine. Pour red wine with bottle as close to the glass as possible without touching the brim of the glass. Fill glass to no more than one-half full. (Photo courtesy of Oneida LTD. Silversmiths.)

White or Rose Wine Service—white wines should be served chilled (50° F; 10° C). After the hostess has ordered the wine, the waiter/waitress, captain, or wine steward should place the unopened bottle in a wine bucket with ice, service cloth draped over the bucket, and a stand for the bucket.

1. *Present* the wine after removing the bottle from the ice and wiping the water from the bottle. Show the bottle as with red wine.
2. *Open* the wine as with red wine.
   Note: The bottle may be replaced in the bucket before opening. This is as acceptable as holding the bottle in one's hands, or resting on the table.
3. *Serve* the wine as with red wine. Insure you are using the proper glass (i.e., Rhine wine glass, all-purpose glass, etc.).
   a. Fill to no more than three-fourths full.
   b. Replace the bottle in the wine bucket, draped with a clean service cloth.
   c. Place bucket and stand to the right of the hostess (if possible) and insure that the bucket is not in an aisle.

Champagne or Sparkling Wine Service—champagne may be served during any portion of the meal and is a delightful accompaniment to any food. Handle gently so as not to increase the internal pressure. It should be served well-chilled (no more

Figure 11.6 Presenting the bottle of wine to the guest. Cradle the bottle by holding the bottom of the bottle with the service cloth and the neck as shown.

Figure11.7 Cutting the foil. Foil should be cut below the bulge. This prevents the wine from touching the foil as this may impart off flavors.

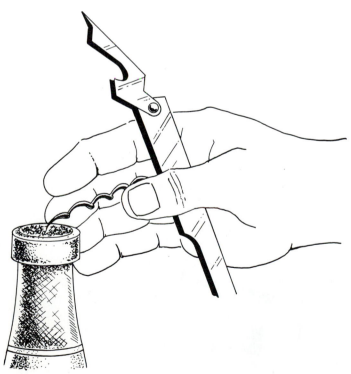

Figure 11.8 Inserting the corkscrew. The forefinger and the middle finger should be used to steady the screw. This also gives the server more strength where needed. The screw should be started into the cork at an angle (as shown in this figure) and after piercing, the screw should be moved vertically so that the cork-screw can be driven down the center of the cork.

Figure 11.9A Drawing the cork. One hand or finger should be used to steady the lever on the brim of bottle while the other hand is used to draw the cork out of the bottle. Do not remove cork totally at this motion.

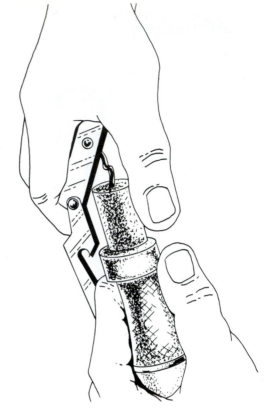

Figure 11.9B Drawing the cork. With the fingers and the thumb, wiggle the cork out for the last one quarter to one half inch. Do not let it pop.

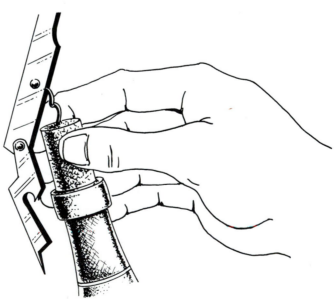

Techniques and Procedures

Figure 11.10 Serving the wine. Cradle the bottle in one hand and expose the label to the guest being served. Pour red wine with the neck of the bottle as close to the brim of the glass as possible, but without touching. Pour white wine from two inches above the brim of the glass. Simultaneously twist the bottle (counterclockwise for right hand pouring) when you stop pouring.

Figure 11.11 Replacing a white wine in the ice bucket. Place the bottle of wine in the bucket and drape a clean napkin or cloth over the bottle.

Figure 11.12A Champagne service. The foil need not be completely removed as shown here. However, as soon as the wire is moved (either by untwisting or breaking) the top of the cork must be controlled by the other hand and never released until the cork has been removed.

Figure 11.12B Removing the champagne cork. The cork should be held firmly with one hand, and the bottle should be twisted (by holding the bottom) with the other hand. The bottle should be at a 45° angle.

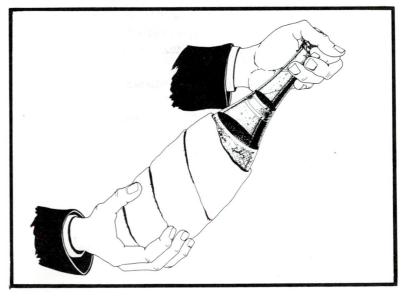

than 50° F). Bring an ice bucket, etc., as with white wine. A champagne tulip glass is recommended for champagne service.

1. *Present* the champagne (unopened) as with white wine.
2. *Open* the champagne with caution, as the pressure can send the cork flying. Wrap the bottle in a towel and tilt at a 45° angle.
   a. *Locate* the wire twist and place your thumb on the cork.
   b. *Remove* the wire (break or untwist) and foil in one action while *still holding the cork.*
   c. *Grip* the cork firmly and twist the bottle to loosen. Continue to hold at a 45° angle.
   d. *Allow pressure* to push cork out, and place to the right of the host.
3. *Serve* the champagne as with wine by allowing the host to sample a small portion.
   a. Begin with person on host's right and continue as with wine service.
   b. *Pour in two motions* by allowing foam to subside and refilling the glass to three-quarters full.
   c. Replace bottle in wine bucket as with white wine.

Decanting should be performed on red wines that have thrown a sediment. Decanting means to pour wine from its bottle to another container from which it will be served. Sediment is a deposit of dead yeast cells (harmless), which imparts a bitter taste and makes the wine appear dull or cloudy. Decanting also gives any wine a chance to breathe or oxidate. This rids the wine of the sulphur taste that it may have. After the wine has been ordered:

1. *Select* the proper bottle from storage using caution not to shake the bottle and place the bottle in a wine basket.
2. *Present* the wine in the basket. After the hostess has approved, set wine on service cart to the right of the hostess.
3. *Open* the bottle while it is still in the basket. The basket should not be used for service.
   a. Cut and remove *all* of the foil using care not to dislodge the sediment.
   b. Wipe the cork and the exposed glass.
   c. Draw and wipe as with red wine. Use caution not to rotate the bottle while inserting the corkscrew as the

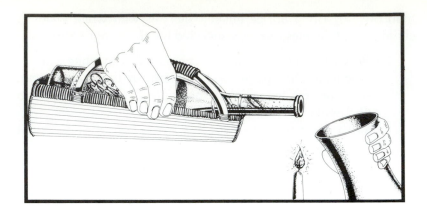

Figure 11.13 Decanting. The bottle and the basket should be held in one hand, and the decanter should be held in the other hand. Use caution with the candle as it should not be directly under the neck of the bottle lest it heats the wine.

sediment may be disturbed. When the corkscrew is inserted through the cork, it may not be in the most convenient location, but *do not move the bottle.*

    d.   Light the candle, but insure that the flame does not heat the wine, but that the light is visible through the neck. (The candle should be offset from under the neck of the bottle.)

4. *Decant* by pouring the wine from the bottle to the decanter. Pour a few drops into the decanter; stop pouring and swirl the wine in the decanter. Pour this wine into an extra glass. Then:

    a.   Pour wine into the decanter in a steady, slow stream.

    b.   Use a continuous motion or the wine will wash back into the bottle and mix with the sediment.

    c.   Stop pouring when the sediment begins to pass through the neck.

5. Allow the wine to rest for a short time if possible before serving; old (maturized) wines can go bad very quickly. Continue service as listed in serving the wine in Red Wine Service.

Note: The basket and bottle should be placed on the hostess's right.

Equipment Required for Wine and Champagne Service:

    Wine, wine glasses (proper type, extra as required), corkscrew (professional lever-type preferred), service cloth, wine bucket and stand (ice), decanter (clear glass preferred), wine basket (wicker or silver) candle and holder, matches, underliner for decanter (silver for fine service).

	°C °F	
	21-69	
	20-68	
	19-66	
	18-64	Full-bodied, Mature Red Wine
	17-63	e.g., Bordeaux
Red Burgundy Wine	16-61	
	15-59	
Full-bodied White Wine Port,	14-57	
Madeira	13-55	
	12-54	
Sherry	11-52	Light Red Wine
	10-50	
Dry White Wine	9-48	Rose Wine
Champagne	8-46	
	7-45	
Sweet Sparkling Wine	6-43	Sweet White Wine
	5-41	
	4-39	
	3-37	
	2-35	
	1-33	
	0-32	

Figure 11.14 Temperature chart for wine service (Adapted from Hugh Johnson's POCKET WINE BOOK. Mitchell Beazley Publishers Limited: London, 1977. p. 17).

To convert °F to °C:
Subtract 32 from °F and multiply by 5/9:
_____ °F − 32 × 5/9 =
_____ °C

To convert °C to °F:
Multiply °C by 9/5 and add 32:
_____ °C × 9/5 + 32 =
_____ °F

Proper method for carrying bottles of wine and wine glasses to the table

Wine glasses may be carried inverted with the waiter/waitress inserting the stem of the glass between his/her fingers and by holding the base of the glass. Single wine bottles should be cradled or carried with two hands. Holding the neck of a wine bottle with one hand is improper. A cocktail tray may also be used to carry both bottles of wine and wine glasses simultaneously.

When carrying a rose, white wine, or sparkling wine to the table, the bottle may be placed in the wine bucket with ice, water, and a service cloth, and this entire set-up may be brought to the table in this form. The ice bucket should be three-fourths filled with ice and half filled again with water. Water will increase the contact of the cold medium on the wine, and it will also allow the bottle to be submerged easily in the bucket.

Banquet wine service differs from à la carte wine service, since the wines have been chosen in advance of the function. The wines are not opened in the presence of the guests, and are simply poured for the guests. It is helpful if one person is designated to serve only wines. The number of people one person can serve efficiently will vary, but an efficient wine steward should be able to pour wine efficiently for upwards of forty guests.

The wine to be used for a large banquet should be checked well ahead of the function. If the wine has turned, the beverage manager, or someone acting in his stead, will be able to purchase an additional supply. The operator may find it difficult to locate three cases of a particular wine on a moment's notice. Since the wines for banquets are opened in the back of the house and there are usually many bottles, an automatic corkscrew is recommended. With two swift motions the cork can be removed from the bottle.

Sales Tips

Without repeating the factors discussed in chapter 7, it is essential that the service staff know something about wines. In reality, it is only necessary for the service staff to know the wines on the establishment's wine list, what those wines taste like, how the names are pronounced, and which wines accompany or complement the foods on the menu. The best way to teach the service staff about the wines is to have regular and frequent tasting (not drinking) sessions. Entree items should also be served, and the wines should be tasted with the food. Some operators serve a few wines to close their regular meetings with the service personnel. The service staff must know how to open wines. A successful method for teaching waiters/waitresses how to open wines is to purchase a corker,[2] save empty wine bottles and corks, cork empty bottles (or bottles filled with water), and have each person practice until he/she is competent.

In a standard commercial restaurant, as compared to an elite, elegant restaurant, only a few wines should be featured; each wine listed should have a brief description of the wine, and the

2. Available from local wine suppliers store or through mail order.

type foods the wine best complements. All wines, except for rare or some vintage wines, should be kept readily available. Controls are essential, but the guest or the waiter/waitress should not be inconvenienced. Additionally, prompt wine service may mean selling another bottle. Bin numbers are very helpful for storing wines, but are also useful on the wine list. The guest does not have to wrestle with clumsy pronunciation (Pouilly Fuisse) and communication between the guest and the waitress, and in turn the bartender, is facilitated.

Wines should be priced realistically. Wine is a plus sale when nothing else can be sold! Stanley Wolfe of Paul Masson Wines said that no one has ever made a cent from tap water. Several rules of thumb have been suggested by some reputable wine experts:

1. Double the price for wines *costing* less than four dollars ($4) and add one dollar to that figure for the selling price.
2. For wines costing between four and six dollars, the mark-up should be seventy-five percent of cost plus one dollar (i.e., a six-dollar wine should sell for eleven dollars and fifty cents).
3. For wines costing more than six dollars, the mark-up percentage should be decreased as the *dollar profit* is more meaningful than percentage profit (i.e., a ten-dollar wine can be sold for fifteen dollars and the operator will still make a comfortable profit).
4. Find out what local package stores sell the wine you have on your list for. Add a few dollars (two or three only) for *your* selling price. Remember that your guests have a good idea of what the wine sells for in the package store, and they may feel "ripped off" if you try to make too much profit (excellent for rare wines).
5. One suggestion was to never have a wine on the list that is more expensive than the most expensive menu item. Obviously, this would not apply to an elite restaurant offering fine wines, for very few entrees cost one hundred dollars!
6. There should be an inexpensive wine on the wine list that is no more expensive than the least expensive, main course menu item.

Know and have the service staff know the proper size bottle to recommend, although the waiter/waitress should never suggest a small bottle. At approximately three ounces per glass:

Split or *small* (6.3 ounces or *187 ml*) — 2 glasses (one or two guests)

Half Bottle, Tenth or *Medium* (12.7 oz. or *375 ml*) — 4 glasses (one or two guests)

Bottle, Fifth or Regular (24.5 oz. or *750 ml*) — 8 glasses (up to four or five guests)

Some Helpful Hints When a Guest Rejects Wine

If a guest rejects a wine (costing less than ten dollars) that the waiter, manager, or hostess feels is still a good wine, the wine should be exchanged without comment. This wine can be used for cooking or for the staff to build morale. *Another bottle of the same wine should not be brought to the guest.* A different wine should be offered with a comment such as "we probably have a bad shipment of XYZ wine, why don't you try the ABC wine instead."

When a very expensive wine is ordered by a strange (non-regular) guest, the waitress should take note. The manager or hostess should intercede and explain what a fine wine he/she has ordered. Perhaps she could strike up a conversation with the guest and ask politely if he/she has ever had a "Chateau Mouton" before. While explaining that the taste may be quite different than what the guest is used to, the manager should explain that if she determines that the wine is *not* sour, the guest is obligated to pay.

For medium-priced wines, the operator must make her own determination on how to handle the situation. In other words, how much loss can the operation absorb for rejected wines?

Some restaurant operators assume *all* the risks of a bad bottle of wine younger than twenty-five or thirty years old. Moreover, most reputable distributors will give credit to the restaurant for a bad bottle.

Spirits and Beverage Service

As with wines, a good manager must know his product before he/she can recommend sales techniques to the service personnel. The intent of this section is to increase the reader's knowledge about distilled spirits, and the service of these spirits. It is beyond the scope of this text to discuss beverage management planning, bar design, beverage cost control, beverage promotion, or a complete history of distilled spirits. The reader should be aware of the books on beverage and bar management listed at the end of this chapter.

Whiskey is basically a spirit or potable beverage obtained from the distillation of a fermented mash of grain and aged in wood.

The production of whiskey is a natural process and the skilled distiller guides the spirit through the four natural processes for the finished beverage. *Mashing* is the first process, which prepares the grain for fermentation. The grain is allowed to sprout and this is combined with a cooked mash, which is converted to fermentable sugars. *Fermentation* is the second process where yeast (a living organism) consumes the sugar, and the by-product of the yeast feeding on the sugar produces alcohol (and carbon dioxide [CO_2]). The product is then *distilled,* which is simply heating the product in a pot still or continuous still until the alcohol vaporizes. The alcohol vapors are cooled and condensed as whiskey. This whiskey is colorless and harsh and needs to be *aged.* When placed in charred oak barrels, the whiskey takes on an amber color, it loses some of its impurities, and the flavoring agents (congeners) mellow during the aging process.

Bourbon is a "distinctive product of the United States" by congressional resolution and must be distilled from a fermented mash containing no less than fifty-one percent (51%) corn, not to exceed 160 proof (160°). It must then be aged in *new* charred oak barrels for a minimum of twenty-four months; and before bottling, not reduced to below 80°. *Sour mash whiskey* is a bourbon, but producers of this product feel that it is superior to bourbon. "A minimum of twenty-five percent of the volume of the fermenting mash must be stillage (cooled, screened liquid recovered from the spent mash of a previous distillation)."[3] Some major commercial brands of bourbon are: Wild Turkey, Bourbon Supreme, Ten High, Jim Beam, Old Grand Dad, I.W. Harper, Old Crow, Dant & Dant, Waterfill & Frazier, and Old Taylor. *Rye* is basically the same product as bourbon; however, rye is used in lieu of corn.

SPIRIT CONTAINER-SIZES

Minature or *Minature* (1.7 fluid ounces or *50 ml*)

Half Pint or *Small* (6.8 fluid ounces or *200 ml*)

Pint or Medium (16.9 fluid ounces or *500 ml*)

3. Paul Beals, "Distilled Spirits and the Beverage Operator," *The Cornell Hotel and Restaurant Administration Quarterly*, 17, no. 3 (November 1976):78.

Fifth or *Regular* (25.4 fluid ounces or *750 ml*)

Quart or *Large* (33.8 fluid ounces or *1.0 liters [1,000 ml]*)

Half Gallon or *Extra Large* (59.2 fluid ounces or *1.75 liters*

Tennessee whiskey is a distinctive type of American whiskey because of its unique production methods, and it is recognized as such by law. After distillation, the spirits of Tennessee whiskey are filtered through maple charcoal before aging. It is claimed that this filtering process eliminates the unwanted harsher elements of the spirit and imparts its own unique character to the whiskey. The two legal distilleries in Tennessee are Jack Daniel's and Geo. A. Dickel, and each produces Tennessee sour mash whiskey.

Blended whiskey (by Federal standard of identity) is "a mixture which contains at least twenty percent by volume of 100° straight whiskey and . . . whiskey or neutral spirits." Some major brands are: Seagram's 7 Crown, Kesslers, Calvert, Fleishman's Preferred, and Imperial. *Canadian Whiskey* is "a distinctive product of Canada in compliance with the laws of Canada regulating the manufacture of whiskey for consumption in Canada." Canadian whiskey is light whiskey, as it is taken off the still at or above 160°, and cannot be called "straight"; therefore it is called "blended Canadian whiskey." Some major brands are: Canadian Club, Seagrams V.O., Black Velvet, Wiser's Deluxe, and O.F.C.

Irish whiskey is generally taken off the still at a high proof and is therefore a light spirit. It is a distinctive product of Ireland and contains no distilled spirits less than three years old, although it is aged seven years before bottling. It also must be designated "blended Irish whiskey" and cannot be called "straight." Some major commercial brands of Irish whiskey are: Old Bushmills, Dunphy's, Jamesons', and Paddy Irish.

Scotch whiskey is a distinctive product of Scotland and carries with it the same identity as that of Irish whiskey. But Scotch carries the characteristic "peat reek" or smoky flavor, which is developed from the drying of the sprouted barley over peat fires Recently single malt Scotch whiskey has become a popular drink; it differs slightly from the blended Scotch whiskeys, but still has the characteristic smoky flavor. Single malt Scotches are Glenlivet and Glenfiddich. Some popular blended Scotch whiskeys are: Teacher's, Dewar's, Lauder's, Cutty Sark, Chivas

Regal, J & B Rare, Johnny Walker (Red and Black), Haig & Haig Pinch and Five Star, Black & White, Usher's, Ballantines, Highland Queen, Grand Old Parr, Vat 69, Usher's Green Stripe, Ambassador Deluxe, and Highland Cream. Scotch drinkers are loyal to their brand.

Vodka is "neutral spirits distilled from any material at or above 190°, reduced to not more than 110°, and not less than 80°, and after such reduction in proof, so treated as to be without distinctive character, aroma, or taste." In other words, vodka is not supposed to taste like anything! Different distillers have their own techniques for producing *even a more tasteless* tasteless spirit. Perhaps this characteristic has given rise to the great sales boom that vodka and the other "white goods" are enjoying. Some major commercial brands are: Smirnoff, Gilbey's, Stolichnaya, Romanoff, Gordon's, Popov, Wolfschmidt, and Hiram Walker.

Gin (dry gin) is a redistillation of neutral spirits (in the United States distilled at or above 190°) which are flavored with juniper berries (required by law) and other botanicals (cocoa, Cassia bark, anise, calamus, lemon and orange peel, licorice, coriander, caraway, orris root, etc.). "English gin makers typically use a spirit distilled at a lower proof in their processes, resulting in a finished product with a more pronounced flavor than its American counterpart."[4] The Dutch gins: Genever, Holland, or Schiedam, are consumed *ice* cold or on the rocks and have a more pronounced, full-flavored, and full-bodied taste as compared to the flavor of the dry gins from England and the United States. Some major commercial brands are Bols Genever, Booth's, Beefeater, Gilbey's, Walker's, Old Mr. Boston, Seagram's, Tanqueray, Gordon's, and Calvert. Gin drinkers are considered the fussiest of the drinking public.

Rum is "any alcoholic distillate from the fermented juice of sugar cane, sugar cane syrup, sugar cane molasses, or other sugar cane products distilled at less than 190°, in such a manner that the distillate possesses the taste, aroma, and characteristics generally attributed to rum; and includes mixtures solely of such distillates." In other words, rum tastes like rum! Rum does not have to be mashed as the sugars are fermentable and can be consumed by the yeast. There are two types of rum on the market: the light rums from Puerto Rico, the Virgin Islands, and other

4. Beals, "Distilled Spirits," p. 83.

Spanish-speaking Caribbean Islands; and the dark (molasses flavored) rums from Jamaica, Barbados, and other English-speaking areas. Light rum mixes well with anything; and, except for vodka, leads all other distilled spirits in sales volume. There are some amber-colored rums (called Añejo) that should not be confused with the dark rums of Jamaica or Barbados. These rums have been aged in wooden casks and take on an amber color (i.e., similar to bourbon). They are mellow in flavor and are usually used for sipping rather than mixing. Some major commercial brands of light rums are: Bacardi, Ron Rico, and Don Q. The dark Jamaican type rums include Lemon Hart, Myer's, and Appleton brands.

"*Brandy* is a potable spirit obtained from the distillation of wine or a fermented mash of fruit, which usually has been suitably aged in wood."[5] Fermentable sugars are available naturally from the grape; and after distillation, brandy is aged "usually three to seven years."[6]

Cognac is brandy that is distilled in the Cognac region in France. In other words, all Cognac is brandy, but not all brandy is Cognac. Cognac is labeled or otherwise marked with stars (3 star, 5 star, etc.) with coded letters (V.S.O.P.) or with the words "Fine Champagne" or "Grande Fine Champagne." Only the "champagne" designations are related to quality and the grapes to produce the product must come from the Grand Champagne or Petite Champagne sections of Cognac. The stars and other letters refer only to relative quality from one producer. For example, Courvoisier V.S.O.P. is a finer product than Courvoisier V.S.; it cannot, however, be compared on the basis of the lettering above, to Delamain or Hennessey.[7] Other than those listed above, some other Cognacs and brandies include The Christian Bros., Camus, Remy Martin, Napolean, and Martell.

Armagnac is brandy from France, but it does not come from the Cognac region. *Apple Jack* and *Calvados* are hard ciders or brandies made from apples. There are many other fruit flavored brandies (i.e., Kirsch from cherries), as well as coffee-flavored brandy (not a coffee liqueur), and other flavored brandies.

Mixed drinks or cocktails can be divided into five basic categories: high-balls, low-balls or on the rocks cocktails, cream

5. Harold J. Grossman, *Grossman's Guide to Wines, Spirits, and Beers.* New York: Scribner's, 1964, p. 228.
6. Beals, "Distilled Spirits," p. 84.
7. Beals, "Distilled Spirits," pp. 84–85.

drinks, and lemon or fruit drinks. A high-ball is a distilled spirit and a mixer such as soda, ginger ale, cola, etc. High-balls are served appropriately in high-ball glasses while low-balls are served in on-the-rocks glasses. Some examples of high-balls are rum and Coke, Seven and Seven, gin and tonic, while low-balls may include scotch on the rocks and other similar drinks. Cocktails are usually served in "up" or cocktail glasses and include martinis, Manhattans, gimlets, and gibsons. Cream drinks are basically spirits, light cream, and flavorings, and are shaken. Some examples include brandy alexander, grasshopper, and golden cadillac. Lemon drinks or fruit drinks typically include all the sours and the collins drinks as well as daquiris and margaritas. Lemon drinks can be further sub-divided into short fruit or tall fruit drinks. Lemon drinks are almost always shaken and may be served in cocktail glasses or sour glasses (when served up), or on-the-rocks in on-the-rocks glasses. Two shakers should be used in mixing, as cream and lemon drinks both are shaken and should not be mixed. The shakers used for cream drinks must be rinsed after each use.

Abbreviated Checklists for Service Personnel

The following checklists may be given to service personnel as a supplement to an introduction to beverage service.

Mixers

Bitter Lemon—Schweppe's
Bitters—Angostura, Holland House (orange)
Club Soda—Canada Dry, Schweppe's
Cola—Coca Cola, Pepsi Cola, Royal Crown Cola
Cranberry Juice
Cream—Use light cream only, heavy cream dulls the flavor
Eggs—Yolk can be used for body in a mixer, but generally only egg whites are used.
Ginger Ale—Canada Dry, Schweppe's
Grapefruit—Fresca, Squirt, Wink
Grapefruit Juice
Grenadine—Giroux, Wupperman's, Holland House
Hot Sauce—Tabasco
Ice Cream—Can be substituted for light cream
Lemon Lime—Seven-Up, Upper 10, Sprite, Mountain Dew
Milk
Orange Juice

Simple Syrup—Sugar water

Super Fine Sugar—Used to sweeten drinks, not as a garnish

Sweetened Lime Juice Extract—Rose's lime juice

Tomato Juice and Tomato Juice Cocktails—Holland House, Mr. & Mrs. T, Snap-e-tom, V-8, common tomato juice brands

Tonic (Quinnine water)—Schweppe's, Canada Dry

Vichy (Natural mineral water)—Imported, Perrier, Vichy, Evian, Domestic—Saratoga, Quevic

Worcestershire Sauce—Lea & Perrin's, Heinz, French's

Bar Garnishes

Carrots (stick)—Bloody Mary's (occasionally)

Celery (stick)—Bloody Mary's (occasionally)

Cherries—All Collins, all Sours, Slings, Fizzes, Planter's Punch, Kiddie Cocktails, Old Fashioned (sometimes), Rob Roys (sweet—sometimes)

Cocktail Onions—Gibson, Bloody Caesar

Confectionary Sugar (10x)—Use as garnish only, not to sweeten

Lemon (slice)—Old Fashioned (garnish or muddled)

Lemon (twist)—Martinis (extra dry or on request), all Dry Manhattans, Perfect Manhattans, all Rob Roys, Mist, Dubonnet cocktails, Campari, Vermouth on Rocks; ask if desire twist with aperitif

Lime (wedge or a squeeze)—Bloody Mary, Virgin Mary, Gimlet, Gin and Tonic, Cuba Libra, Gin Ricky

Olives (Spanish)—Martinis, occasionally Dry Manhattans

Oranges—Same as cherries

Pineapple (stick)—Planter's Punch, Mai-Tai

Nutmeg—Brandy Alexander

Common Bar Terms

Aperitif—Appetizer; usually appetizer beverage

Back Bar—Location of call and premium brands

Bitters—A flavoring used in mixing drinks

Call Liquor—A liquor ordered by brand name, but not a premium brand (e.g., Johnny Walker Red)

Decanter—A container into which wines or spirits are decanted from their original containers for service

Frappe—Iced. Term for service of liqueur with finely cracked ice

Garnish—Fruit, onion, olive, etc., in a cocktail

High-ball—A drink of alcoholic liquor and water or a carbonated beverage served in a tall glass

House Liquor—Liquor used by the establishment. Usually not a well-known brand

Jigger—A jigger refers to the portion used at the particular establishment. The size of a jigger may vary from establishment to establishment.

Muddler—A wooden tool used for crushing fruit or cracking ice for cocktails

On-the-Rocks—A drink, other than a High-ball, that requires ice cubes in it.

Perlick—Portable draft beer dispensing machine (brand name)

Premium Brands—Top-of-the-line brands (e.g., Johnny Walker Black)

Up—Any drink that is served without ice cubes.

Shaker—The glass and stainless steel container used for thorough blending of drinks.

Shot—Refers to a standard

Stirrer or Swizzle Stick—Used in any cocktail or mixed drink *with ice in the drink*.

Strainer—Used to pour a drink out of a shaker glass, but not allowing any ice to pour out.

Top Shelf—Same as premium brands

Well or House Well—Same as house liquor

Spirits

Aperitif—An appetizer usually a beverage.
Major commercial types: Pernod, Dry Sherry (Widmer's, Taylor, Dry Sack) Campari, Lillet, Byrrh, White or Red Vermouth (Cora, Tribuno, Martini and Rossi, Cinzano), Dubonnet (red or white)

Apple Jack—Hard cider—"Laird's"

Brandy—A potable spirit obtained from the distillation of wine or a fermented mash of fruit, which usually has been suitably aged in wood.

Major Commercial Brands:

Cognac—Courvoisier, Napolean, Remy Martin, Hennessey, Delamain

Note: All Cognac is brandy, but all brandy is not Cognac (must be from Charente, France).

Brandy—The Christian Bros., Hiram Walker

Gins—Redistillation of pure alcohol with the juniper berry.

Major Commercial Brands:

Gordon's, Walker's, Tanqueray, Gilbey's, Beefeater's, Booth's, Calvert, Seagrams, Fleishman's

Liqueurs or Cordials—An alcoholic beverage prepared by combining a spirit (usually brandy) with certain flavorings (herbs, bitters, and spices) and then adding sugar syrup for sweetening.

Major Commercial Brands:

Galliano, Drambuie, Cointreau, Cream de Menthe (green or white), Tia Maria, Kahlua, Cream de Cacao, Grand Marnier, Triple Sec, Southern Comfort, Peter Heering, B & B, Forbidden Fruit.

Rums—Any alcoholic distillate from the fermented juice of sugar cane, sugar cane syrup, sugar cane molasses, or other sugar cane products distilled at less than 190 proof, in such manner that the distillate possess the taste, aroma, and characteristics generally attributed to rum, and includes mixtures solely of such distillates.

Major Commercial Brands:

Barcardi, Ronrico, Myer's Don Q.

Whiskies—A potable beverage obtained from the distillation of grain.

Bourbon—Distilled from fermented mash of rye, corn, wheat, and malted barley or malted rye grain.

Major Commercial Brands:

Wild Turkey, Jim Beam, Old Grand Dad, Four Roses, I.W. Harper, Old Crow, Ten High, Early Times, Ancient Age, Jack Daniels (Black)

Rye—Meadow Brook, Old Overholt, and Rittenhouse

Canadian—Canadian Club, Seagrams V.O., Black Velvet, Windsor Supreme, Canadian Mist

Irish—Old Bushmills, Jameson's

Scotch—Teacher's Dewar's, Cutty Sark, Chivas Regal, J & B, Usher's, Johnny Walker (black or red), Haig, Black & White, Ballantines, Lauder's

Tennessee—Jack Daniel's (black or green)

Vodka—is neutral spirits distilled from any material at or above 190 proof reduced to not more than 110 and not less than 80 proof, and after such reduction in proof, so treated as to be without distinctive character, aroma, or taste.

Major Commercial Brands:

Smirnoff, Gordons, Popov, Wolfschmidt, Gilbey's, and Walker's

Other Spirits

Akvavit (Aquavit)—made from grain or potatoes and flavored with caraway seeds. Aalborg is the only approved export from Sweden.

Bitters—distillation and infusion of aromatic seeds, herbs, barks, roots, and fruits blended on a spirit base.

Major Commercial Brands:

Campari, Cynar, Angostura

Tequila—distilled from pina or pineapple of the century plant cactus

Major Commercial Brands:

Jose Cuervo, Ole, Tequila Sauza, Two Fingers

Cocktails — Their Ingredients: Garnishes

Bacardi—a daiquiri with grenadine: none

Black Russian—Kahlua and Vodka: none

Bloody Mary—Tomato juice, worcestershire, Tabasco, salt, pepper, Vodka: squeeze of lime

Bourbon—none

Brandy Alexander—light cream, dark cream de cacao, brandy: nutmeg

Collins—Lemon mix with Gin, Club Soda: orange and cherry Vodka, Bourbon, Sloe Gin, Rum, John—made with whiskey

Daiquiri—Lemon mix, light Rum: none

Frappes—Liqueur poured over crushed ice: none

Gibson—Same as Martini, Gin with White Vermouth: pickled cocktail onion

Gimlet—Gin with Rose's Lime Juice: squeeze of lime Vodka Gimlet—substitute Vodka for Gin

Gin Fizz—Gin, lemon juice, sugar, club soda: cherry

Golden Cadillac—Galliano, White Cream de Cacao, or Triple Sec and Cream: none

Grasshopper—Light cream, green Cream de Menthe, light Cream de cacao: none
Harvey Wallbanger—Screwdriver with Galliano Liqueur
Kir—White wine with Cream de Cassis (currant)
Manhattan—Bourbon or Blended Whiskey with Sweet Vermouth, bitters optional: cherry
   Dry—Substitute Dry for Sweet Vermouth: lemon twist
Margarita—Unsweetened lemon juice, Triple Sec, Tequila: salt rimmed edge
Martini—Gin with Dry Vermouth: olive or lemon twist
   Extra Dry—Gin with dark or Dry Vermouth: lemon twist
   Vodka—Vodka with Dry Vermouth: olive or lemon twist
Mists—Scotch or Bourbon poured over crushed ice: twist of lemon
Old Fashioned—Sugar, bitters, club soda or water, Blended Whiskey: muddled (optional), orange, lemon, cherry
Perfect Manhattan—Bourbon or Blended Whiskey with Dry and Sweet Vermouth: lemon twist
Perfect Martini—Gin with Sweet and Dry Vermouth: twist or olive
Pink Lady—Cream, Grenadine, sugar, Gin
Pink Squirrel—Light cream, Cream de Almond, light cream de Cacao
Rob Roy—Manhattan using Scotch instead of Bourbon
   Sweet, Dry, and Perfect: lemon twist
Roy Rogers—A Shirley Temple
Rusty Nail—Drambuie and Scotch: none
Salty Dog—Vodka, grapefruit: salt rimmed high-ball glass
Screwdriver—Vodka and orange juice
Shirley Temple—Nonalcoholic Grenadine, ginger ale: cherry
Sidecar—Unsweetened lemon mix, Triple Sec, Brandy: sugar coated rim
Singapore Sling—Gin, lemon mix, club soda, Grenadine and Cherry Brandy (Kirsch)
Sours—Whiskey and lemon mix: orange and cherry
   Can be made with Bourbon, Scotch, Vodka, Gin, Rum, Apricot, Tequila: same garnish
Stinger—Brandy with White Cream de Menthe: none
Virgin Mary—Bloody Mary without Vodka
White Russian—Cream, Kahlua, Vodka

Liqueurs or Cordials

Liqueurs or cordials—synonomous terms—were originated by alchemists whose special elixirs were marketed as medicinal cures for diseases, to extend life and as aphrodisiacs. The flavorings and the sugar (by law 2.5 percent by weight) were used to mask the flavor of an inferior spirit. A liqueur is a combination of spirits and flavorings and sugar syrup and have replaced brandy, in some areas, as an after-dinner drink. The flavorings are added by one of three methods or a combination of these methods:

Infusion or maceration method is similar to the making of tea, where the flavoring agents are steeped or soaked in the spirit until the spirit has extracted the color, aroma, and flavor of the fruits. Infusion or maceration is used primarily in the making of fruit-flavored liqueurs.

Percolation method is identical to the making of coffee, where the spirit is passed over and over the flavoring ingredients until almost all of the flavor and aroma is extracted. This method is used primarily for making the plant liqueurs such as Benedictine, Drambuie, Cream de Cacao, Cream de Menthe, and Triple Sec.

The distillation method is also used to produce the plant liqueurs and this procedure is similar to the production of gin. Leaves, seeds, and other flavoring agents are placed on a tray and the spirit picks up the flavor as it passes the flavoring agents.

There are five categories or types of liqueurs: (1) *Fruits* are the most popular flavoring agents used in liqueurs and some types include strawberries, blackberries, peaches, apricots, and cherries. (2) *Peels* are also used extensively and the most popular are the oranges from Curacao. (3) *Seeds,* such as aniseed (anisette) and apricot pits (amaretto) are also used to flavor liqueurs. (4) *Herbs* are used to flavor liqueurs; but with few exceptions (Chartreuse and Benedictine), the herbs do not predominate the flavor. (5) *Cremes* such as Creme de Menthe (mint leaves) and Creme de Cacao (cacao bean) are usually the sweetest liqueurs.

Some of the more popular liqueurs listed alphabetically (P indicates proprietary brand; all others are generic liqueurs):

Advocaat—Egg nog brandy 40°

Akvavit—Rye and caraway 90°

Amaretto—Almond Flavored 56°

Anisette—From aniseed; taste like licorice 50-60°

Benedictine (P)—Herb liqueur from secret formula 86°

B & B (P)—Benedictine and brandy

Chartreuse (P)—Herb liqueur from France; secret formula; yellow 86° and green 110°

Cherry Herring/Peter Herring (P)—Cherry-flavored liqueur 50°

Chocolat Suisse (P)—Chocolate liqueur 60°

Cointreau (P)—A triple sec 80°

Curacao—Peel from green oranges of Curacao 50-60°

Drambuie (P)—Highland malt scotch and heather honey 80°

Forbidden Fruit (P)—Grapefruit flavored 64°

Galliano (P)—Italian herb liqueur

Grand Marnier (P)—French orange Curacao liqueur 80°

Grenadine—Alcoholic 25° or nonalcoholic from pomegranates

Irish Mist (P)—Irish whiskey and honey 80°

Kahlua—Mexican coffee-flavored liqueur 53°

Kummel—Caraway flavored 80-86°

Ouzo—Greek aniseed flavored liqueur 92°

Peppermint Schnapps—Light mint liqueur 60-70°

Pernod (P)—Absinthe type

Rock and Rum—Rum and rock candy

Rock and Rye—Rye whiskey and rock candy

Sabra (P)—Israeli chocolate, orange liqueur 60°

Sloe Gin—From sloe berry 60°

Strega (P)—Famous Italian herb liqueur 80°

Tia Maria (P)—Jamaican coffee-flavored liqueur 63°

Triple Sec—Orange-flavored liqueur 60-80°

Vandermint (P)—Dutch chocolate mint liqueur 60°

Cream Liqueurs (from 40°-80°)

Almond or Noyaux—Fruit stones

Ananas—Pineapple

Bananas

Cacao—Brown or white

Cafe—Coffee

Cassis—Black currant

Fraises—Strawberries

Framboises—Raspberries

Menthe—Mint

Mandarine—Tangerines

Noisette—Hazel nuts

Noix—Walnuts

Noyaux—Fruit stones
Prunelle—Plums
Rose—Rose petals and vanilla
Vanille—Vanilla
Violette—Violets

Fruit-Flavored Liqueurs and Brandies (generic)

Apricot
Blackberry
Cherry
Coffee
Cranberry
Peach
Ginger

Beer and Ale

Beer is one of the oldest beverages known, and beer is a standard beverage in every country. In fact in some countries, beer is the safest beverage to consume, as the water used must be pure before the brewing process begins. Beer is made from barley which is malted (sprout) to change the starch to fermentable sugars. The wort, liquid (water) from the mashing process, is filtered and then boiled for several hours and flavored with hops. Rice or other adjunct grains may be added to lighten the brew. After the wort is filtered again, it is allowed to ferment where the carbon dioxide (gas) is collected (to be added back later). The beer is stored (lagered) at very cold temperatures for one to three months where the solids are precipitated (i.e., collect at the bottom). The beer is then carbonated from the (previously) collected CO_2.

Beer is a fermented beverage made from malted barley and other starchy cereals.

Malt liquor has a higher alcoholic content than beer. It is aged longer, higher priced, more bitter, and hoppier than beer.

Ale is fermented at a higher temperature (the yeast remains on top), which gives it a full-bodied flavor. It is more bitter and slightly more expensive than beer.

Bock beer is a heavy brew; darker and sweeter than beer. A dark malt (carmelized) that has been heated more; bock beer is becoming obsolete.

Stout is a very dark, bitter beer product with a licorice flavor.

Draught beer is unpasteurized (most beer is pasteurized at 140° F) and must be kept refrigerated or it will spoil. Canned or bottled draught beer is unpasteurized, and it is passed through millipore filter.

Some beer products are kroezened which is the adding of yeast after fermentation has begun, and others use beechwood chips to aid the clarification process. *Premium* is an arbitrary term now since many beers are distributed nationally. The nationally distributed brands, however, command a higher price even though transportation costs may be the same or *even less!* There are several low-calorie beers on the market that have achieved wide acceptance among beer drinkers. Incidentally, 80 percent of the people who drink beer drink over a six-pack a night. For those operations that sell a lot of beer, it behooves management to serve a good beer. What are some of the critical factors for determining the quality of beer?

Critical Factors in Determining the Quality of Beer

Age (delivery)—demand a fresh product from your supplier. An old product (oxidized) has a cardboard taste. All beer is dated and you should obtain a code card from your wholesaler.

a. Draught—30 days at wholesaler and cannot exceed 60 days at retailer or keg must be destroyed.
b. Cans and bottles may be held for 60 days. If you hold longer than this, you could be serving bad beer.
c. Delivery man and you must rotate your stock.
   In storage and in the restaurant.
   In cooler where actually serving the guest.
   Delivery should be made in refrigerated trucks or at least insulated ones as temperature should not rise above 50° F.
   Hand trolleys should be used to move beer to prevent agitation.

Temperature (storage)—Best storage temperature for beer is 38° F. Yet, if you are in a warm climate (e.g., Texas), perhaps 35° F would be better. Best serving temperature is approximately 40° F.

Pressure in the draught lines should be at twelve to fourteen pounds per square inch. Lines should be flushed regularly and always after changing kegs. Lines are flushed by running water through the lines until clear; the keg is connected and the top opened until beer begins to flow.

Beer must be served in a "beer clean glass." Use the proper and compatable detergents (chemical energy), and use the proper procedure for washing (i.e., brushes, mechanical energy). The two methods for washing are: (1) three steps—detergent, rinse, disinfectant; (2) two step—detergent, disinfectant. How can you tell if you have a "beer clean glass?" Bubbles in the head should be small, and head should stay on top until the bottom of the glass. Bubbles should not adhere to side or bottom of glass. Dirt, grease, etc., takes the CO_2 out of solution. *Lacing* is the foam that clings to the side of the glass when you drink and should be present in a "beer clean glass." Pizza operations or other operations where there may be a lot of grease in the foods require special care. If hand washing is used, tanks may need changing every two hours.

Draught beer should be dispensed by getting a rolling action at bottom of glass. Be aware of the distance of glass from the faucet, and of the angle of the glass to the faucet. The glass should be tilted slightly and then moved to the vertical position as the glass fills. Bottled beer should be served by pouring the beer *down the center of the glass.* Beer should not be trickled down the side of the glass.

Beer Glassware

Mugs are durable and eye appealing for certain types of operations. In certain elegant dining rooms, mugs would not complement the decor of the room. Straight shells or pilsner glasses should be used; however, straight shells (tall footed pilsner glasses) are not good for draught beer. Stemware looks nice, but breakage may be excessive.

Abbreviated Checklist for Service Personnel

Beer and Ale
Definitions:
Beer is a generic name embracing all malt beverages. Specifically, it is a brewed and fermented beverage made from malted barley and other starchy cereals, flavored with hops.
Ale is an aromatic malt or cereal brew, usually fuller-bodied and more bitter than beer.

Stout is a very dark ale with a strong malt flavor, a sweet taste, and a strong hop character.

Domestic

National (Premium) Brands

Budweiser, Miller, Schiltz, Old Milwaukee, Michelob, Pabst, Blue Ribbon, Carling Black Label, Ballantine (ale), Lowenbrau (light, dark) Tuborg.

Imported

Canada—Molson's (beer, ales), Labatts, O'Keefes, Red Cap Ale

Denmark—Carlsberg

England—Bass Ale, Whitehead Ale

Germany—Wurzburger Hofbrau, St. Pauli Girl

Holland—Heineken's, Amstel

Ireland—Guinness Stout

Japan—Kirin, Asaki (not sake)

Mexico—Carta Blanca

Philippines—San Miguel

Low Calorie—Schiltz Light, Miller Lite, Anheuser Natural Light, Michelob Light. Many breweries are now producing low calorie beer.

Serving Beer and Cocktails

Standard service for cocktails and beer requires the use of a cocktail or hand-held tray. Guests should be served from the right side with the waiter's right hand, and in the center of the cover. The tray should be carried in the left hand (see Task Procedures in chap. 9). A cocktail napkin should be placed in front of the guest *just prior* to serving the cocktail. The practice of leaning over the guests' table and placing cocktail napkins around when the guests first order is not recommended.

Bottled beer should be served to the guest by pouring the beer down the center of the glass. When decanter service for cocktails or spirits is used, the procedure differs slightly.

Decanter Service for Cocktails

When decanters are used for cocktails, the spirit should be poured into the glass (with or without ice already in the proper glass), and the mixer added to the guest's desires. This should be accomplished on the tray while the waiter holds the tray with his left hand and performs this operation with his right hand. The high-ball or cocktail is then served in the center of the cover on a cocktail napkin.

Some operations use supreme dishes with ice to serve cocktails from a decanter. The cocktail glass and a small, four- or six-ounce decanter is placed on ice in a supreme dish and carried to the guest's table on a cocktail tray. A cocktail napkin should be placed in the center of the cover (with the crest, if any, facing the guest) and the proper glass should be centered on the napkin. The supreme dish with the decanter in it should be placed to the right and slightly above the cover. The waiter may remove the decanter from the supreme dish, circle the bottom of the decanter on the rim of the supreme dish (for show and also to remove water), and pour the spirit, appetizer, or dessert wine for the guest.

Banquet Service

It is difficult to determine whether portable bars are necessary for servicing banquet operations without knowledge of the particular facilities. Certain advantages become apparent however. (1) Any room may become a cocktail lounge. (2) Several outlets (bars) may be available in a large room (advantageous for cash bar). Anytime one is served, rather than serving himself, the caliber of service is improved. Additionally, whenever preparation (cocktails) is performed away from the guest's view, the caliber of service is also superior. With these two thoughts in mind, an elegant banquet would have no bars visible, and each guest would be served by a waitress. Yet service bars may be some distance from the party and a temporary set-up may be required.

Conclusion

The study and service of wines, spirits, beers and ales, and cordials is exhaustive and no attempt has been made to cover everything. It is important for the service manager and his/her staff to know about the products being sold, whether food or beverage. A review of this chapter will acquaint one with the basics on wine, beers, and spirits.

Questions

1. How are wines classified?
2. What are the five major categories of wines? List three examples of each.
3. How are wines named?
4. Recall the procedure for serving red wine, white wine, and sparkling wine.
5. How should you decant a maturized wine? Why take the foil completely off?
6. How does *pouring* a sparkling wine differ from pouring a still wine?
7. Why is Scotch not considered "straight" whiskey?
8. What is bourbon, vodka, rum? Why are these products so different?
9. Distinguish between ale, beer, stout, and bock beer.
10. What are the ways that flavorings are added to cordials?
11. What five major ingredients (categories) are used to flavor cordials?
12. What are the five categories of mixed drinks?

References for Further Study

Bar-Server Magazine. *Pouring for Profits.* Hiram Walker Incorporated.

Beals, Paul. "Distilled Spirits and the Beverage Operator." *The Cornell Hotel and Restaurant Administration Quarterly* 17, no. 3 (November 1976):78-84.

Bespaloff, Alexis. *The Signet Book of Wines.*

Grossman, Harold J. *Practical Bar Management.* Ahrens Publishing Co.

Grossman's Guide to Wine, Spirits, and Beers.

Lichine, Alexis. *The Encyclopaedia of Wines.*

Old Mr. Boston Distillers. *The Deluxe Bartender's Guide.*

Pronunciation Guide

Menu Terminology

Agneau (ahn-yó)—Lamb

Aigre (aý-grr)—Sour

A la Carte—Food prepared to order; each dish priced separately

A la King—Served in cream sauce containing mushrooms, green peppers, pimentos

A La Mode—Usually refers to ice cream on top of pie, but may refer to other dishes served in a special way, such as beef a la mode, which calls for a scoop of mashed potatoes.

Amande (ah-mawnd)—Almond

Amandine (ah-maun-deén)—With almonds

Americaine (ah-mair-ee-kén)—American style

Ananas (ah-nah-nah)—Pineapple

Anchois (awn-schwáh)—Anchovy

Andalouse (awn-dah-loos)—With tomatoes and peppers

Antipasto—Italian name for hors d'oeurves; assortment of appetizers such as salted or pickled fish, olives, anchovies, peppers, etc.

Artichaut (ahr-ti-shów)—Artichoke

Asperges (ah-spaýrge)—Asparagus

Aspic (ah-spéek)—Decorated jellied piece

Aubergines (oh-bare-zheén)—Eggplant

Au Buerre (o-búrr)—With butter

Au Gratin (oh-grah-tán)—Food covered with a sauce, usually cheese, sprinkled with crumbs and baked

Au Jus (oh-joó)—With natural gravy

Au Lait (oh-laý)—With milk

Bake—To cook by dry heat, usually in oven

Baked Alaska—Brick ice cream on cake

Baste—To moisten a roast with water, drippings or seasoned sauce while it is roasting to prevent drying out

Bearnaise (bair-nez)—In America, a sauce similar to Hollandaise, fortified with meat glaze, and with tarragon flavor predominating

Bechamal (báy-shaw-mel)—Cream sauce

Beurre (burr)—Butter

Beurre Noir (burr nwáh)—Browned butter

Bien Cuit (be-en-kwí)—Well-done (meats)

Bifteck (bíf-teck)—Beefsteak

Bisque (beesk)—Thick, rich soup

Blanc (blawnk)—White

Blanchi (Blahn-shée)—Blanched

Blanquette (blawn-két)—Stew with white wine

Blintzes—Thin pancakes rolled around a filling of cream cheese, chopped meat or fruit

Boeuf (böff)—Beef

Bombe (bomb)—Ice cream molded in globular form

Bonne Femme (bon fém)—Literally means *good wife*. Term used to indicate simple family-style or home-style.

Bouillabaisse (bwée-yuh-baze)—Fish stew

Bouilli (bu-yée)—Boiled; to cook with moist heat, with liquid (at its boiling point) as a surrounding medium

Bouillon (bwee-yawn)—Broth

Bouquetiere (boo-ket-yér)—With mixed vegetables

Bourguignonne (boor-geen-yawn)—With onions and red burgundy wine

Braise—To cook slowly in a small amount of liquid

Brochettes (broshetté)—Meat broiled on skewers

Brouille (bru-eé)—Scrambled

Broil—To cook by exposing food to direct intense heat

Brunoise (broon-wáz)—Small diced or shredded vegetables sauteed in butter or fat

Cafe (kah-fáy)—Coffee

Canard (kah-nahr)—Duck

Canape (kah-nah-páy)—Sliced bread used as the base for foods to make small open-faced sandwiches

Caneton (kah-nuh-tawn)—Duckling

Carre (káh-ray)—Rack

Carte de Jour (cárt-du-zhur)—Menu of the day

Celeri (se-le-rée)—Celery

Cepe (sep)—A variety of mushroom

Cervelle (sir-vél)—Brain

Cerises (sir-rée-say)—Cherries

Champignon (shaw-peen-yaẃn)—Mushroom

Chantilly Cream—Dessert of vanilla whipped cream

Chapon (shah-pawn)—Capon

Chasseur (sha-súr)—Sauteed with mushrooms, shallots, and white wine

Chateaubriand (sha-tó-bree-yawn)—Thick filet mignon

Chaud (show)—Warm, hot

Chou-Fleur (shoo-flúre)—Cauliflower

Chowder—Thick soup usually made of clams, oysters, or fish; New England style: with milk, cream; Manhattan style: with tomatoes

Choux de Bruxelles (shoo-duh-bresael)—Brussel sprouts

Chutney—Relish, sweet and highly seasoned, made of chopped vegetables and/or fruit

Cochon (ko-shawn)—Suckling pig

Compote (kawn-pawt)—Stewed fruit

Consomme (kawn-saw-máy)—Clear soup

Coquille (ko-kée)—Shell for baking

Creme (krem)—Cream

Creme Fouettee (krem-fo-et-táy)—Whipped cream

Crepe (krep)—Pancake

Crevette (kruh-vét)—Shrimp

Crisson (kree-sawn)—Watercress

Croquette (kro-két)—Patty of meat

Croutons (kroo-tawns)—Diced, fried bread floated on top of soup or used in salads

Cuisine (kwe-zeén)—Kitchen

Deep Fry—To cook in fat as a surrounding medium

Dejeuner (day-zhoo-náy)—Breakfast, lunch

De Jour (du-zhúr)—Of the day

Demitasse (day-me-tás)—A small cup or spoon; black coffee served in small cup

Diable (dee-abl)—Deviled

Duchesse (du-chéss)—Potatoes mixed with egg and forced through a pastry tube

Echalotes (esh-a-lót)—Shallots

Eclairs (ek-lares)—French choux paste filled with cream and iced

Ecrevisse (ay-kruh-veéce)—Crayfish

Encasserole—Baked or served in an individual dish

En Papillote (en pah-pee-yote)—Baked in an oil papered bag

Entree (én-tray)—Originally, food served between heavy courses; now, generally, the main dish

Entremets (awn-truh-méh)—Sweet; desserts

Epinard (ay-pee-nahr)—Spinach

Escargots (es-kahr-go)—Snails

Faisan (fay-zawn)—Pheasant

Farce (fahrce)—Ground meat

Farci (fahr-seé)—Stuffed

Filet (fee-láy) — boneless ribbon

Fillet Mignon (fee-lay me-nyon) — Tenderloin of beef, choicest cut

Fillet (fill-it) — Tenderloin of beef, mutton, veal, or pork without the bone

Flambe (flawn-báy) — Flamed

Florentine (flaw-ren-teén) — With spinach

Foie (fwa) — Liver

Foie de Veau (fwa-du-vó) — Calve's liver

Foie Gras (fwa-gráh) — Goose liver

Fondue (fawn-dóo) — Melted cheese

Fricassee (free-kah-sáy) — Chicken or veal stew

Frit (free) — Deep fat fried

Froid (frwah) — Cold

Fromage (froh-mahge) — Cheese

Fume (foo-máy) — Smoked

Galantine (gäl-än-teén) — Boned meat, fish or poultry stuffed and pressed in a symmetrical shape

Garni (gahr-née) — Garnished

Gateau (gah-tóe) — Cake

Gelee (zhuh-láy) — Jelly

Gigot (zhee-gó) — Leg of lamb

Glace (glah-sáy) — Glazed, iced, frosted

Goulash — Stewed beef or veal seasoned with paprika (Hungarian specialty)

Gratine (grah-tee-náy) — With breadcrumbs

Grill — To cook by direct heat, normally over a heavy cast steel or aluminum grill plate

Haricot (ah-ree-kó) — Bean

Haricot Vert (ah-ree-ko-ver) — String bean

Hollandaise (aw-lawn-déz) — Sauce made with egg yolk, melted butter, and lemon

Homard (oh-már) — Lobster

Hors d'oeuvres (or-durve) — Pre-dinner tidbits

Huitre (wheatr) — Oyster

Jambon (zhahm-báwn) — Ham

Jardiniere (zhahr-dan-yér) — With vegetable

Julienne (zhool-yén) — Thin strips

Jus (zhoo) — Juice, gravy

Kabob — Pieces of meat (usually lamb or beef) broiled on a skewer

Lait (lay) — Milk

Langouste (lawn-goóst) — Sea crayfish or rock lobster

Langue (lang) — Tongue

Legume (lay-goóm) — Vegetable

Lyonnaise Potatoes — Sauteed with onions

Maitre d'Hotel (maytr-doe-téll)—With spiced butter

Marinate—To allow food to soak or steep in a marinade so flavoring is absorbed

Marmite (mahr-méet)—Pot; stew

Meringue (meh-ráng)—Beaten egg white

Meuniere (moon-yér)—Pan fried and served with brown butter

Mignon (mee-yawn)—Dainty

Minestrone (mi-na-stró-ne)—Italian vegetable soup with noodles and cheese

Mornay (mornáy)—Cheese sauce

Mousse (moose)—Whipped foam

Naturel (nah-tew-rél)—Plain

Noir (nwah)—Black

Noisette (nwah-zét)—Hazelnut

Nouille (noo-eé)—Noodle

Oeuf (uf)—Egg

Oignon (awn-yáwn)—Onion

Pain (pan)—Bread

Panache (pah-násh)—Mixed vegetables

Paner (paney)—Covered with bread crumbs

Pate (pah-táy)—Meat pie

Patisserie (pah-tee-súh-ree)—Pastry

Peche (pesh)—Peach

Petit (puh-tée)—Small

Poire (pwahr)—Pear

Pois (pwah)—Peas

Poisson (pwah-sáwn)—Fish

Pomme (paum)—Apple

Pomme de Terre (paum-duh-tér)—Potato

Potage (pah-táhge)—Soup

Pot au Feu (paw-toe-fóo)—Boiled beef with a variety of vegetables and broth served as a meal

Poulet (poo-láy)—Chicken

Printaniere, a la (preen-taun-yér)—meat dishes garnished with early spring or mixed vegetables

Proscuitto (pra-zhóoto)—Italian ham specially processed, very salty, often served with melon

Provencale, a la (pro-ven-sál)—Describes preparation characterized by tomato and garlic mixture

Puree (poo-ráy)—Sieved food

Quennelle (kuh-nél)—Forcemeat

Quiche (keesh)—Tart or piecrust filled with egg yolks, cream, and cheese, and baked (served hot)

Ragout (rah-góo)—Stew

Ris (ree) —Sweetbreads (see sweetbreads)

Riz (ree) —Rice

Roast —Originally, to cook on a spit; now the same as baking when applied to meat

Rognon (rawn-yawn) —Kidney

Rossole (rus-soul) —Browned

Roti (ro-tee) —Roasted

Risse (roos) —Russian

Salade (salahd) —Salad

Saumon (saw-mone) —Salmon

Saute (saw-táy) —Pan fried

Selle (sell) —Saddle

Shallots —Onion-like plant whose bulbs resemble garlic but are milder

Sorbet (sawr-báy) —Sherbet (ice)

Souffle (soo-fláy) —Whipped pudding made of egg whites and baked in the oven

Steep —To soak in a liquid below boiling point to extract flavor

Sweetbreads (ris) —The thymus gland of a young animal (calf) used for food; choice delicacy

Table d'hote (tah-bla-doé) —Meal served in several courses at set price

Tasse (tahce) —Cup

Tortue (tor-toó) —Tortoise, turtle

Tournedos (toor-nuh-dó) —Two small tenderloin steaks

Tripe (tryp) —Lining of beef stomach

Truite (trew-eét) —Trout

Truffles (troof) —Fungus-like mushrooms which grow underground, chiefly in France

Veau (vo) —Veal

Vapeur (va-púrr) —Steamed

Veloute (vuh-loo-táy) —White sauce made from fish, chicken, or veal stock

Vichyssoise (vee-shee-swáhz) —Hot or cold potato and leek soup

Vin (və) —Wine

Vinaigre (vin-ay-grr) —Vinegar

Vinaigrette (vee-nay-grét) —Dressing with oil, vinegar, and herbs

Volaille (vo-lié) —Poultry

Vol Au Vent (vole-oh-vawn) —Patty shell

Pronunciation Guide for Wine

Alsace (Ahl-zahss) —Region in northeastern France

Anjou (Ahn-zhóo) —Area in the Loire Valley

Appelation Contrôlee (Ah-pel-ah-s'yohng Kohn-tro-láy) — Guarantee of place and quality

Asti Spumante (Áh-stee Spoo-mahn-tee)—A sparkling white wine from Piedmont in Italy

Auslese (Owss-leh-zeh)—Select picking of fully-ripened grapes

Avignon (Ah-veen-yong)—Major city in Cotes du Rhone

Bandol (Bahn-dohl)—A red wine from Cotes de Provence

Barbaresco (Bar-ba-ress-ko)—Red wine from Piedmont

Barbera (Bar-béh-ra)—Red wine/grape from Piedmont

Bardolino (Bar-doh-lée-no)—A Veronese red wine

Barolo (Ba-ró-lo)—A fine red wine from Piedmont

Batard-Montrachet (Ba-tar-Mohng-ra-sháy)—White Grand Cru in Puligny-Montrachet

Beaujolais (Bo-sho-láy)—Major red wine region of Southern Burgundy

Beaune (Bone)—The capital of Burgundy

Beerenauslese (Beh-ren-owss-leh-zeh)—Individually selected over-ripe grapes

Bereich (Bay-rye'kh)—A smaller district within a Gebeit (Germany)

Bernkastel (Behrn-kas-tel)—The chief vineyard city of the Middle Moselle

Bernkasteler Doktor (Behrn-kast-ler Dohk-tór)—World-famous vineyard in Bernkastel

Blanc (Blohng)—White

Blanc Fume (Blohng Fu-may)—The Sauvignon Blanc from the Loire

Blanchot (Blawng-shó)—Grand Cru in Chablis

Bocksbeutel (Box-boy-tel)—The flat-sided squat bottle used in Franconia (similar to Mateus bottle)

Bordeaux (Bor-dóh)—Major city in Gironde

Brouilly (Broo-yée)—Largest commune in Beaujolais

Cabernet Sauvignon (Ka-behr-nay So-veen-yohng)—The most important grape of Bordeaux

Campania (Kahm-pahn-ya)—A department in southern Italy

Carbonnieux (Kar-bohn-yúh)—A classified growth in Graves (white)

Chablis (Sha-blée)—White wine region north of the Cote d'Or

Chambertin (Shawm-behr-tahng)—Red Grand Cru in Gevrey-Chambertin

Champagne (Shawm-pine)—The vineyard region northeast of Paris

Charmes (Sharm)—White Premier Cru in Meursault

Chassagne-Montrachet (Sha-sign-Mohng-ra-sháy)—White wine commune in the Cote de Beaune

Chateau (Sha-tōr)—Named vineyards in Bordeaux

Chateauneuf-du-Pape (Sha-toh-nuhf du Pahp)—Red wine area in the Cotes du Rhone

Cheval Blanc (Shuh-vahl Blohng)—A First Great Classified Growth of St. Emilion

Chevalier-Montrachet (Shuh-vahl-yáy Mohn-ra-sháy)—White Grand Cru in Puligny-Montrachet

Chianti (K'yahn-tee)—Famous red wine from Tuscany

Chianti Classico (K'yahn-tee Kla-see-ko—Superior Chianti

commune (ko-múne)—Vineyard area in the Cote d'Or

Corvo (Kor-vo)—A fine "chateau-bottled" red wine (Sicily)

Cote Chalonnais (Koht Sha-lohn-náy)—Northwestern region of Southern Burgundy

Cote de Beaune (Koht duh Bóne)—The southern region of the Cote d'Or

Cote de Beaune-Village (Koht duh Bóne-Vee-láhj)—Appellation for Cote de Beaune (red)

Cote de Brouilly (Koht duh Broo-yée)—A superior commune in Beaujolais

Cote Maconnais (Koht Ma-ko-nay)—North central region of Southern Burgundy

Cote de Nuits (Koht duh N'wee)—Northern region of the Cote d'Or

Cote de Nuits—Villags (Koht duh N'wse-Vee-láhj)—Appellation for Cote de Nuits (Red)

Cotes de Provence (Koht duh Pro-vawńss)—The wine region of Provence

Cote d'Or (Koht dor)—The heart of the Burgundy region

Cotes du Rhone (Koht du Rohn)—Vineyard region in the Rhone Valley

Coutet (Koo-tay)—A classified first growth in Sauternes

Criots (Les) (Cree-yó)—White Grand Cru in Puligny-Montrachet

Dom Perignon (Dohm Pay-reen-yohng)—The Benedictine monk famous in Champagne

Edelbeerenauslese (Eh-del-behr-en-owss-leh-zeh)—Extraordinary individual overripe grapes

Eiswein (Icé-vine)—Perfectly ripened, partially frozen grapes

Emilia-Romagna (Ay-meél-ya Ro-mahn-ya)—A department in north central Italy

Est! Est! Est! (Est Est Est)—A delightful white wine from Montefiascone

Frascati (Fra-ska-tee)—A strong red wine from Latium

Fuisse (Fwee-sáy)—White wine village in the Cote Maconnais

Gamay (Ga-máy)—A red wine grape used mainly in Beaujolais

Gevrey-Chambertin (Zhev-ray-Shawn-bair-teng)—The largest commune in the Cote de Nuits

Gewurztraminer (Guh-vurts-tra-mee-ner)—A superior quality Traminer

Gironde (Zhee-rawńd)—The major river of Bordeaux

Givry (Zhee-vrée)—A commune in the Cote Chalonnais

Goldtropfchen (Gólt-trupf-shen)—The famous vineyard in Piesport (Moselle)

Graves (Grahv)—A red and white wine district of Bordeaux

Haut-Brion (Oh-Bree-yohńg)—A classified first growth in Graves (red)

Hermitage (Air-mee-tahzh)—Red wine area in the Cotes du Rhone

Himmelreich (Hím-mel-rye'kh)—The most famous vineyard in Graach (Moselle)

Hipping (Híp-ping)—Most famous vineyard in Nierstein (Rheinhesse)

Inferno (Een-faír-no)—A fine red wine from Valtellina (Lombardy)

Johannisberg (Yo-há-niss-bairg)—Town in the Rheingau

Kabinett (Ka-bee-nétt)—First grade of Qualitatswein Mit Pradikat

Lacryma Christi (La-kree-ma Krée-stee)—A still or sparkling white wine from Campania

Lafite-Rothschild (La-feet- Rohts-sheéld)—A classified first growth in Medoc (Pauillac)

Lambrusco (Lahm-bróo-sko)—A slightly carbonated, sweet red wine from Emilia

Lascombes (Lahs-kawḿb)—A classified second growth in Medoc (Margaux)

La Tache (La Tahsh)—Red Grand Cru in Vosne-Romanee

Latour (La-toor)—A classified first growth in Medoc (Pauillac)

La Tour Blanche (La Toor Blawnsh)—A classified first growth in Sauternes

Lenchen (Lén-shen)—The most famous vineyard in Oestrich (Rheingau)

Leognan (Lay-oh-n'yńg)—A principal parish in Graves

Leoville-Barton (Lay-oh-veél Bar-tohńg)—A classified second growth in Medoc (St. Julien)

Montagny (Mohng-tahn-vée)—A commune in Cote Chalonnais

Montrachet (Le) (Mohng-ra-sháy)—White Grand Cru in Puligny-Montrachet

Monts des Milieu (Mohng day Meel-yúh)—A Premier Cru in Chablis

Moselblumchen (Mó-sel-blum-chen)—A blended wine— Liebfraumilch of the Moselle

Moulin-a-Vent (Moo-leng-ah-Veng)—The best known commune in Beaujolais

Mouton-Rothschild (Moo-tohng-Roht-sheél)—A classified second growth in Medoc (Pauillac)

Muscadet (Muss-ka-dáy)—Vineyard region of the Loire Valley

Musigny (Les) (Mu-zeen-yée)—Red Grand Cru in Chambolle-Musigny

Nebbiolo (Nebb-yó-lo)—A red wine grape of Italy

Nierstein (Néer-shtine)—A vineyard village of the Rheinhesse

Nuits St. Georges (N'wee Seng-Zhorzh) — A red wine commune in Cote de Nuits

Orvieto Abbocatto (Orv-yay-toh Ahb-bo-ká-toh) — Slightly fruity white wine from Umbria

Orvieto Secco (Orv-yáy-toh Sék-ko) — Dry white wine from Umbria

Pauillac (Pohl-yahk) — A principal parish in the Haut-Medoc

Pavie (Pa-vée) — A first great classified growth in St. Emilion

Pessac (Pess-sahk) — A principal parish in Graves

Petit Chablis (Puh-tee-Sha-blée) — A lesser appellation in Chablis

Petit-Village (Puh-tee Vee-lahzh) — A first growth in Pomerol

Petrus (Pay-truss) — A great first growth in Pomerol

Piedmont (Peéd-mont) — A region in northeast Italy

Piesport (Peéss-port) — Vineyard village of the Middle Moselle

Pinot Chardonnay (Pee-nó Shar-doh-nay) — The noble white grape of Burgundy

Pinot Noir (Pee-nó N'war) — The noble red grape of Burgundy

Pomerol (Po-may-ról) — A red wine district of Bordeaux

Pommard (Po-már) — The best known commune in Cote de Beaune

Pouilly-Fuisse (Poo-yée-Fwee-sáy) — Famous white wine from Cote Maconnais

Pouilly-Fume (Poo-yée-Fu-máy) — The important wine from the Loire Valley

Preuses (Les) (Pruhz) — A Grand Cru in Chablis

Provence (Pro-vengss) — The vineyard region of the French Riveria

Puligny-Montrachet (Pu-leen-yée Mohng-ra-shay) — White wine commune in Cote de Beaune

Qualitatswein (Kua-lee-taits-vine) — Superior German table wine (quality wine)

Rheims (Rengss) — The capital of the Champagne region

Rheingau (Rine-g'ow) — A vineyard area on the Rhine

Rheinhesse (Rine-hess-seh) — A vineyard area on the Rhine

Rheinpfalz (Palatinate) (Rine-pfahlz) — A vineyard area on the Rhine

Richebourg (Le) (Reesh-boórg) — Red Grand Cru in Vosne-Romanee

Riesling (Rees-ling) — The noble grape in Alsace and Germany

Rieussec (R'yuh-sék) — A classified first growth in Sauternes

Romanee (La) (Ro-ma-náy) — Red Grand Cru in Vosne-Romanee

Romanee-Conti (La) (Ro-ma-náy — Kohn-teé) — Red Grand Cru in Vosne-Romanee

Romanee-St. Vivant (Ro-ma-náy Seng-Vee-vahng) — Red Grand Cru in Vosne-Romanee

Rose d'Anjou (Ro-zay dahn-zhóo) — A Vin Rose from Anjou (Loire)

Rudesheimer Berg (Róo-dess-him-er Bairg) — Finest vineyards in Rudesheim (Rheingau)

Rugiens (Les) (Ru-zhéng) — Red Premier Cru in Pommard

Ruwer (Ru-ver) — A vineyard area of the Upper Moselle

Saar (Zar) — A vineyard area of the Upper Moselle

Saint-Amour (Seng Ta-moor) — The northernmost commune in Beaujolais

Saint-Marc (Sahng-már) — A classified great growth in Barsac (Sauternes)

Santenay (Sahng-tuh-náy) — Southernmost commune in the Cote de Beaune

Santenots (Les) (Sahn-tuh-nó) — Red Premier Cru in Volnay

Sassella (Sahs-sél-la) — A fine red wine from Valtellina (Lombardy)

Saumur (So-mur) — An important white wine of the Loire

Sauternes (So-taírn) — White wine region of Bordeaux

Sauvignon Blanc (So-vee-yohng Blahng) — Major white wine grape of the Graves

Scharzhof (Shárts-hohf) — A famous estate in Wiltingen (Saar)

Schloss Johannisberg (Shlohss Yó-ha-nis-bairg) — Most famous vineyard of Johannisberg (Rheingau)

Schloss Vollrads (Shlohss Fóhl-rahts) — Most famous vineyard of Winkel (Rheingau)

Sekt (Sekt) — Sparkling wine from Germany

Semillon (Say-meel-yohng) — Major grape of the Sauternes

Sicily (Sís-sil-ly) — Island region at southern tip of Italy

Soave (So-aĥ-vay) — A Veronese white wine

Sonnenuhr (Zoh-nen-oor) — Most famous vineyard in Wehlen (Moselle)

Spatlese (Shpáyt-leh-seh) — Late-picked fully-ripened grapes

Steinberg (Shtíne-bairg) — Most famous vineyard in Hattenheim (Rheingau)

Steinwein (Shtíne-vine) — The generic name for Franconian wines

St. Emilion (Seng-tay-meel-yohng) — Red wine district of Bordeaux

St. Estephe (Seng-tes-téff) — A principal parish in the Haut-Medoc

St. Julien (Seng-zhul-yeńg) — A principal parish in the Haut-Medoc

Strasbourg (Strahss-boórg) — The capital of Alsace

Sylvaner (Sil-vá-ner) — White wine grape used in Alsace and Germany

Syrah (See-rá) — Red wine grape of the Cotes Du Rhone

Tafelwein (Táh-fel-vine) — Ordinary German table wine (table wine)

Tavel (Ta-vél) — Vin Rose commune in the Cotes du Rhone

Teurons (Les) (Toor-ohńg) — Red Premier Cru in Beaune

Tiergarten (Teér-gar-ten) — An important vineyard in Trier (Ruwer)

Traminer (Trá-min-ner) — White wine grape used mainly in Alsace

Trier (Trée-yer) — An important city on the Moselle

Trockenbeeren (Tró-ken-be-ren) — Semi-dried or shriveled grapes

Trockenbeerenauslese (Owss-leh-zeh) — Select picking of shriveled grapes

Tuscany (Túss-ca-nee) —A department in central Italy

Valmur (Vahl-mur) —A Grand Cru in Chablis

Valpolicella (Vahl-po-lee-chél-la) —Veronese red wine

Vaudesir (Voday-zéer) —A Grand Cru in Chablis

Verdicchio (Vair-deék-yo) —A pale white wine

Verona (Veh-ró-na) —A region in Northern Italy

*** Vieux-Chateau-Certan** (V'yuh-Sha-tóh-Sair-tahng) —A great first growth in Pomerol

Villefranche (Veel-frawnsh) —Main city of Beaujolais

Vin Rose (Veng Ro-záy) —A light rose-colored wine

Vin Santo (Veen Sahn-toh) —A white dessert wine from Tuscany

Volnay (Vohl-náy) —Red wine commune in Cote de Beaune

Volnay-Santenots (Vohl-nay Sahn-tuh-nó) —Red Premier Cru in Volnay

Vosne-Romanee (Vone Ro-ma-náy) —Red wine commune in the Cote de Nuits

Vougeot (Voo-zhóh) —Red wine commune in the Cote de Nuits

Vouvray (Voov-ráy) —Important white wine in the Coteaux de Touraine (Loire).

Wurzburg (Vúrts-boorg) —The main city of Franconia

Yquem (d') (Des-kem) —The classified superior first growth (Sauternes)

Zeller Schwarze Katz (Tséll-er Shvar-tseh Kahtz) —The "black cat" wine from Zell (Moselle)

*Denotes Chateau

Table Arrangements

There are any number of arrangements that can be made with standard size tables that are available on the market: rectangular, round, oblong or oval, serpentine, quarter-round, half-round, trapezoid. When tables are to be used as display tables (e.g., buffet or gift tables) they should be draped (i.e., a ruffled or straight cloth should be attached from the edge of the table and this should extend to the floor). The front side of a head table should also be draped.

Tables used for eating, discussion, conference, etc., or where guests will be seated should not be draped, and the tablecloth should extend a minimum of ten inches beyond the table's edge. The tablecloth should not touch the floor. For large banquets tables may also be placed on elevated platforms. This will break up the monotony of the room, and will provide thoses guests at the rear of the room with a better view of the head table and speaker.

For conferences or meetings, tables should be set with water glasses and water pitchers as well as ashtrays and matches. It would be foolish to specify the number of ashtrays required as different groups will have different habits, and the total time the participants will spend in the room without breaks must be taken into consideration. Additionally the number of staff servicing the meeting will determine the number of ashtrays and amount of water that should be preset. For large functions, tables with water or other refreshments may be set at strategic locations around the room.

The author recommends that a plan (to scale) be drawn for each function room and each banquet room which includes obstructions (e.g., columns, permanent fixtures, etc.). The sketch should also show dimensions, entrances (for guests and staff) or any other pertinent information. A template may be cut out (to the *same* scale as the plan drawing) that depicts each table style owned or used by the property. It is much easier to arrange tables on paper than it is to have set up and then have to move a banquet round because it does not fit.

As with dining room setup, a minimum space of two feet or twenty-four inches long by fifteen inches deep should be allowed for each person for any function, and the space between the backs of two chairs must also not be less than two feet.

The following table arrangements depict standard tables, and can be selected for buffets, gift tables, head tables, small banquets, conferences, dinner meetings, or just meetings. Endless combinations can be sketched, and those depicted below may be increased in size by the symmetric addition of more tables.

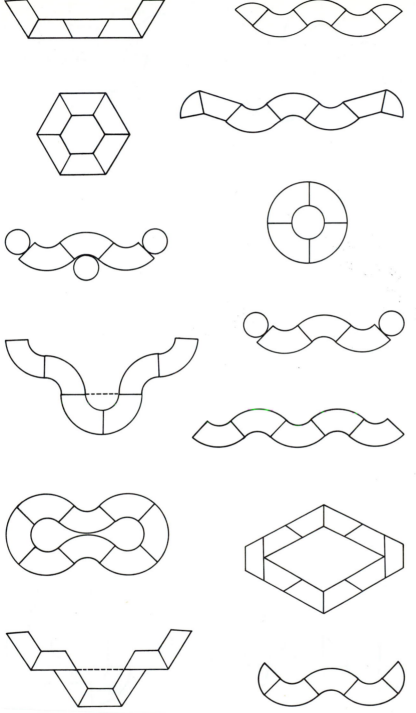

Figure B.1 Table arrangements for buffet tables, gift tables, head tables, small banquets, conferences, dinner meetings, meetings

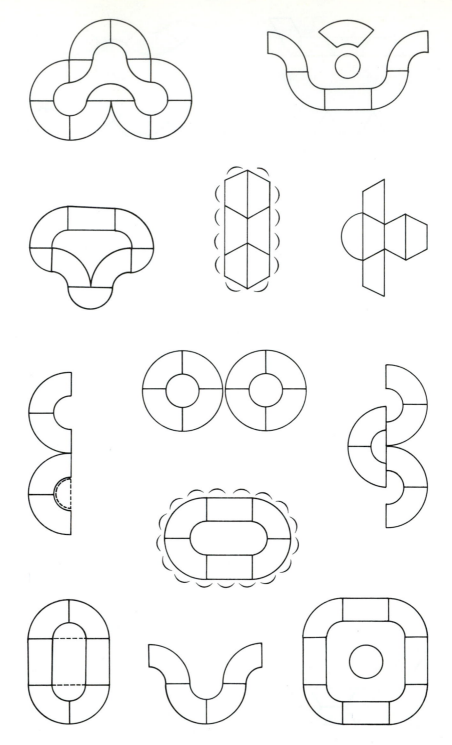

Appendix **C**

Napkin Folding Guide

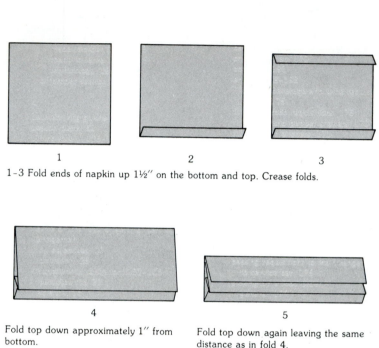

1
2
3

1–3 Fold ends of napkin up 1½″ on the bottom and top. Crease folds.

4

Fold top down approximately 1″ from bottom.

5

Fold top down again leaving the same distance as in fold 4.

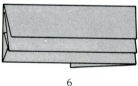

6

Fold right side of napkin under or behind napkin on the reverse of the louvre.

7

Fold left side of napkin under as with fold 6. Place either in center of cover or to left of cover (informal) under silverware. This fold looks best when the two bottom louvres are approximately 1″ in width and the top louvre is 3″ in width. You may choose to have all louvres equal in width.

Figure C.1 The Cumberbund

284

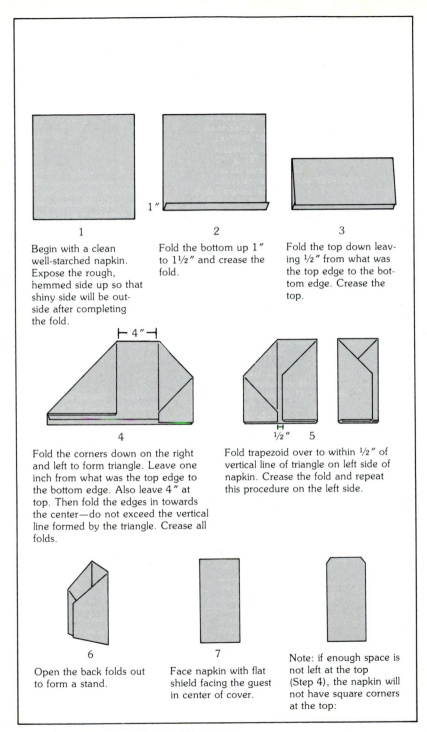

Figure C.2 The Escutch-
eon

1

Begin with a clean
well-starched napkin.
Expose the rough,
hemmed side up so that
shiny side will be out-
side after completing
the fold.

2

Fold the bottom up 1″
to 1½″ and crease the
fold.

3

Fold the top down leav-
ing ½″ from what was
the top edge to the bot-
tom edge. Crease the
top.

4″

4

Fold the corners down on the right
and left to form triangle. Leave one
inch from what was the top edge to
the bottom edge. Also leave 4″ at
top. Then fold the edges in towards
the center—do not exceed the vertical
line formed by the triangle. Crease all
folds.

½″ 5

Fold trapezoid over to within ½″ of
vertical line of triangle on left side of
napkin. Crease the fold and repeat
this procedure on the left side.

6

Open the back folds out
to form a stand.

7

Face napkin with flat
shield facing the guest
in center of cover.

Note: if enough space is
not left at the top
(Step 4), the napkin will
not have square corners
at the top:

Figure C.3 Single Fan

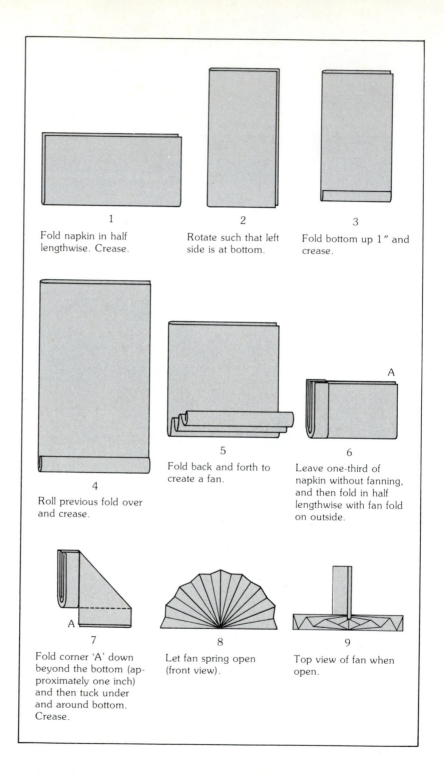

1
Fold napkin in half lengthwise. Crease.

2
Rotate such that left side is at bottom.

3
Fold bottom up 1″ and crease.

4
Roll previous fold over and crease.

5
Fold back and forth to create a fan.

6
Leave one-third of napkin without fanning, and then fold in half lengthwise with fan fold on outside.

7
Fold corner 'A' down beyond the bottom (approximately one inch) and then tuck under and around bottom. Crease.

8
Let fan spring open (front view).

9
Top view of fan when open.

Figure C.4 The Double Fan

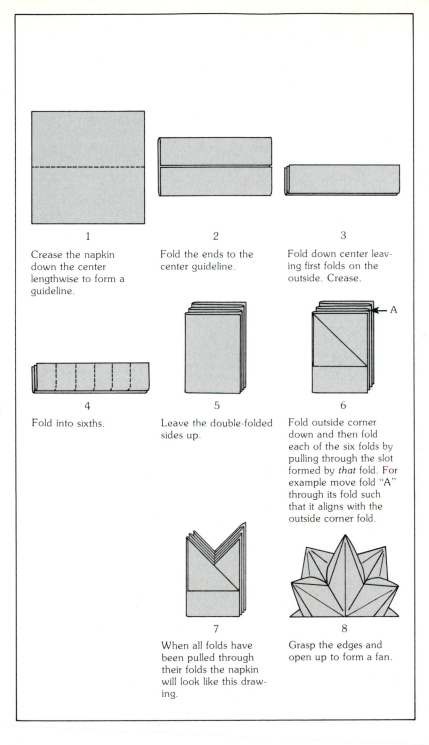

1

Crease the napkin down the center lengthwise to form a guideline.

2

Fold the ends to the center guideline.

3

Fold down center leaving first folds on the outside. Crease.

A

4

Fold into sixths.

5

Leave the double-folded sides up.

6

Fold outside corner down and then fold each of the six folds by pulling through the slot formed by *that* fold. For example move fold "A" through its fold such that it aligns with the outside corner fold.

7

When all folds have been pulled through their folds the napkin will look like this drawing.

8

Grasp the edges and open up to form a fan.

Figure C.5 The Ruffled
Double Fan

1-4. Follow steps as listed for the double fan.

Top View

Front View

5

6

7

Leave the single folded
sides up (opposite side
from the double fan).

Pull the *single folds* out
to form a ruffle on
either side of the
straight center fold.

Spread fan centered in
the cover.

Figure C.6 The Sailboat

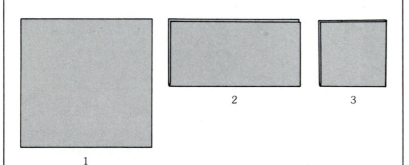

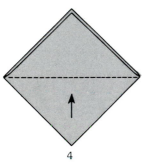

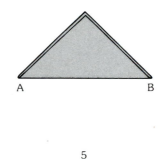

1-3. Fold into quarters.

4

Turn napkin with single folds up. This is the same as 3, but not in the same proportion.

5

Fold bottom up and form a triangle.

A   B
6

Fold corners A and B down as indicated.

AB
7

Tuck corners A and B under napkin (6) and then squeeze ends together; such that A and B touch each other.

AB
8

Pull each single fold up one at a time to form sails while clasping ends A and B to hold together.

Figure C.7 Robin Hood's Hat

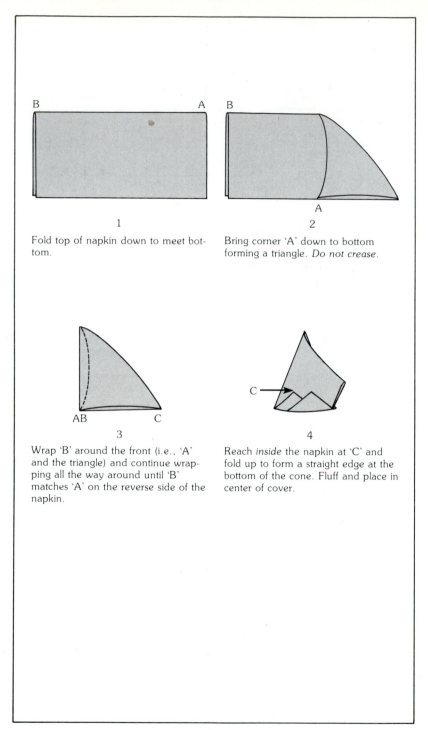

1

Fold top of napkin down to meet bottom.

2

Bring corner 'A' down to bottom forming a triangle. *Do not crease.*

3

Wrap 'B' around the front (i.e., 'A' and the triangle) and continue wrapping all the way around until 'B' matches 'A' on the reverse side of the napkin.

4

Reach *inside* the napkin at 'C' and fold up to form a straight edge at the bottom of the cone. Fluff and place in center of cover.

Figure C.8 Fleur De Lis

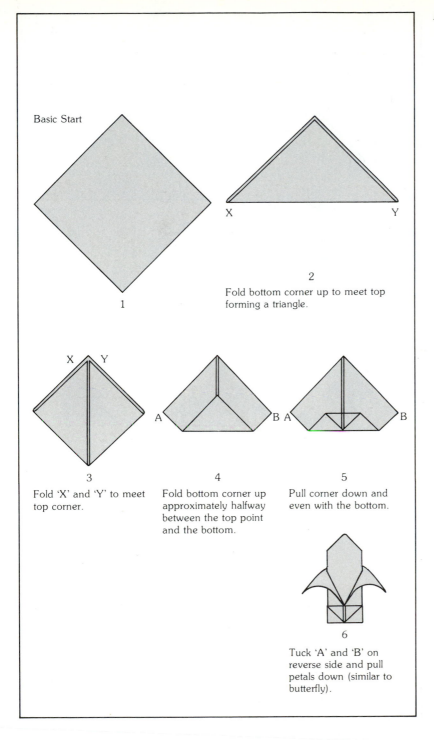

Basic Start

1

2
Fold bottom corner up to meet top
forming a triangle.

3
Fold 'X' and 'Y' to meet
top corner.

4
Fold bottom corner up
approximately halfway
between the top point
and the bottom.

5
Pull corner down and
even with the bottom.

6
Tuck 'A' and 'B' on
reverse side and pull
petals down (similar to
butterfly).

Figure C.9 Luncheon Fold

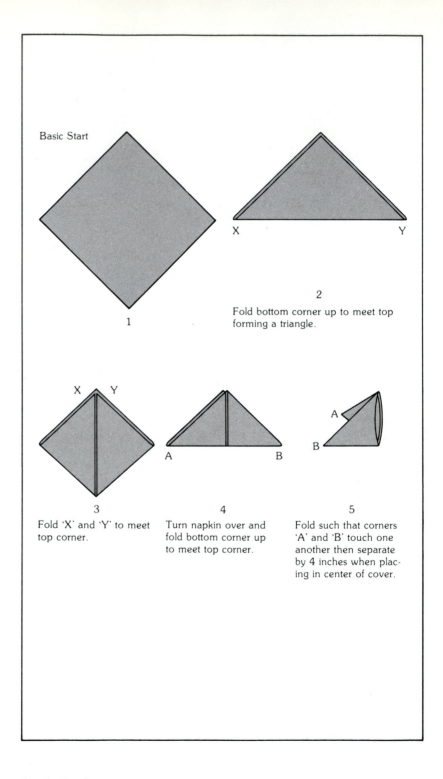

Basic Start

1

2
Fold bottom corner up to meet top forming a triangle.

3
Fold 'X' and 'Y' to meet top corner.

4
Turn napkin over and fold bottom corner up to meet top corner.

5
Fold such that corners 'A' and 'B' touch one another then separate by 4 inches when placing in center of cover.

Figure C.10 Bishop's Hat

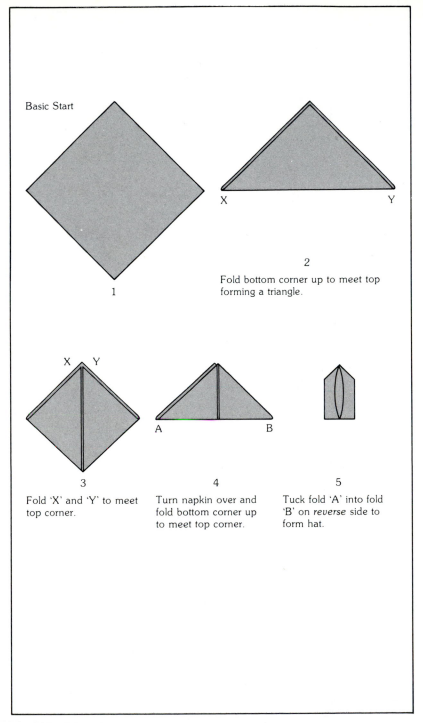

Basic Start

1

2
Fold bottom corner up to meet top forming a triangle.

3
Fold 'X' and 'Y' to meet top corner.

4
Turn napkin over and fold bottom corner up to meet top corner.

5
Tuck fold 'A' into fold 'B' on *reverse* side to form hat.

Figure C.11 Butterfly

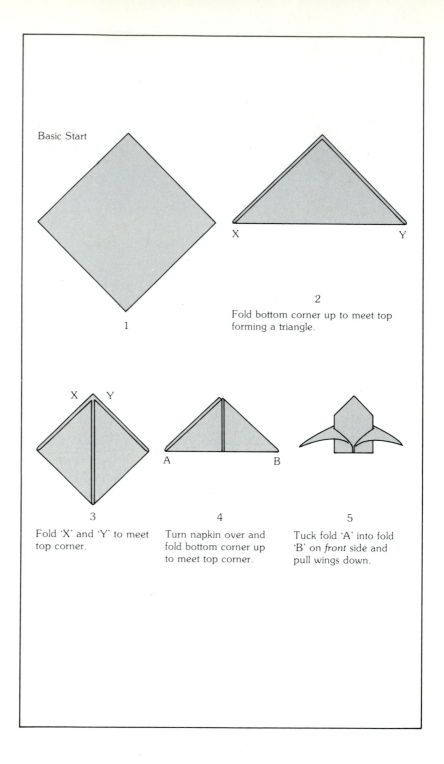

Basic Start

1

2
Fold bottom corner up to meet top forming a triangle.

3
Fold 'X' and 'Y' to meet top corner.

4
Turn napkin over and fold bottom corner up to meet top corner.

5
Tuck fold 'A' into fold 'B' on *front* side and pull wings down.

Metric Conversions for Weights and Measures in the United States and England

Weights and Measures in the United States and Great Britain and Metric Systems

For most purposes the modern units used for measures and weights in the United States are the same as those used in Great Britain. The major exception is in the measurement of capacity. In the following tables, therefore, there are three systems for liquid capacity—U.S., British, and metric—instead of the two major systems—U.S.-British combined and metric.

The S.I. system (*Systeme Internationale*), a refinement of the long-used metric system, will in time become the universal system of measurement. Britain is already committed to a complete transfer to this system, and the United States has approved transfer on a voluntary, industry-by-industry, basis.

LENGTH

United States
Great Britain   *Metric or S.I.*

		10 millimeters = 1 centimeter
12 inches	= 1 foot	10 centimeters = 1 decimeter
3 feet	= 1 yard	10 decimeters = 1 meter
1,760 yards	= 1 mile	10 meters = 1 dekameter
5,280 feet	= 1 mile	10 dekameters = 1 hectometer
6,080 feet	= 1 nautical mile	10 hectometers = 1 kilometer

AREA

United States
Great Britain   *Metric or S.I.*

144 square inches   = 1 square foot   100 square centimeters = 1 square decimeter
9 square feet   = 1 square yard   100 square decimeters = 1 square meter (centare)
4,840 square yards = 1 acre   100 square meters   = 1 square dekameter (are)
43,560 square feet = 1 acre   10,000 square meters   = 1 hectare
640 acres   = 1 square mile   100 hectares   = 1 square kilometer

VOLUME AND DRY CAPACITY

United States
Great Britain   *Metric or S.I.*

1,728 cubic inches   = 1 cubic foot   1,000 cubic centimeters = 1 cubic decimeter
27 cubic feet   = 1 cubic yard   1,000 cubic decimeters = 1 cubic meter
1 dry pint   = 33.6 cubic inches   1,000 cubic meters   = 1 cubic dekameter
1 dry quart (2 pints)   = 67.201 cubic inches   1,000 cubic dekameters = 1 cubic hectometer
1 peck (8 quarts)   = 537.6 cubic inches   1,000 cubic hectometers = 1 cubic kilometer
1 bushel (4 pecks)   = 2,150.42 cubic inches

WEIGHT

United States
Great Britain
(avoirdupois weight)   *Metric or S.I.*

437.5 grains   = 1 ounce   1,000 milligrams = 1 gram
16 ounces   = 1 pound   1,000 grams   = 1 kilogram
100 pounds   = 1 cental   100 kilograms   = 1 quintal
2,000 pounds   = 1 short ton   1,000 kilograms = 1 metric ton
2,240 pounds   = 1 long ton

(Also in Great Britain)
14 pounds   = 1 stone
2 stones   = 1 quarter
4 quarters   = 1 hundredweight
20 hundredweights = 1 long ton

LIQUID CAPACITY

United States

16 fluid ounces	=	1 pint
2 pints	=	1 quart
4 quarts	=	1 gallon
5 fifths	=	1 gallon

1 fluid ounce	=	1.8 cubic inches
1 pint	=	28.88 cubic inches
1 quart	=	57.75 cubic inches
1 gallon	=	231 cubic inches

*1.2 American gallons = 1 imperial gallon

Great Britain

20 fluid ounces	=	1 imperial pint
2 imperial pints	=	1 imperial quart
4 imperial quarts	=	1 imperial gallon*

1 fluid ounce	=	1.735 cubic inches
1 imperial pint	=	34.68 cubic inches
1 imperial quart	=	69.35 cubic inches
1 imperial gallon	=	277.4 cubic inches

Metric or S.I.

10 milliliters	=	1 centiliter
100 centiliters	=	1 liter
100 liters	=	1 hectoliter
10 hectoliters	=	1 kiloliter

1 milliliter	=	1 cubic centimeter
1 liter	=	1,000 cubic centimeters
1 hectoliter	=	100,000 cubic centimeters

Temperature Conversions

Degrees Fahrenheit (°F) to Degrees Celsius (°C)*

°F	°C		°F	°C		°F	°C
+ 0	− 17.78		+ 60	+ 15.56		+ 120	+ 48.87
1	17.22		61	16.11		121	49.44
2	16.67		62	16.67		122	50.00
3	16.11		63	17.22		123	50.56
4	15.56		64	17.78		124	51.11
+ 5	− 15.00		+ 65	+ 18.33		+ 125	+ 51.67
6	14.44		66	18.89		126	52.22
7	13.89		67	19.44		127	52.78
8	13.33		68	20.00		128	53.33
9	12.78		69	20.56		129	53.89
+ 10	− 12.22		+ 70	+ 21.11		+ 130	+ 54.44
11	11.67		71	21.67		131	55.00
12	11.11		72	22.22		132	55.56
13	10.56		73	22.78		133	56.11
14	10.00		74	23.33		134	56.67
+ 15	− 9.44		+ 75	+ 23.89		+ 135	+ 57.22
16	8.89		76	24.44		136	57.78
17	8.33		77	25.00		137	58.33
18	7.78		78	25.56		138	58.89
19	7.22		79	26.11		139	63.44
+ 20	− 6.67		+ 80	+ 26.67		+ 140	+ 60.00
21	6.11		81	27.22		141	60.56
22	5.56		82	27.78		142	61.11
23	5.00		83	28.33		143	61.67
24	4.44		84	28.89		144	62.22
+ 25	− 3.89		+ 85	+ 29.44		+ 145	+ 62.78
26	3.33		86	30.00		146	63.33
27	2.78		87	30.56		147	63.89
28	2.22		88	31.11		148	64.44
29	1.67		89	31.67		149	65.00
+ 30	− 1.11		+ 90	+ 32.22		+ 150	+ 65.56
31	0.56		91	32.78		155	68.33
32	0.00		92	33.33		160	71.11
33	+ 0.56		93	33.89		165	73.89
34	1.11		94	34.44		170	76.67
+ 35	+ 1.67		+ 95	+ 35.00		+ 175	+ 79.44
36	2.22		96	35.56		180	82.22
37	2.78		97	36.11		185	85.00
38	3.33		98	36.67		190	87.78
39	3.89		99	37.22		195	90.56
+ 40	+ 4.44		+ 100	+ 37.78		+ 200	+ 93.33
41	5.00		101	38.33		205	96.11
42	5.56		102	38.89		210	98.89
43	6.11		103	39.44		215	101.67
44	6.67		104	40.00		220	104.44
+ 45	+ 7.22		+ 105	+ 40.56		+ 225	+ 107.22
46	7.78		106	41.11		230	110.00
47	8.33		107	41.67		235	112.78
48	8.89		108	42.22		240	115.56
49	9.44		109	42.78		245	118.33
+ 50	+ 10.00		+ 110	+ 43.33		+ 250	+ 121.11
51	10.56		111	43.89		255	123.89
52	11.11		112	44.44		260	126.67
53	11.67		113	45.00		265	129.44
54	12.22		114	45.56		270	132.22
+ 55	+ 12.78		+ 115	+ 46.11		+ 275	+ 135.00
56	13.33		116	46.67		280	137.78
57	13.89		117	47.22		285	140.56
58	14.44		118	47.78		290	143.33
59	15.00		119	48.33		295	146.11

Water freezes

$\begin{bmatrix} 32°F \\ 0°C \end{bmatrix}$

Ethyl alcohol boils

$\begin{bmatrix} 173°F \\ 78.5°C \end{bmatrix}$

Water boils

$\begin{bmatrix} 212°F \\ 100°C \end{bmatrix}$

The formula used to derive the table is:
$$°C = 5/9 [°F − 32]$$

*Degrees Celsius was formerly called degrees Centigrade. The change was made to honor Anders Celsius (1701-1744) in accordance with the scientific custom of naming units of measurement after famous scientists who have contributed to that field.